Hunter S. Thompson is a humble man who writes books for a living and spends the rest of his time bogged down in strange and crazy wars. He is the author of many violent books (see below) and brilliant political essays, which his friends and henchmen in the international media have managed for many years to pass off as "Gonzo Journalism".

The reasons for this are myriad, and we will speak of them later. In the meantime Dr. Thompson lives the life of a freelance country gentleman in Woody Creek, Colorado, and exists in a profoundly active Balance of Terror with the local police authorities. He is currently at work on *99 Days: The Trial of Hunter S. Thompson* and a long-awaited sex book, *Polo Is My Life*.

Also by Hunter S. Thompson in Picador

Generation of Swine
The Great Shark Hunt

Dr. Hunter S. Thompson

SONGS OF THE DOOMED

More Notes on the Death of the
American Dream

GONZO PAPERS VOL. 3

published by Pan Books

First published in the United States of America 1991 by Summit Books,
a division of Simon & Schuster Inc.
This paperback edition first published in Great Britain 1991 in
Picador by Pan Books Ltd,
Cavaye Place, London SW10 9PG
9 8 7 6 5 4 3 2 1
© Hunter S. Thompson 1990
ISBN 0 330 32179 X
Printed and bound in Great Britain by
Butler & Tanner Ltd, Frome and London

Grateful acknowledgement is made for the following permissions:
Extract from *Anatomy of Melancholy* courtesy of AMS Press. "I
Knew the Bride When She Used to Rock and Roll" written by
Nick Lowe, © 1977 by Rock Music company, used by permission.
Extract from *The Great Gatsby* by F. Scott Fitzgerald reprinted by
permissin of Charles Scribner's Sons, an imprint of Macmillan
Publishing Company, copyright 1925 by Charles Scribner's Sons,
renewed 1953 by Frances Scott Fitzgerald Lanahan. "Warning Is
Issued on Cocaine Use with Sex After Man Loses Limbs," by
Lawrence K. Altman, June 3, 1988; copyright © 1988 by The New
York Times Company; reprinted by permission. Letter; "Final
Analysis: Gerald Goldstein, Esq." copyright Gerald Goldstein,
used by permission. "D. A. Snags Thompson in Sex Case" and
"Thompson Hit with 5 Felonies" copyright David Matthews-Price,
used by permission. "Hunter Hails Legal Triumph for Americans"
copyright Mark Huffman, used by permission. "American Pie"
words and music by Don McLean © copyright 1971, 1972 by
Music Corporation of America, Inc., and Benny Bird Music; rights
administered by MCA Music Publishing, a Division of MCA Inc.,
New York, NY 10019; used by permission. Extract from *The Quiet
American* by Graham Greene copyright © 1955 by Graham
Greene; reprinted by permission of Viking Penguin, a Division of
Penguin Books USA Inc. Extract from "Where Are You Tonight?"
written by Michael Timmins © 1990 Paz Junk Music and BMG
Songs, Inc., used by permission; all rights reserved. "Sacred Elegy
V" from *George Barker Collected Poems* reprinted by permission
of Faber & Faber Ltd.

With special thanks to Catherine Sabonis-Chafee, my Top Gun, who did most of the work and endured more real fear and loathing in ninety-nine days than most people see in a lifetime and laughed like a warrior in the constant shadow of doom, jail, and pure craziness . . . well, well, well . . . The infamous "woman called Cat" turned out to have solid gold balls

And once again, to my cruel and relentless editor, David McCumber, the fearless Doctor of Deadlines, who put this book together under truly heinous pressure

> **"When the going gets weird,
> the weird turn pro"**
> **—HST**

PUBLISHER'S NOTE

The author has asked that the publisher contribute a note to this latest
work. This is it: Thanx, Doc.

J.H.S.
N.Y.C., *August 1990*

To all the friends and strangers and even enemies
who answered the Great Roll Call when I was
seized by rabid scum who tried to put me in prison

CONTENTS

Editor's Note   II

AUTHOR'S NOTE

Let the Trials Begin   15
Electricity   24
Last Train from Camelot   30

NOTE FROM RALPH STEADMAN   33

THE FIFTIES: Last Rumble in Fat City

Tarred and Feathered at the Jersey Shore   37
Saturday Night at the Riveria   40
Prince Jellyfish   42
   Hit Him Again, Jack, He's Crazy   42
   Interview   51
   Cherokee Park   57
Fleeing New York   63

THE SIXTIES: What the Hell? It's Only Rock and Roll . . .

Letter to Angus Cameron   69
The Rum Diary   70
Revisited: The Puerto Rican Problem   102
The Kennedy Assassination   105
Back to the U.S.A.   106
Hell's Angels: Long Nights, Ugly Days, Orgy of the
   Doomed . . .   107
Midnight on the Coast Highway   110
Ken Kesey: Walking with the King   112
LSD-25: *Res Ipsa Loquitor*   113

Chicago 1968: Death to the Weird   115
First Visit with Mescalito   119

THE SEVENTIES: Reaping the Whirlwind, Riding the Tiger

Iguana Project   131
Never Apologize, Never Explain   136
Vegas Witchcraft   137
High-Water Mark   140
Fear and Loathing   142
Lies—It Was All Lies—I Couldn't Help Myself   143
Ed Muskie Doomed by Ibogaine: Bizarre Drug Plot Revealed   144
Washington Politics   147
Summit Conference in Elko: Secret Gathering of the Power
    Elite   148
Opening Statement: HST   153
Rolling Stone: Abandon All Hope Ye Who Enter Here   159
Dance of the Doomed   161
Checking into the Lane Xang   162
Whooping It Up with the War Junkies   166
Confidential Memo to Colonel Giang Vo Don Giang   177
Memo to Jim Silberman on the Death of the American Dream   179
Letter to Russell Chatham   185

THE EIGHTIES: How Much Money Do You Have?

Welcome to the '80s   189
Bad Craziness in Palm Beach: I Told Her It Was Wrong . . .   191
Sugarloaf Key: Tales of the Swine Family   207
The Silk Road   211
    Fishhead Boys   211
    Overview   215
    The Murder of Colonel Evans   220
Letter to Ralph Steadman   227
Letter to Ken Kesey   234
Last Memo from the National Affairs Desk   235
Memo from the Sports Desk   241
Via Certified Mail   243
The Dukakis Problem: Another Vicious Beating for the New
    Whigs   245

Secret Cables to Willie Hearst   250
  Re: Qaddafi   250
  Re: The Column   250

San Francisco Examiner Columns

The New Dumb   254
Fear and Loathing in Sacramento   257
  Strange Ride to Reno   259
  Omnia Vincit Amor   261
  The Death of Russell Chatham   264
Whiskey Business   266
I Knew the Bride When She Used to Rock and Roll   269
Community of Whores   271

Return to the Riviera Cafe   274
Avery: Making Sense of the '60s   276
German Decade: The Rise of the Fourth Reich   279
Turbo Must Die   281
Memo to Jay Johnson, Night Editor, *San Francisco Examiner* 283
Warning Issued on Cocaine   286

WELCOME TO THE NINETIES: Welcome to Jail

Editor's Note   289
Nothing But Crumbs   290
Arrest Warrant and Charges   292
Beware   295
This Is a Political Trial . . .   296
Thompson Hit with 5 Felonies   297
Memo to Hal Haddon: Attack Now   297
The Art of Hitting the One Iron   299
Motion and Order to Dismiss the Case   300
Hunter Hails Legal Triumph for Americans   301
Press Release, Owl Farm, 5/31/90   303
Final Analysis: Gerald Goldstein, Esq.   305
**A Letter to *The Champion*: A Publication of the National
  Association of Criminal Defense Lawyers, Keith Stroup,
  Executive Director**   310
Later That Year . . .   312
Author's Note   314

EDITOR'S NOTE

Shortly before this book went to press, we were stunned and profoundly demoralized by a news bulletin out of Aspen—along with murky AP wire-photos—saying that Dr. Thompson had been inexplicably seized, searched, and arrested on nine felony counts and three bizarre misdemeanor charges of brutal sex and violence. Initial reports from the Pitkin County Sheriff's Department were hazy and incoherent, but Thompson's alleged attorney told reporters that "The Doctor is probably guilty of these crimes and many others, which means he could go to state prison for at least sixteen years."

It seemed impossible, but so what? Moments after his arrest, Thompson posted $2,000 cash bail and flew out to California on a private Learjet to deliver a series of lectures on "Journalism and the Law," despite efforts by local police authorities to prevent him from leaving the state without an ankle-strap body beeper that would cause him to radiate high-pitched beeping signals every fifteen seconds and would suck blood from the arch of his foot every two hours "for drug-abuse testing and other criminal evidence."

He disappeared, nonetheless, in the company of a key female witness, and remained incommunicado for many days until he was finally tracked down in a bungalow at the Beverly Hills Hotel by his old friend and colleague Raoul Duke, who flew in from Shanghai on a U.S. military jet to head the search for Thompson and force him to deliver his book manuscript on schedule, in accordance with a seven-year-old contract that made no provision for jailing and criminal seizure of the author by half-bright white-trash cops in a troubled rural district.

Duke agreed to return from China, after long years of exile, to head the Operations wing of Thompson's legal defense and also compel delivery of the doomed and desperate writer's final chapter. In a hastily called press conference at the Polo Lounge on Sunset Boulevard, Duke told reporters to "stand back. This is victory or death. That is all ye know and all ye need to know."

*Fiend behind the fiend behind the fiend behind the
Fiend. Mastodon with mastery, monster with an ache.
At the tooth of the ego, the dead drunk judge:
Wheresoever Thou art our agony will find Thee
Enthroned on the darkest altar of our heartbreak
Perfect. Beast, brute, bastard, O dog, my God!*

—GEORGE BARKER, *SACRED ELEGY V*, 1943

AUTHOR'S NOTE

WOODY CREEK, JULY 1990

LET THE TRIALS BEGIN

"He that goes to law holds a wolf by the ears."
—Robert Burton, *Anatomy of Melancholy*

I WANDERED INTO A library last week and decided to do a quick bit of reading on The Law, which has caused me some trouble recently. It was a cold, mean day, and my mood was not much different. The library was empty at that hour of the morning. . . . It was closed, in fact, but not locked. So I went in.

Far up at the top of the long stone staircase I could see a small man gesturing at me: waving at me, shouting. . . . But his voice sounded crazy and scattered, like the screeching of a cat or the sound of beer bottles exploding in a garbage compactor. The only words I could hear were *OUT* and *NIGHT*.

When I got about halfway up the stairs I stopped and raised both hands. "Don't worry!" I shouted. "Police!"

He shuddered and fell back, saying nothing. His eyes were huge and a shudder ran through his body as I approached. "No problem," I said to him. "Just routine police work." I flashed my gold *Special DEA Agent* badge at him, then reached out to shake hands, but he moaned suddenly and leaped away . . . and as he collapsed awkwardly on the cold marble floor I saw that his left ankle was encircled by a heavy steel band that was strapped to a black box.

"What the fuck is *that* thing?" I asked him, reaching down to help him up. But he scuttled away again; and then he hissed at me.

"*You* know what it is!" he whimpered. "You filthy murdering *pig!*"

"What?" I said. "Are you crazy?" Then I jumped down on him and grabbed his foot so I could bring him a little closer. He uttered another sharp, terrified cry as I slid him across the smooth floor and pulled his ankle up to where it was right in front of my eyes.

"Be quiet," I said. "I want a look at this thing in good light." He struggled briefly, but I quickly stepped over his leg and hyperextended his knee until he went rigid, then I braced him and examined the box. It was a standard-issue Body Beeper with a lock-on ankle bracelet— one of the New Age tools now available to law enforcement agencies everywhere, for purposes of electronic House Arrest for those who have been brought *within The System,* but for whom there is no room in the overcrowded jails, pens, and prisons. The United States of America has more people locked up than any other country in the world, including Cuba and South Africa. Our prison system from coast to coast is bulging at the seams, and hundreds more are being crammed in every day—more and more of them saddled with the *mandatory Sentences* and *No Parole* Provisions that came in with the first Reagan Administration, which began only ten years ago, but it seems like twenty or thirty. . . .

Indeed. But that is another very long story and we will save it for later. . . . So let's get back to the library and my new buddy, the unfortunate Prisoner that I seized and captured by accident at four o'clock in the morning when I caught him wandering aimlessly through the hallways of a massive public building with his eyes bulged out and his spine like rubber and probably his nuts on fire, too, because he had nothing to say for himself and no excuse for anything.

He was a loser. A wimp full of fear, with no pride and sure as hell no Money. . . . But I let him go, anyway and we talked for a while in the Mens Room about his problem. We were both nervous, so I went out to the car and got a bag of warm beers out of the car, along with a wooden pipe about half-full of good marijuana.

Soon we were both in a better mood, and I told him I was not really the Police, but just another good old boy with a yen to Read Law for a while and a few hours to spare before my next court appearance.

He was a first-time offender from Phoenix, serving work-release time in the Library on a six-year Attempted Rape charge that happened when he wandered into the Ladies Room at the airport and got in a fight with two Mexican women who said they were paid police informants and turned him in as a Sex Offender when the airport police finally ran him down in a false doorway at the far end of the Lost Luggage hangar and dragged him away in handcuffs to the Red Carpet Club where they subjected him to a loud and humiliating Strip Search and beat him on the kidneys with iron gloves.

He was innocent, he said, but it made no difference. . . . When they finally got him to jail he was charged with nine felonies including Aggravated Assault on a Police Officer, Gross Sexual Imposition and

Possession of 2,000 Marijuana Seeds that fell out of the lining of a suitcase he had borrowed from his son, for the trip.

That night he was beaten severely in the holding cell by a gang of sodomites who took all his cigarettes and then kicked him into a coma.

After thirty-three days in the jail hospital, he was assigned to a public defender who laughed at his case and called him "shiteyes" and said it was all a matter of money.

Ten weeks later, he was assigned to another lawyer who said he had no choice but to plead guilty and take his medicine like a man.

"I was lucky," he said. "I almost got sixteen years." He grinned happily and stared vacantly into my eyes.

"As it is now, I'll only have to do five."

He was broken; a niggardly shell of a man, so afraid of the Law and the Cops and the Courts that he felt lucky and grateful to be serving only five years instead of sixteen—even though he was innocent. But now, after two long years on his knees *within The System,* he no longer missed standing up.

It made me nervous, so I started pacing around in circles on the white tile floor and jabbering distractedly at him from time to time. . . . I was thinking; my mind was running at top speed, scanning and sorting my options. They ranged all the way from Dumb and Dangerous to Crazy, Evil, and utterly wrong from the start.

"Do you keep any whiskey in this place?" I asked him. "We need whiskey. My brain is getting hazy."

He stared at me for a moment. Then he smiled vaguely and stood up. "Sure," he said. "I think I can put my hands on a pint of Old Crow." He chuckled. "What the hell? I could use some whiskey, myself." He slid down off the marble washbasin where he'd been sitting and shuffled out of the room. He moved quickly and almost gracefully, but the ugly black box on his ankle slowed him down and caused him to walk with a limp.

I sat on my own basin and drank our last warm beer. What the hell am I doing here? I wondered. I am a Doctor of Journalism and a Man of The Cloth. Why am I slumped in a bathroom at the Public Library at four o'clock in the morning? Drinking whiskey and smoking marijuana with a soul-dead convict who might be taken back in jail at any moment?

"What's your name?" I asked him as he returned with a half-finished pint of whiskey in a brown bag.

"Andrew," he said. "They call me Andy."

"Okay, Andrew," I said. "Give me that whiskey and stand back. We are on the brink. Yes. I have an idea."

He tossed me the bottle and I drank deeply, then handed it back to him. "Don't worry about having this stuff on your breath when they come for you," I said. "I have a new electric toothbrush out in the car that will sterilize your whole Thorax in ten seconds. I also have some very fine cocaine downstairs in the car, which you might want to use when your eyes start looking like they do now. . . ." I slapped him on the leg and hit the Old Crow again. "Hot damn, Andrew!" I barked at him. "We are *warriors.* The time has come to *rumble!*"

He said nothing. The bottle of whiskey was tilted high over his face, and I could see that he was finishing it off. . . . So what? I thought. We can always get more. The whiskey stores opened at seven, and I didn't have to be in court until ten. There was plenty of time to do anything we wanted. Many wrongs could be righted in five hours if we had the right tools. . . .

"Well, Andrew," I said to him in a high-pitched mournful voice. "I hate to be the one to tell you this . . . I don't want to hurt you, but—"

"No!" he shouted. "Please don't kill me!"

I seized him quickly by the hair and jerked him off balance. His eyes rolled back in his head and then he went limp. "Stop whining!" I snapped. "I just want to tell you about a *legal* axiom."

"Bullshit," he croaked. "You're a goddamn vicious maniac!" He jerked out of my grasp and leaped away, then he braced on the balls of his feet, bashed me in the stomach with a frenzied right hook. "You bastard!" he screamed. "Get away from me! You're a paranoid psychotic!"

"We are going to Court, Andrew. We are champions! We will crush them like cheap roaches! TODAY'S PIG IS TOMORROW'S BACON!" I spun suddenly and hurled my green beer bottle so fast across the room that it exploded against the wall like a glass bomb before he even saw it happen. *BANG!* Whirling like Quisenberry and catching a runner on the nod at second. . . . Fantastic speed and accuracy, no reason at all, but Andrew went crazy with joy and I had to subdue him physically and give him a chance to calm down. It was almost dawn. "Where are the telephones?" I asked him. "Where is a Fax machine? We will kill the ones who eat us, and eat the ones we kill!"

We had no choice.

I moved quickly for the door, but he stopped me. "Wait a minute," he said. "We're almost out of whiskey."

He was right. The Old Crow pint was empty except for a few drops down in one corner, and the bars would not open for three hours.

"Don't worry," he said. "I know where there's more. Upstairs in the president's office."

"Wonderful," I said. "We can't run out of whiskey at a time like this. Go get it. We'll need everything we can get our hands on, before this thing is over."

He chuckled and tried to sprint off, but the thing attached to his ankle made him stumble. "Goddamnit!" he screamed. "I'd *kill* to get rid of this thing!"

"Don't *say* that," I snapped. "We are innocent men! We are working within the system . . . and besides, I think I have some good crank outside in the car."

He went upstairs to loot the president's office, and I went down those long marble steps, once again, to where my jeep was parked in front of a fireplug on the street. Hot damn! I thought. This will be a very fast day. . . .

It was still raining. There was no other sound on the street. Only rain in the elm trees and the fast lazy slap of my brand-new white low-cut Chuck Taylor All-Stars on the sidewalk. I felt like a polar bear, and I wanted to hear some music.

The big weird jeep was still there, lurking peacefully under the trees and almost invisible in the mist and the hanging Spanish moss. . . . It was huge, but it had no color. It came from the factory with no paint— only a dull stainless steel finish that soon faded to a filthy shade of yellow and millions of tiny reddish pits all over the hood and the doors and even the Panzer-style undercarriage.

"These holes are *not rust*," the pompous little factory rep assured me. "What you see here is priceless chemical *development* that was applied to this vehicle only after fifty-five years of careful research at our secret Color Color Lab in the Milanese Alps. . . . So you *must* be patient," he warned. "This process takes *time*. It involves the slow liberation of Astro-Bacteria, which is frequently *lethal* to laymen. And which did, in fact, end the life of the tragic genius who first invented it, a man named Squane from Austria."

Well . . . maybe so, I figured. It was ugly and pitted all over with millions of festering poison pits, which boiled and bubbled constantly and infected all those who touched it. . . .

But it was a full-bore Lamborghini hot rod, a monstrous thing that weighed 5,000 pounds with bulletproof glass and twelve cylinders with a top speed of 125 miles an hour and a .50-caliber machine-gun mount behind the driver's seat. . . . One night on the Big Sur Highway I beat a Porsche 928 from the Carmel Bridge to Nepenthe by nine minutes, mainly because I beat her like a cheap hound on the curves. It was a small woman driving the 928 and she went all to pieces when I passed her at 110 on the Bixby Creek Bridge and then squeezed her into the sand dunes. . . .

Why not? It happened to *me* once—in Sacramento, when some Japs in a brute Lamborghini ran me down on The Parkway like I was standing still, then bashed me repeatedly at top speed until I finally lost control. . . . It was one of the ugliest moments of my life and I'll never forget it. Those tattooed swine! I should have had them locked up, but I was helpless.

After that, I got one of my own, for $150,000.

But that is another story, and I was too busy that day to even think about it. Dawn was coming up and it was still raining and I had to be in court at 9 o'clock and, ye gods, I still had this freak to deal with— this gutless zombie with a beeper on his leg who obviously needed help, and somehow I was it.

How had it happened? I slid into the Lambo and locked the heavy armored door behind me. . . . What dangerous craziness had plunged me into this situation? All I'd wanted to do was hang out in the library for a while and read some Law.

But somehow I wound up with Andrew on my hands. They had railroaded him into jail for five years, and now I was his only hope. One way or another, I had to get him into a courtroom situation where he'd be able to confront The System on its own mean terms. Put him on the Attack, instead of always on his knees. . . . Right. And we needed to get that goddamn beeping manacle off his leg.

Indeed. But first things first. Calm down, cool beer, and relax with elegant music . . . and yes, ah ha, the *Crank*. Andrew was looking a bit limp, and we would both need special energy for the ordeal I knew was coming. . . . Once I broke him out of jail, as it were, I would be responsible for him until my lawyers took over. They were good, and I felt sure they could get him a new trial. Never mind this *jail* bullshit. He was innocent. He never had a chance. . . . But no more. The worm had turned. My man Andrew was about to know what if felt like to go into court like a warrior and beat the swine to death with their own rules.

I felt good about this, very calm and focused as I buried my face in a silver bowl of pure speed and snorted until my whole head went numb and my eyeballs seemed to be fusing together. . . . I punched the music up to 600 watts and felt the jeep shudder nicely as Lyle Lovett came on. . . . Thank god this thing is soundproof, I thought, or we might have a serious police problem.

Which is something I like to avoid. But it is getting harder and harder. These are bad times for people who like to sit outside the library at dawn on a rainy morning and get ripped to the tits on crank and powerful music.

As I walked back to the library I remembered Bobby Kennedy's words: "The only thing necessary for the triumph of evil is for good men to do nothing."

But not *me*, Jack. Whatever I was doing that morning, it was sure as hell not "nothing." I was about to pluck an innocent victim from the jaws of The System. . . . Hell yes! I thought. Thomas Jefferson would be proud of me today, and so would Bobby Kennedy. . . .

The crank was taking hold, which caused me to think rapidly in odd mathematical terms and suddenly understand that Thomas Jefferson had been dead only 142 years longer than Bobby Kennedy which is not a long time in places like Egypt and Cambodia and approximately the same, in fact, as the life expectancy of the average American woman by the year 2015.

I was brooding on these things as I bounded up the long gray steps and found Andrew fretting nervously on his slab in the Main Floor Executive Men's Room. He had some rumpled-looking Xerox pages out in front of him, but he quickly gathered them up as I entered.

"Where the fuck have you been?" he snarled. "I'm about to go crazy! They expect me back at the jail in twenty minutes. I'm doomed." He eyed me sullenly and lifted a quart bottle of Southern Comfort to his lips, sucking it down his throat so fast that his eyes rolled back in his head and I thought he was passing out.

"You bastard!" I yelled. "Give me that goddamn bottle! I want you on your toes when we go to court. You're about to face a life or death situation!"

"Screw you," he said. "You're crazy as a goddamn loon. I should have had you arrested the minute I saw you."

I gave him a quick Pre-Frontal Lift and bounced him off the mirror, then I seized the whiskey bottle from his hand as he slumped to the floor. . . . "Get a grip on yourself, Andrew," I said.

I gave him a rolled-up hundred-dollar bill and watched him snort almost half of our whole stash into his head like a bullet. He choked desperately for a few seconds, then leaped to his feet and fixed me with a wrong and unnatural grin. I could see that he was going sideways. "You fool," I said. "You took too much."

"Fool?" he screeched. *"Nobody* calls me a *fool."* He laughed distractedly and lurched at me, but I shoved him away.

"Calm down," I said. "We have serious business to do."

"Business?" he shouted. "What kind of *business?"* He lunged at me again, but I could see that he was going into spasms. "You *business* bastard!" he jabbered. "I know what kind of *business* you're in! *Yeah!* Take care of business, Mister *Businessman!"* Then he scrambled up to his wet marble ledge above the urinals again, clinging to a pipe with one hand and fumbling in his pocket with the other.

"Be careful!" I said. "We'll *both* be fucked if you fall down and split your goddamn skull before we get to court."

He stared at me for about twenty seconds, saying nothing. Then he reached down, demanding the whiskey, and unfolded the wad of Xerox pages that he'd been reading so intensely when I came back from my run to the Jeep.

"What court?" he yelled. "What are *you*—the *judge?"*

Ye gods, I thought. What now? This poor fool had been in jail for so long that he can't handle the crank and the whiskey and freedom all at once.

"Who *are* you?" he screamed. "What do you do for a *living?"*

"Never mind that," I said. "Right now I'm your *skyhook*—so come off that goddamn ledge and let's get some of this stuff on paper. We don't have much time."

"Paper?" he screeched. "What are you—some kind of *writer?"* He laughed harshly. "You want *paper*, shiteyes? I'll give you some goddamn paper." *Yeah!* I'll give you *writing*, you asshole! If you think you're a goddamn writer, get ready to drop to your knees."

Then he lifted the crumpled pages up to his eyes and started to read, but I cut him off.

"What *is* that stuff?" I asked. "Give it to me."

He smiled disdainfully and jerked the papers out of my grasp. *"Stuff?"* he said. "You call this *stuff?"*

"Okay," I said. "What is it?"

He hesitated, then smiled happily. "This is my *writing!"* he said. "This is *my* stuff! This is probably the best *stuff* ever written in English! And it's *mine!* I wrote it when I was in jail—like Ernest Hemingway."

"Ernest was never in jail," I said. "At least not like you. He never swept floors in a library at night with a beeper strapped to his ankle." It was cruel, but I felt the time had come to rein him in, to flog him back to reality. But he was getting hysterical, so I let him read on.

"Stand back!" he yelled. "I am the most amazing writer in the world! I wrote this one night in the jail *library*, when nobody else was watching!"

"Wonderful," I said. *"Read* your crazy shit."

He hurled the whiskey bottle at me, but it missed and went into the stalls, where it exploded against a wall and left glass all over the floor. . . . Jesus, I thought. This place will be a bitch to clean up in the morning—or even explain. Well, I guess I can't rightly explain this mess. Don't ask *me* how it happened. I swear. This place is normally so *clean* this time of the morning. . . . We have convicts at night, you know. They clean the whole library, spic and span. But good God almighty. It's so ugly and horrible now that I can't stand to even see it!

Andrew ignored the explosion and began reading his work, in a loud and menacing voice. He had obviously done this more than once, probably in solitary confinement. . . . I listened curiously as he launched into the thing and started to get wound up. It was something about electric storms and Benjamin Franklin. But I was not really listening. My mind was on *court*.

Meanwhile Andrew raved on, rolling his eerie phrases like a man gone wild in a trance, and I began to pay more attention. . . . Jesus! I thought. This is pretty good stuff. I recognized a certain *rhythm*, a weird *meter* of some kind that reached me even if I wasn't listening. . . . It was strange. I had a feeling that I knew it all from somewhere, but I couldn't quite place it. . . .

Soon I felt a queer humming all over my body, like falling into music, and for a long minute or two I actually *liked* Andrew again. He definitely had a feel for words, almost like an idiot-savant. By the time he was halfway through I was ready to give him money.

I was listening carefully now. He called his screed "Electricity" and this is how it went:

ELECTRICITY

They laughed at Thomas Edison.

IT HAS BEEN RAINING *a lot recently. Quick thunderstorms and flash floods . . . lightning at night and fear in the afternoon. People are worried about electricity.*

Nobody feels safe. Fires burst out on dry hillsides, raging out of control, while dope fiends dance in the rancid smoke and animals gnaw each other. Foreigners are everywhere, carrying pistols and bags of money. There are rumors about murder and treachery and women with no pulse. Crime is rampant and even children are losing their will to live.

The phones go dead and power lines collapse, whole families plunged into darkness with no warning at all. People who used to be in charge walk around wall-eyed, with their hair standing straight up on end, looking like they work for Don King, and babbling distractedly about their hearts humming like stun guns and trying to leap out of their bodies like animals trapped in bags.

People get very conscious of electricity when it goes sideways and starts to act erratic . . . eerie blackouts, hissing, and strange shocks from the toilet bowl, terrifying power surges that make light bulbs explode and fry computer circuits that are not even plugged in. . . . The air crackles around your head and you take a jolt every time you touch yourself. Your lawyer burns all the hair off his body when he picks up the cordless phone to dial 911.

Nobody can handle electricity gone amok. It is too powerful. . . . Ben Franklin was never able to lock a door again after the day lightning came down his kite string and fused that key to his thumb. They called it a great discovery and they called him a great scientist; but, in fact, he bawled like a baby for the rest of his life every time he smelled rain in the air.

I find myself jerking instinctively into the classic self-defense stance of a professional wire wizard every time I hear rain on the roof. That is an atavistic tic that I picked up many years ago in my all-night advanced intelligence electronics class at Scott AFB, on the outskirts of east St. Louis—where I also learned about pawnshops, oscillators, and full-bore lying as a natural way of life.

The stance was the first thing we learned, and we learned it again every day for a long, crazy year. It is as basic to working with serious electricity as holding your breath is to working underwater. . . .

Lock one hand behind your back before you touch anything full of dissatisfied voltage—even a failed light bulb—because you will almost certainly die soon if you don't.

Electricity is neutral. It doesn't want to kill you, but it will if you give it a chance. Electricity wants to go home, and to find a quick way to get there—and it will.

Electricity is always homesick. It is lonely. But it is also lazy. It is like a hillbilly with a shotgun and a jug of whiskey gone mad for revenge on some enemy—a fatal attraction, for sure—but he won't go much out of his way to chase the bugger down if ambush looks a lot easier.

Why prowl around and make a spectacle of yourself when you can lay in wait under some darkened bridge and swill whiskey like a troll full of hate until your victim appears—drunk and careless and right on schedule—so close that you almost feel embarrassed about pulling the trigger.

That is how electricity likes to work. It has no feelings except lone-liness, laziness, and a hatred of anything that acts like resis-tance . . . like a wharf rat with its back to the wall—it won't fight unless it has to, but then it will fight to the death.

Electricity is the same way: it will kill anything that gets in its way once it thinks it sees a way to get home quick. . . .

Zaaappp!

Right straight up your finger and through your heart and your chest cavity and down the other side.

Anything that gives it an escape route. Anything—iron, wire, water, flesh, ganglia—that will take it where it must go, with the efficiency of gravity or the imperative of salmon swimming upriver. . . . And it wants the shortest route—which is not around a corner and through a muscle mass in the middle of your back, but it will go that way if it has to.

Some people had to have their loose hand strapped behind them in a hammerlock with rubber cords, just to keep their hearts from ex-ploding and their neck nerves from being fried like long blond hairs in a meat fire when the voltage went through. But sooner or later they learned. We all did, one way or another.

One night—perhaps out of boredom or some restless angst about the fate of Caryl Chessman or maybe Christine Keeler—I connected a 50,000-volt RF transformer to one end of the thin aluminum strap on the Formica workbench that ran around three sides of the big classroom; and then I grounded the strap to a deep-set screw in a wall socket.

Severe shocks resulted when the generator jumped its limiter and began cranking out massive jolts and surges of RF voltage. A 50,000-volt shock ran through my stomach, just below my navel, burning a long, thin hole that I can still pull a string of dental floss through on wet nights.

It was horrible, and still is, but it was also a massive breakthrough; and I will never forget the warped joy I felt when the first surge of electricity went through them. They squawked at each other and flapped their arms like chickens. . . .

My own pain was nothing compared to the elation of knowing that I had just made an unspeakably powerful new friend—an invisible weapon that could turn warriors and wizards into newts, and cause them to weep.

Washington, D.C., 1989

About halfway through I suddenly came out of my coma and started feeling so weak and crazy and maybe drunk with terrible speed hallucinations that I had to lean against the wall. . . . It was too horrible to understand all at once.

That dirty, evil, thieving little bastard! That treacherous rotten little *sot!* I was stunned by the flat-out criminal insanity of it. . . . Jesus, I thought. We don't get many moments like this in life. It was an original experience.

Incredible. No wonder I had a feeling all along that I'd heard or maybe seen Andrew's proud gibberish somewhere before. It was *mine*. I had *written it*, word for word, for one of my long-ago *Examiner* columns that I thought got killed at the last moment, before it went to press and out on the syndicate wire. . . .

Well . . . shit happens. Once a thing gets loose on the wire it can turn up almost anywhere. Even in the hands of some filthy little pervert like Andrew—who had his own warped reasons for plagiarizing it all by himself in the jail library at night.

But he was clearly sick and dangerous. He was a liar and a thief and a rapist who was probably incurable. . . . In some states they have Castration Programs for foul balls like this: Chop out the hormones, turn them into eunuchs with fat little hands and glistening eyes and wispy hair on their necks who don't mind admitting they're wrong.

My brain felt crazy, but my body was stone rigid. I felt like I'd just been shot in the nuts from behind, then went into shock, or at least a state of No Pain, but I hung on and stared straight back at his dirty, poisonous, treacherous, ugly little eyes.

They were small and rheumy with drink and cheap speed. Or maybe crack and PCP. . . . God only knows. You can get anything you want in prison these days, and he was in truth a Dope Fiend and a shameless thieving whore with a bad whiskey jones and the morals of a slut on acid.

Fuck you, Andrew, I said to myself. You're *doomed*. You are a rotten lying degenerate and if there is any real justice in this world you will stay in a filthy backwater prison for the rest of your goddamn life and rats will gnaw through your skull. . . .

I stared at him, but he was grinning like a newborn sheep. His mind was somewhere else. Lost and gone, like some kind of Pod with no pulse. . . . He was ugly and *wrong*. Deeply wrong, and now I knew what had to be done. The truthless little swine had left me no choice. He was evil. . . .

"Not bad, Andrew," I said finally. "Not bad at all. Who wrote that stuff?"

"Me," he said cheerfully. "*I* wrote it."

I shrugged and stood up, then I snorted the rest of the crank and took him by the arm. "Let's go, Andrew," I said. "It's time to go to court."

He followed me out of the library and down to the street. It was still raining. When we got to the jeep I gave him a chamois to bite on while I seared the hardened steel strap off his leg with electric bolt cutters and then sent him back out on the street and told him to hurl the whole beeping evil contraption through the only window in the library that was still lit up—the Executive Men's Room, where we'd spent most of this hideous night.

Seconds later I heard the crash, and then he came loping out of the darkness with a waterhead grin on his face. "Good work, Andrew," I said. "That was a very shrewd move. Now they'll think you're still somewhere *in the library*. They'll be looking for you all day."

He giggled and slapped his thighs. "Fuck those pigs!" he said. "Their brains are *pitiful!* They'll never look for me in *court*, will they?"

I smiled but said nothing. There was no need for it. The die was cast. The fat was in the fire. This giddy little rapist was about to have his day in court.

It was early and we still had an hour to kill, so I drove around for a while and listened to Bob Dylan songs while I took the big Lambo through Cherokee Park at speeds that caused Andrew to lose his grip again. He wept and jabbered and cursed me as I aimed the huge tank of a jeep down narrow roads full of S-curves at 100 miles an hour without ever touching the brakes.

Then I drove downtown on River Road and hit what looked like the entrance to the old Jeffersonville Bridge at a hundred and fourteen or fifteen. . . . But the bridge had been changed somehow, or maybe demolished, and we almost went into the river. When we finally got jammed in a maze of bent steel and old wooden girders, I looked down and saw that we were just over the spot where my old friend Muhammed Ali had stood when he came back to Louisville after winning the 1960 Olympics and threw his Gold Medal into the Ohio River just after accepting the Key to The City from the mayor, my friend Harvey Sloan, and who still denies it ever happened.

"All history is gossip," said Clare Booth Luce.

"Judge Marshall has made his decision," said Andrew Jackson. "Now let him enforce it."

Right, and so much for all that. I backed off the bridge and drove slowly over to Courthouse Square, where the lawyers were gathering for breakfast. . . . My own people were not there yet, so we ordered some poached eggs and fatback and then I grabbed a well-dressed lawyer out in the parking lot and shook him down for some speed, which I snorted at once in a doorway just across from the old county jail.

Andrew was useless, but I ignored him. It was almost nine and business was picking up at the metal detector gates leading into the courtroom. "Let's go," I said. "It's time."

On the way to the security checkpoint I handed him a baggie full of crank and a steel Knife'n'Knuckles tool that I knew would be seized at Security. "Here," I said. "Take these things and I'll meet you inside. I have to go through the Press gate, where the cops do a full body search on *everybody*. . . . Yes. So you take this stuff and go through the Visitors' gate. They don't search anybody down there. Just stroll right through and my lawyers will be there to meet you with all the papers."

"Hot damn," he said. "We'll bust these pigs wide open. I can hardly wait to get up there on the stand and tell the *real* story about what they did to me."

"Don't worry, Andrew," I said. "There is damn little Justice in this world, but you're about to get your share of it."

"Yeah," he muttered. "It's about goddamn time."

I nodded. He was still about 88 percent drunk and he was still wearing his blue *JeffCo Jail* coveralls. The crank had worn off a long time ago, and now he was getting sloppy. There was a stupid kind of

White Trash arrogance in his manner, and his eyes were like two little holes poked into his skull with a cheap screwdriver. . . . I was beginning to hate the sight of Andrew. He was dumb and ugly and loud; a bonehead rapist with a big mouth and a mean spirit. So I busted him. It was easy. . . .

As we approached the courtroom I could see that my old friend Rodman, the bailiff, was in charge of Security at the Press/Media gate. Wonderful, I thought. We are about to witness an outburst of brainless violence. . . . Rodman once played fullback for Male High when they won the State Championship three years in a row, but in recent years he had fallen on hard times and now he worked mornings for the court and sold drugs to lawyers in the alleys around Courthouse Square at night. He was a huge brute with no sense of humor and no morals at all. He appeared to be asleep as I checked myself through the metal detector and whacked him on the side of his head with a rolled newspaper. . . . "Wake up Rodman," I said. "Your time has finally come!"

"O, God," he moaned. "What now?"

"Good news," I said. "You're about to make a huge arrest. Is your gun loaded?"

"You bet," he said. "I'm hungry to kill somebody. I need money."

"Never mind money," I said. "You'll be a hero and get *promoted*. Or killed. There *will* be shooting."

"O, Jesus," he hissed. "What's happening?"

"Big news," I said. "A vicious armed rapist just escaped from the county jail and he's trying to get into your courtroom to blow the judge's head off."

"God almighty!" he said. "Where is the bastard?"

"Right over there," I whispered, pointing to Andrew as he stood nervously in line at the Spectators' gate, where a crippled teenage bailiff called "Missy" was aggressively searching everybody who came through the gate, unaware that she was about to confront an armed psychotic rapist with nothing to lose.

Rodman took one look at the situation and leaped into action. He drew his gun and raced across the hall like a fullback and hit Andrew from behind, just as the stupid little pervert slithered into the gate and set off every bomb-detector siren in the courthouse. . . .

Andrew never had a chance. Rodman got him in a death-grip Full Nelson while the teenage bailiff kicked him repeatedly in the groin until he finally sank to his knees and screamed desperately for help as Rodman pistol-whipped him from behind, then dragged him to his feet just as I got there and hooked Andrew twice in the groin before he even saw who I was. So I hit him again. before Rodman could put him in manacles. . . . Other courthouse bystanders joined in—stomping and whooping as they swarmed over him. He was like a rubber chicken, kicking and jerking and screaming as I moved closer and closer to the Beating Area and tried to catch his eye, but it was impossible. They were swollen shut, and I had a feeling he didn't want to talk to me anyway, if only because he was bitter.

On my way out of the courthouse I stopped by his cell and had to push my way through the crowd, so I could speak with him personally. . . .

"You'll have plenty of time to write your *stuff* now," I said quietly. "You'll be in jail for the rest of your life."

He stared through the bars at me, but his eyes were like split grapes and his shoulders were so slumped that they almost *touched* in the shadows under his chin. He was ruined, he was finished. . . . He was doomed.

I wanted to kill him. And I knew I could, but it would be wrong. . . . Indeed. I was tired of murder, and tired of scum like him. How many times can a zombie rapist like Andrew be allowed to work his foul will with impunity, before we *know* he has to be murdered?

But not by me. I was weary. I was lonely. And I was weak in a different way, this time. I had lost my tolerance, especially for poison lizards like Andrew.

On my way out, I paused long enough to give him a quick beating on both sides of his ugly truthless head. . . .

And then I left, with no noise, and walked back to the hotel in the rain. It was midnight, and I was running late on my deadline for the column, which I finally composed on a voice-writer in a frenzy of hate, disillusion, and fear:

LAST TRAIN FROM CAMELOT

OCTOBER IS THE cruelest month of any election year, but by then the pain is so great that even the strong are like jelly and time has lost all meaning for anybody still involved in a political campaign. By that time, even candidates running unopposed have abandoned all hope of victory and live only for the day when they will finally be free to seek vengeance on all those treacherous bastards who once passed themselves off as loyal friends and allies and swore they were only in it because they all shared the same hopes and dreams. . . .

October in the politics business is like drowning in scum or trying to hang on through the final hour of a bastinado punishment. . . . The flesh is dying and the heart is full of hate: the winners are subpoenaed by divorce lawyers and the losers hole up in cheap motel rooms on the outskirts of town with a briefcase full of hypodermic needles and the certain knowledge that the next time their names get in the newspapers will be when they are found dead and naked in a puddle of blood in the trunk of some filthy stolen car in an abandoned parking lot.

Others are not so lucky and are doomed, like Harold Stassen, to wallow for the rest of their lives in the backwaters of local politics, cheap crooks, and relentless humiliating failures. By the time Halloween rolls around, most campaigns are bogged down in despair and paralyzed by a frantic mix of greed and desperation that comes with knowing that everything you have done or thought or worked for or believed in for the past two years was wrong and stupid.

There are never enough seats on the last train out of the station. . . .

MEMO FROM SKINNER

Doc, don't call me anymore. I quit. Politics is a disease for dirty little animals. We were wrong from the start. . . .

I had a dream last night. It scared me worse than anything that ever happened to me. It was so horrible and so real that I woke up screaming and burned all that skin off the back of my hand, but I was so crazy I never even noticed it. I didn't even feel it when that bitch bit me in the face.

Hell, that was nothing. This time I saw the devil and it scared the s--- out of me. He tried to get his hands on my throat but I kept stabbing him.

And then I saw all those people running out of the White House and screaming about murder. I thought they had killed Bush, but it turned out that Bush had murdered Quayle. Shot him with a Luger.

The night cook said she had heard them screaming and fighting all night and drunk on whiskey in the Lincoln Room. It was nothing new, but this time George started slapping him around a little bit. He said Quayle was stealing from him. He just stepped back and shot him nine times in the stomach and then gouged out one of his eyes while he was dying.

DEATH TO THE WEIRD

November has finally come and the Fat Lady is about to sing for a lot of people who will call it a hateful noise, even though they always swore they loved music. The campaign is over unless somebody gets assassinated, and even that probably wouldn't make much difference unless it was Jesse Jackson. . . . No riots would erupt if any of the others were croaked. You can't miss what you never had.

> *"The dog sucked his brains out,"*
> *the girl replied. "He's dead."*

San Francisco, 1988

NOTE FROM RALPH STEADMAN

Hunter S. Thompson does not suffer fools gladly. In fact, I have reason to believe that I am the only fool he has indulged like a twin in all his life, but that is a long and other story. All kings need their fool. King Lear's fool was his wisdom and finally his vision. Hunter has both in full measure and needs neither fool nor pretender to forge his destiny and maybe ours.

Nevertheless, as the fool, I am determined to make my presence felt if only on the tattered endpapers of his third cumbersome volume of scrofulous prose and put the record straight. It was *I* who darkly saw what he needed to know in Kentucky and it was *I* who raged against the coming of the light in Miami and at the Watergate hearings. It was *I* who knew for certain that America was sick at heart and it was *I* who discovered the dark legend of Hawaii through Robert Hough's book of Captain Cook's voyage and realized that Hunter may be the reincarnation of LONO—the God returned after 1500 years of wandering like a lovesick child to save his people—and his beloved American Constitution. Make no mistake about that, for he is your saviour and he is guardian of all you profess to hold dear. In his weirdness he illuminates the faults in your reason and etches the silhouettes of your antics against a pure white background like Balinese shadow puppets.

For better or worse he sees inside the blackness of those silhouettes searching for the soul of a nation, united only in its desire to seek individuality in a melting pot. It is a privilege to have him in my life.

Ralph Steadman, 20th July 1990

Most of the big shore places were closed now and there were hardly any lights except the shadowy, moving glow of a ferryboat across the Sound. And as the moon rose higher the inessential houses began to melt away until gradually I became aware of the old island here that flowered once for Dutch sailors' eyes—a fresh, green breast of the new world. Its vanished trees, the trees that had made way for Gatsby's house, had once pandered in whispers to the last and greatest of all human dreams; for a transitory enchanted moment man must have held his breath in the presence of this continent, compelled into an aesthetic contemplation he neither understood nor desired, face to face for the last time in history with something commensurate to his capacity for wonder.

—F. Scott Fitzgerald, *The Great Gatsby*

The
FIFTIES

LAST RUMBLE IN FAT CITY

TARRED AND FEATHERED AT
THE JERSEY SHORE

WHEN I GOT OUT of the Air Force I got a job in Jersey Shore, Pennsylvania, which for some queer reason as an innocent child I believed was on the Jersey shore somewhere. It turned out to be like 400 miles into the mountains and down the road from Penn State. It was an abandoned coal town. The paper was just one of those stupid dailies with big white margins around it, tiny type, no pictures. I had to join the goddamn Elks Club in order to get a drink there on weekends.

I was the sports editor. I had an apartment way out, big gray place, naked bulbs. It was a nightmare, really. I was tolerated, but it was clear that I was weird. It was a given. And I didn't like the publisher who also acted as the editor. He was an asshole. Cheap bastard.

I was a good editor. I did wire copy, wrote headlines, and laid out the paper. I was more concerned with the layout than the writing. I was a layout freak for a long time. That's how I got into taking pictures. I got so dissatisfied with the photographs I was getting—this was in the Air Force—that I began to take them myself. I began to see photographs not for what they portrayed but for how they fit on the page. You know, if I needed a long, thin, dark photograph to balance a four-column, like a banner photo of a football game, of people running, a panoramic thing, I would get what I wanted. One long shot of a guy catching a pass in the end zone. I may have had this one section in my mind even before the game was played and for that picture I needed a picture of a guy reaching very high and just one person so I ended up having to take the pictures myself just so they would fit into my idea of how the sports section should look. I did that in Pennsylvania too.

It was an afternoon paper so I had to be there at seven in the

37

morning. I was finished by two and then what did I have to do? Hang out in the Elks Club. Shoot pool. Afternoons were a hard time in Jersey Shore.

There was one guy that I got along with. He was an academic, kind of an unemployable poet who might lecture once or twice at the local community college. He worked on the paper, writing features. He became my only human contact. He was the best person to talk to in town.

He had a nice farm outside of town. And he had a daughter who worked in Chicago for the Encyclopaedia Britannica. Very pretty, dark-haired girl who had just gotten out of either Northwestern or the University of Chicago. He wanted me to meet her because nobody else in this barren town was between the ages of fifteen and fifty. It was clearly a match of the ages. It was mandatory for him to do this. He thought it was the best thing he had done for both me and his daughter. She was barely off the train when I went to have dinner at. the ranch.

She was a very pretty girl, and on the second night, it may have been the first night, in any case, he and I switched cars for some reason. It was raining, actually, that's why we switched cars. Because his car was better in mud, I guess. On the roads in the rain. I was driving a '49 Chevy myself, which was a little bit shaky. He had no idea what I was going to do. I didn't either. I ended up in the car with his daughter, driving around in a horrible monsoon.

Well, I hadn't seen a human being in about five weeks, didn't have anybody to talk to. I was very pleased, like some guy who'd been given a great present, until I drove the car into the river.

Actually, I didn't drive it in but I got myself stuck on the riverbank, and somehow tried to turn around and the front end slid into the water. It was about two-thirty in the morning and I had to wake up a farmer in the driving, horrible torrential rains. I had to walk about three miles to the nearest house and beat the hell out of it, get some old Dutch farmer up. He was really angry and I don't know how the hell I managed to get him to do it. He didn't know me. He didn't know what I was doing in this weird bog down by the river this early in the morning. He had to put on his rain clothes, get his tractor, and come down there and pull the car out.

I was behind the wheel as he hooked onto the back and started to pull the car back up toward the road. The bastard was in a rage and he was pulling it out as quick as he could. You know how you open the door and look back, you have your one hand on the wheel and *you're looking as you're backing up? The door caught on a log and ripped the door off the side of the car. It was hanging by one hinge so we got it back up on the road but it wasn't quite on the road so he went around to the front, hooked onto the bumper and tore the bumper off. But it too was still hanging.*

So here's the car a mangled wreck full of mud, the front end full of water, but it still runs. I took her and it back to this guy's house and got my own car and went back to this grubby, soot-filled apartment that they'd gotten for me.

I went to work the next day. I had to get there very early, like seven o'clock, to do all the overnight wire stuff for the afternoon paper. At about seven-thirty I was sitting there casually going through the wire copy, the previous day's basketball scores, putting the sports page together for the day and I heard this horrible noise outside in the street from far off. I began to hear this grinding as metal was rending and grinding on concrete. It sounded like someone driving a railroad car down the street set over on its side—like some kind of a G-9 Cat was pulling a piece of junk along the main street of town.

Everybody heard the noise. People got up and said, what the hell is that? So I got up to look out just in time to see the feature writer whose car I'd driven into the river the night before drive into sight with his bumper grinding and sending up sparks, with his torn door off and dragging. He was bringing his car in to show the people what I had done. He could have tied it up, I guess, made less noise, but he wanted to present the spectacle to the editor and publisher and make me pay for it. Ah, it was such a horrible sight. And so was he.

The parking lot for the paper was behind the building so he had to turn in past the front of the building, go around the side, park in back, and come in the back door. I could see his face as he drove past. He was beet-red and I knew heavy trouble was coming so while all the rest of them went around to the back door to see what in the hell had happened to his car, what was wrong with it, I just got up, took my coat off the rack and went out the front door. Didn't even collect my pay. Went straight to the apartment, loaded the car and drove to New York like a bastard.

I'd never been there, never even seen it. I remember being stunned at the New York skyline as I drove over this big freeway, coming across the flats in Secaucus. All of a sudden it was looming up in front of me and I almost lost control of the car. I thought it was a vision.

Woody Creek, March 1990

SATURDAY NIGHT AT THE RIVIERA

IT WAS LIME, the stuff you mix in with concrete.

It was down there beside the furnace. I don't know why, I just picked up this bag of lime, put it on my shoulder, the fifty-pound bag. Through the narrow hall out of the basement, up the winding stairs to the sidewalk on Perry Street.

I was with McGarr, and we both had dates. We walked down toward the Riviera and I noticed that the bag was leaking. It wasn't real bad but it was getting faster.

It was Saturday night, and the Riviera on Saturday night was then and still is jammed. It's a focal point for weekenders from the Bronx and New Jersey, Columbia law students, whatever. It's a triangular-shaped place with a door, like a hundred feet wide in the back and four feet wide at the front door. That's all it is. They have a swinging door. We were walking on the other side of the street. There's a cigar store that's still there. . . .

Anyway, these girls worked for Time magazine. They were friends. We were going over to hear Bob Dylan or something like that. There wasn't anything strange about the situation except that meanwhile this thing is leaking. McGarr says, "What's that in that fucking bag? What are you carrying that bag for?" And I didn't know. I had no reason.

Then—and I don't know what the hell possessed me to do this—I said to McGarr, "Well all right, let's go over and have a beer." We were just walking along and there had been no intention of going to the Riviera. We never went to the Riviera on Saturday night.

And he said, "Are you crazy? What do you mean go and have a beer?" And the girls are saying "No, we can't go in there, it's a mob scene." I insisted and McGarr kind of caught on somehow, as people will. He didn't say anything. At that point I took my watch off and handed it to my date.

And we went in there to have a beer. They wouldn't come with us. They waited in the coffee shop across the street or something.

And there was no end to the people, wall-to-wall people, and I still have this fucking leaking bag. And it's getting worse. You want to *keep in mind, it was in the back, behind me, where it was leaking. As we jostled our way through the bar, the people in there—the sporting crowd, dressed to the nines, Fordham people, like that—they noticed right away. We were three feet inside, maybe six, when people were starting to bitch about it: "Hey! Now, what the shit?? This white shit all over me? Look at this! Get the hell out of here . . . what are you doing?"*

The bar was in front of me . . . and we were still trying to buy a beer. We had to really slide through a crowd, like you get at pari-mutuel windows. And the anger, the muttering behind me growing louder. The place was real long, maybe a hundred and fifty feet long, the bar along one side, the stairs, the main dining room, the music stage back in back. The bar was almost all the way to the front so we had to go only about fifteen feet, maybe twenty. But to find a place at the bar was hard.

As these people behind me were bitching, the bartender noticed there was some kind of problem, and McGarr began slamming a glass on the bar. "Goddamnit, we want a beer." I don't think we ever got one. I think I got a half-empty one that I grabbed and drank, reaching over. The sack was making a horrible mess, it was really going.

And the bartender and the manager were there, and suddenly a great roaring and mumbling began: "FUCK YOU GET OUT OF HERE YOU BASTARDS." Yeah, I remember, a great protest: "FUCK THIS IT'S ALL OVER ME! JESUS WHAT IS THAT SHIT . . . LYE!" They thought it was lye. Hell, I thought it might be lye. Lime, lye, I don't know. Sure. "IT'S FUCKING LYE! IT'S COR-ROSIVE!"

What was I going to do, could I drop it? We were being pushed out and people were starting to swing, and McGarr took a few shots, and I was going backwards toward the door. There were fights going on, bartenders, managers, punches were being thrown, I was hit once or twice, but I still held on to the bag.

When we got to the door I realized this was going to be an igno-minious departure with that whole crowd, I mean that angry crowd of a hundred people fighting—a hundred people wanted to hurt me right then. We were being gotten rid of.

Just as I got to the door I grabbed the bag by those tits where they tie the corners and leaped back there and swung the fucker straight out. I think maybe I was swinging at somebody who had hit me. It burst on the way around. At the end of the swing it just busted loose, emptied in my hands—the rest of the fifty pounds—and they went completely nuts. *The whole place turned white. Turned utterly white.*

The girls who were across the street in the coffee shop said it was the zaniest thing they had ever seen. The doors of the Riviera blew open like this very suddenly and for an instant there we were, backs first, and an eruption of white smoke and people running around inside and people going blind way back inside, way back, like a five-minute walk to the door. It was panic, utter panic.

They beat the shit out of us on the street. The bartender, the patrons, screaming, "LYE! WHY THE FUCK DID YOU . . . YOU DIRTY BASTARD!" Oh, they beat the shit out of me. It was worse than the Hell's Angels. Everybody wanted a piece.

Woody Creek, March 1990

PRINCE JELLYFISH

"Just another lonely country boy grown weary of the night
Just another boy with a sink full of dirty dishes . . ."
—COWBOY JUNKIES, "WHERE ARE YOU TONIGHT"

HIT HIM AGAIN JACK, HE'S CRAZY

"Manhattan . . . is the homeland of the uprooted."
—MALCOLM COWLEY

NEW YEAR'S EVE in Manhattan. A freezing rain blows through the dark streets. Above the city, far up in the mist and rain, long beams of yellow light sweep in great circles through the black air. They are anchored to the Empire State Building—that great phallic symbol, a monument to the proud dream of potency that is the spirit of New

York. And below, in the damp neon labyrinth of the city itself, people hurry: somewhere . . . everywhere . . . nowhere. . . .

Welburn Kemp lay on the couch in his Charles Street apartment, his head propped up on two pillows. He looked at his watch: eight-thirty. Another hour and he could go to the party without feeling uncomfortably early—and obviously alone. In the meantime he drank.

He crossed the room to the tiny kitchen and refilled his glass. On the way back to the couch he paused by the phone and thumbed through a small book full of numbers. He dialed one . . . let it ring several times . . . and hung up in disgust. Goddamn! He thought, I know she doesn't have a date. But he had tried the same number four times already: no answer . . . no answer . . . no answer . . . and no answer. New Year's Eve, and no date.

He felt agonizingly certain that all over the city there were girls without dates: pretty girls, lonely girls, girls who sat by the phone with tears in their eyes, waiting for that last minute call.

But no way to find them. (No way, damnit!) Ah well, get drunk and to hell with it.

It was almost ten when he got up to go. He took what was left of his bourbon, jammed the bottle into his overcoat pocket, and went down the stairs to the street. The rain was just a drizzle now, but it quickly settled in his hair and crept in icy rivulets across his scalp. The bottle in his pocket bounced against his body at every step, and he held it with one hand as he hurried along the street to the subway.

The party was at Harry Kardeman's place on Morningside Drive, over a hundred blocks away. He had met Kardeman in the army, working for the base newspaper at Fort Carson, Colorado. When they got out—only several weeks apart—Kemp had gone to ply his trade in the backwoods of American journalism, and Kardeman had settled down to the intensely quiet life of a Columbia law student. He rarely gave parties, and when he did there was never enough liquor and the people he invited were, in Kemp's opinion, lumps of well-dressed clay. But a party was a party . . . and there would be girls . . . yes . . . girls.

And just then he saw one. He was standing on the curb at Sheridan Square, waiting for the light to change, when he saw her emerge from the subway hole across the street. She was small and a little thin, with a frail, delicate look about her that struck a fatherly chord somewhere deep in his groin. He watched her as she hurried across the street (coming directly at him) and continued to stare when she shifted her gaze slightly and looked him straight in the face. She wore a canvas rainhat, and her eyes looked large and lonely in the shadow beneath the brim. He stood rooted to the spot, unthinking, as she passed by. Then he turned to watch her as she hurried around the corner.

Suddenly it came to him: the girl is alone! All alone on New Year's Eve! She wants me!

He wanted to whirl and follow her, but the rational side of his mind refused to let him move. What if I'm wrong? he thought. I'll make an ass of myself!

But the frustration of looking all day for a date was too much for him. He turned quickly and hurried around the corner after her. She was halfway down the block and he ran to catch up. The bottle bounced wildly in his pocket and he clutched it to his body as he ran.

Fifty feet behind her he stopped running and wondered for a moment what he was going to say. At the corner of Bleecker she stopped for an instant and looked behind her before crossing.

Oh God! he thought. She's going to say something! Panic seized him and his mind groped wildly for words. But no . . . she hurried on . . . and he followed, trying to organize his thoughts as he walked.

He fondled the bottle in his pocket as he planned his approach. "Miss," he would say, tapping her gently on the shoulder, "excuse me, but I couldn't help noticing you were alone."

She would look at him warily, not quite sure of what to say. Girls like this hate to admit they're lonely, he thought, I'll have to be suave and gentle.

"Well I'm alone too," he would say with a frank and disarming smile, "and I'm on my way to a party. I wonder if you'd care to join me."

She would hesitate and he would reassure her: "Nothing wild, of course . . . just a few friends of mine . . . law students at Columbia."

She would smile then, in spite of herself. His calm would overcome her. She would be properly reluctant at first, but a few words of persuasion would be all she needed.

In mulling over his approach he almost ran into her as she turned into a doorway. The near-collision flustered him momentarily, and by the time he recovered his wits she was through the open door and into the hallway. She was opening the door of a ground floor apartment when he stepped into the light of the entranceway. The glare made him squint, and his mind was spinning with excitement as he opened his mouth to speak. He stopped by the door, several feet from her, and smiled as casually as he could.

"Ah . . . good evening," he said.

She looked at him blankly for a moment . . . then turned away and yelled into the apartment: "Jack! Come here quick! There's a guy after me!"

The words echoed in Kemp's mind, but he refused to accept them. No, he thought, no. What's happening here . . . ?

"Pardon me," he said, "but I wonder if . . . ah . . . you see . . . I wonder if you'd like to . . . ah . . ."

His voice failed as he heard something moving inside the apartment. Suddenly a small, muscular man in an olive-drab undershirt burst into the hall, yelling "Where is he? *Who's* after you?" He carried a thick leather belt in his hand, a vicious-looking thing that dangled by his side as he looked at Kemp, standing a few feet away in the entrance.

"Whaddeyou want?" he roared.

Kemp's mind felt numb. He stammered, but it sounded like the gibberish of a fiend.

At the sound of Kemp's voice, the man roared again: "You sonofabitch! Get outta here!"

Kemp still could not move. No, no, he thought. This can't be!

The girl pointed at him: "He's crazy!" she screamed. "He followed me clear from the subway!"

The girl's scream sent the man into action; he snarled wildly and lashed out with the belt. Kemp bolted for the doorway, but the strap caught him across the shoulders as he leaped into the street. *Swaacckkk!*

It nearly knocked him down. His knees went rubbery and he screamed in terror. Over his shoulder he saw the man lash out again. *Swaacckkk!* It caught him on the arm this time, wrapping itself around his elbow. He jerked away, nearly hysterical with fear and confusion, and lurched backward against the building. The man came at him again, still snarling and the girl screamed behind him: "Hit him again, Jack! He's crazy!"

As Kemp turned to run the lash caught him on the back of the head. Pain shot through his body and he uttered a long, high-pitched chattering whine that rattled up the street. He felt himself moving, running with desperate speed toward the corner. He was still unable to comprehend this terror, this insane misunderstanding. No . . . no . . . why . . . ? The man was running after him, screaming hoarsely: "You filthy bastard!" The strap swished through the air behind him, just missing his neck. The bottle was bouncing . . . almost out of his pocket . . . and he gripped it against his stomach . . . running now in a low, awkward hunch and breathing heavily. Screams echoed in the street behind him and he gasped for breath. He ran for two blocks before he realized the man was no longer chasing him.

As he lurched around a corner he spotted a cab half a block away. He shouted: "Cab! *Cab!*" It pulled over to the curb and he sprinted the last twenty yards.

As he fell exhausted into the back seat the driver turned with a curious look. "What's wrong, buddy?" he asked. "You all right?"

"Quick, get going!" Kemp gasped. "They're after me."

"Who's after you?" the driver said quickly. "The cops?"

"No, no!" Kemp said. "A man with a whip! A lunatic . . . quick, hurry on!"

The driver shrugged his shoulders and the cab moved slowly away from the curb. Fearfully, Kemp peered out the rear window, but the street behind them was quiet.

"Where to?" the driver asked.

Kemp relaxed. "Morningside Drive," he said, "corner of a Hundred and Twentieth."

Now moving through traffic, through tunnels of neon sparkling in the rain. Up Eighth Avenue, past Penn Station, the Port Authority Bus Terminal, Madison Square Garden . . . then through the Puerto Rican section: wide streets lined with delicatessens, cheap clothing stores, pawn shops, and miles of dark tenements . . . finally past Columbia, tires bumping on the damp bricks, and now at the corner of Morningside Drive. A dollar-ninety, quarter tip, and into the rain again.

In the lobby Kemp felt his shoulder: no pain, but the back of his head was still sore. Probably used the buckle end, he thought. Jesus, what a god-awful thing!

A tubercular old woman rode up with him in the elevator, hacking and coughing into a withered hand. Kemp tried to hold his breath, but couldn't. He breathed carefully, trying for clean air. When they got to the fifth floor he leaped into the hall and took a deep breath. The old woman continued upward with her flock of germs.

The apartment was full of people he'd never seen. He pushed through the crowd and left his overcoat in one of the bedrooms, then went to the kitchen to mix a drink. Christ, he thought, I *need* a drink! Getting beaten with a leather whip is enough to give a man pause. And for no reason, either . . . just trying to be nice.

Kardeman was in the kitchen, talking with two girls. He shouted happily as Kemp came through the door. "Welburn! About time you got here—where've you been?"

"I was attacked on the street . . . by a man with a whip."

"Oh? Well . . . get yourself a drink, there, and join the party." He hesitated: "Ah . . . say, Kemp . . . don't you have a date?"

"No, sorry."

"Well, keep away from mine," Kardeman said with a smile, "the rest are fair game." He introduced the two standing with him: one was giggling stupidly and the other had no ears. Kemp stared, unable to believe it, but . . . ah yes . . . there they were, flat and tiny against her head.

"Kemp's going to write the great American novel some day," Kardeman told the girls. They nodded appreciatively and Kardeman smiled. He had a faintly chubby face, with small, intelligent eyes and short blond hair. The beer fat was beginning to show at his beltline, giving him that healthy, rounded sort of look that old ladies invariably remark upon: "My, how well you look, Harry." His family lived on Long Island, but he preferred to live in the city while he went to school.

Kemp moved into the living room, nodding here and there to people he knew. The apartment was full of law students: "A flogs B, then pleads regression from tort. In the meantime B dies from another flogging, this time by C . . . what? . . . Ah ha! But Powell says . . ."

Smoke . . . music . . . conversation . . . tweed coats and cordovans . . . girls moving here and there, standing, drinking, laughing, having a good time.

Kemp stood in a corner, feeling self-conscious and too sober. In the dining room was a table full of bottles, none of them empty. Kemp recognized the honor-system setup: you put your bottle on the table and drank from no other. His bottle was almost empty; he eyed the liquor table with a mixture of guilt and greed . . . all that liquor, enough to drive a man straight out of his mind . . . sucking it up like a maddened beast . . . rubbing it all over his body. . . .

Kemp was the only stag. He felt them watching him . . . fearing him . . . keeping their dates close at hand. The fools, he thought. *They know*.

He was joined in his corner by Jay Gold, the law school's answer to James Murray. Gold was immaculate in his new black suit, well-creased and precision-neat as always. His date was drunk, passed out on the coats in the bedroom.

"Flunked two out of five last time," he was saying. "What the hell . . . why worry about these things . . . ?"

They strayed into a group of intense young men discussing the possibility of a nuclear attack. Their dates nodded wisely and stared into their drinks. Someone laughed and someone else joined. The music was louder and Kemp went back for another drink.

His bottle was light—maybe two more drinks—but he filled the glass with bourbon. Back in the living room he spotted Gold talking to a girl he'd seen earlier; a tan, Creole-looking girl, lean and sensuous in a dark blue dress.

Gold eyed him strangely as he approached. "I thought you'd passed out, Kemp."

"No, Gold, I can't really say that I have. Uh . . . What's this I hear about your date being sick?"

"The soaking sweats," Gold replied. "She gets them every New Year's Eve."

The girl looked alarmed: "The soaking sweats?" she asked.

"It's psychosomatic," Gold said, "a result of severe tension . . . usually in the womb."

The girl looked at him with a puzzled smile.

"How is she?" Kemp asked.

Gold laughed. "All right, Kemp," he said. "You've made your point. This is Ann Farabee." Kemp smiled and Gold continued: "Ann, this is Welburn Kemp."

Ann Farabee smiled. Her eyes sparkled, large and brown above high cheekbones.

"You aren't from New Orleans, are you?" Kemp asked.

"No," she said. "Why?"

"Just a wild guess," Kemp said.

"Are you from New Orleans?" she asked.

"No," he said. "Nashville."

Gold turned to go. "Excuse me," he said. "I think I'll check on my date."

Kemp turned to the girl: "Do you have a date?" he asked.

"Of course I do," she said with a short laugh. "Somewhere."

"But you don't have a drink," he protested.

"Oh, I had one," she said, glancing around as if she might find it floating beside her in the air. "It's here somewhere."

"I'll get you one," Kemp said. "Come on."

"Who are you with?" he asked on the way to the kitchen.

"A boy named David Bibb."

"A law student?" Kemp asked.

"Yes," she said. Then she turned to look at him. "Don't you have a date?"

"No," he replied. "I tried to get one, but I was beaten with a whip on my way to pick her up."

"You're kidding!" she exclaimed.

"Not at all," he assured her. "It was terrifying!"

"But where?" she asked. "Who . . . ?"

"Some lunatic," Kemp said. "Jumped out of a doorway half-naked and started beating me with a big strap."

"Great Scott!" she cried. "What did you do?"

"Oh, I handled him," Kemp said modestly. "I know a little judo . . ."

"It's just unbelievable!" she exclaimed.

"Well he won't be beating people for a while," Kemp said quietly. "When I left him he could hardly breathe."

She murmured sympathetically.

Kemp saw himself standing off a whole pack of lunatics with whips, cutting them down like weeds with the back of his hand . . . nimble and quick, silent and deadly. . . . "Attack *me,* will you!" . . . whap! . . . slash! . . . screams of pain . . . now standing above a ring of prostrate bodies, wiping the blood off the back of his hand with a handkerchief.

"You didn't get hurt, did you?" she asked.

He laughed. "I'm fine," he said as he handed her the drink, "just fine."

He felt a twitching in his groin as he watched her turn to put her drink on the table. She was not as tall as she'd looked when he first saw her, but her body was slim and willowy. He could see the faint outline of muscles stretching beneath the flesh on her arm as she lit a cigarette. He thought about offering her a light, but it was too late. She dropped the match in an ashtray on the table, and turned back to find Kemp staring intently at her legs.

He jerked his glance upward and their eyes met. Kemp flushed slightly but said nothing. Her expression was blank, but her eyes seemed (to Kemp) like dark coals of smoldering sensuality. He turned away, unable to meet her gaze any longer. I wonder where her date is, he thought. Maybe he's passed out.

"Who is this Bibb character?" he asked suddenly.

She looked down at the floor. "I barely know him," she said with a shrug of her shoulders. "He's a friend of Harry's."

Kemp nodded. Kardeman's friends are all boobs, he thought. Especially the law students . . . this poor girl is stuck with a boob! On New Year's Eve!

She watched him, obviously amused by the pained expression on his face.

I must have this girl, Kemp decided. I want her . . . this boob has no right to such a girl . . . I must get her out of here.

Suddenly the whole apartment was plunged into blackness. Kemp's first thought was of a nuclear attack. Oh Jesus, he thought, not now! Not just when I've found this girl! There were screams in the living room, followed by shouts and laughter. He realized it was only midnight—no bomb. Midnight! he thought suddenly. Where's that girl? I can't see anything! He reached out wildly and felt his hand thump into a body; there was a cry of pain. "Sorry," he said, "who's that?"

"It's me," said a soft voice, "Ann."

"Good Lord," he said, feeling immensely relieved, "I thought you'd run away."

"Are you all right?" he asked. "Did I hurt you?"

"No . . . I'm all right."

He reached out slowly, tentatively, his heart pounding with excitement. He found her arm, let his hand rest there for a moment, then moved it over to her waist. It rested on her hip now, and he could feel the elastic band of her panties beneath his thumb. He pulled very gently and she swayed against him. With his other hand he reached back to put his drink on the table, and heard the clatter of ice cubes and broken glass behind him as it missed the table and burst on the floor.

He felt her long fingers on the back of his neck, pulling him down. A chill of astonished excitement ran through him as her tongue slid gently into his mouth. He pulled her closer, rubbing his hand slowly up and down her back and feeling his fingers bump along the little ridges of her spine. Their tongues touched, bumped together, and his hand slid below the elastic band and pressed in, toward his body. She gasped softly and he felt her fingers tighten on his neck.

Somewhere in the distance he heard voices. The lights came on and people appeared in the kitchen. Reluctantly, he let her pull away. Now there was a voice behind him, asking for a drink . . . no, talking to Ann. "I've been looking for you," it said. Kemp turned and saw him standing there, looking angry and bewildered. It's the boob, he thought. What now?

He moved toward Ann as if to kiss her, but she jumped away. "No," she said. "It's over."

How ridiculous! Kemp thought happily. The boob stared, apparently stunned by the awful failure of his long-awaited moment of abandon. Then he turned to Kemp: "What do you think you're doing?" he mumbled.

"I was kissing your date," Kemp said calmly. "We thought you'd gone home." Ann smiled, and Kemp felt warm and powerful.

Slowly, the boob grasped the meaning of it all. He started to say something . . . stopped . . . turned a pitiful, hopeless half-grin on Ann . . . and walked quickly out of the kitchen.

"I really shouldn't have done that," she said. "Now he'll hate me."

"You?" Kemp said with a laugh. "I wonder how he feels about me!"

She hesitated for a moment, then looked up at him: "Let's go somewhere," she said. "I feel guilty, staying here."

INTERVIEW

For almost six months Kemp had been angling for a job on one of the metropolitan papers. He'd tried them all, from the slimiest, shabbiest tabloids to the gray and haughty *Times*. He had a vision of himself as a reporter—trench-coated, sabre-tongued, a fearless champion of truth and justice. He saw himself working late at night, lonely and feverish at a desk in the empty newsroom, pounding out stories that would rock the city at dawn.

Since early fall he had worked tirelessly to find a reporter's job: writing long letters, shouting into phones, filling out applications—all to no avail. The magazine job was getting on his nerves. He'd been at it for over a year, turning out an endless stream of senseless, unsigned articles: a new plastics plant in Toledo, gaslights make a comeback in Kansas City, dogskin shopping bags the newest thing in novelties, and finally those soggy plums of free publicity—the dashing, dynamic "man of the week" profiles! He winced each time he read his own copy.

In the past six months he'd suffered through at least five "don't call us, we'll call you" interviews, and after each one he seethed with bewildered anger. What was wrong with the bastards? They were shouting from the rooftops for new blood, weeping and mumbling all over the country about journalism going to the dogs, editors lined up twelve deep at the wailing wall, screeching and begging for young talent . . . and here poor Kemp couldn't even get a job as a cub reporter! Insane, by God!

They were trying to freeze him out, by Jesus! They were afraid of him . . . afraid he would show them up for the incompetent half-wits they were! There was no room in their complacent world for a man who despised mediocrity—who would let nothing stand in the way of truth. The great American press was a babbling joke—an empire built on gossip and cliches—a final resting place for rumor-mongers and pompous boobs.

So, while the nation floundered in a bog of half-truths and erotic pap, and the press wallowed in its own foul nest, Kemp plugged away at *Business Age,* stewing in his own bitterness. Day after day he turned out his quota of tripe, waiting impatiently for that call to the battlements, that urgent summons to a higher duty, that day when he would charge into the fray as the legendary reporters of an earlier and more fortunate generation had done before him.

When it finally came, he was surprised at his own apathy. He felt no excitement, no anticipation—just a mild annoyance at the tardiness of his long-awaited summons. It came from a big morning daily, where his application had been on file for at least three months.

A week after New Year's Eve he got a call from the editor's secretary, asking him to come in on Friday for an interview. "Mr. Turner can see you at three-thirty," the voice said. "Would that be all right?"

His excitement mounted as the elevator ascended to the fourth floor, the city room. The atmosphere was a sharp contrast to the dull efficiency of his own office; the hum of conversation, incessant pounding of typewriters, wire machines clacking with urgent regularity—all this gave an air of tension and importance to the place. Things were happening here; it was a throbbing nerve center, a great clearinghouse for up-to-the-minute history. The atmosphere of subdued excitement settled in his brain, driving out the bitterness and the frustration of earlier rejections. He felt that old anticipation now, that sense of purpose; he was about to join a proud and noble team, a profession dedicated to the cause of truth.

The sign on the door said WILLIAM TURNER, MANAGING EDITOR. The secretary told him to go in.

The office was small and bare: two chairs, a desk, and a typewriter. William Turner looked up from a sheaf of papers on the desk. "Kemp?" he said. "Good to see you. Sit down."

Kemp sat, putting his briefcase on the floor beside the chair.

Turner looked at him with a smile. "Are you still available, Kemp?"

"Sure," Kemp said quickly. "My job is about to drive me crazy."

"What are you doing?" Turner asked.

"I'm a staff writer for *Business Age.*"

"Sounds all right," said Turner. "What's wrong with it?"

"It's a little dull," Kemp said. "I'd like to write something besides tripe for a change."

Turner looked at him blankly for a moment, then picked a piece of paper off the desk. Kemp recognized his application, filled out several months before; there was a small note in someone else's handwriting clipped to the front of it.

"I see you went to Washington and Lee," Turner said. "Where's that?"

"Lexington, Virginia."

"What kind of school is it?" Turner asked.

Why you ignorant swine, Kemp thought. It's a barber college! "Liberal Arts," he said, "one of the best in the South."

"Never heard of it," said Turner. "What did you major in?"

"English."

Turner was staring at the application. He was thin, about forty-five or fifty, Kemp guessed, and not very impressive-looking. He looked up. "You don't have much experience, do you?"

"Three years," Kemp said. "Two dailies and a national magazine."

Turner smiled: "That may sound like a lot to you," he said, "but by guild standards it almost makes you a beginner."

"What do you mean, a beginner?" Kemp exclaimed. "I've been working on newspapers for five years!"

"Five?" said Turner. "You list only three on the application."

"I was sports editor of a paper in the army for two years," Kemp explained. "I forgot to put that down."

"Well it wouldn't count, anyway," Turner said with a grin.

"Why not?" Kemp demanded.

"It just doesn't," Turner said. "Experience is determined by the guild scale . . . service papers don't count at all, weeklies count slightly, and dailies count according to their circulation." He glanced again at Kemp's application. "Yours probably amounts to about two years."

Kemp stared sullenly at the floor.

"Hell, for that matter," Turner continued, "I've never even heard of the Blackmoor, Indiana, *Gazette,* or the Creek, Virginia, *Daily Press.*"

"Well, they exist," Kemp snapped. "I have paycheck stubs to prove it."

"Certainly," Turner said quickly, "of course. What did you do, general reporting?"

"Sportswriting," Kemp said. "Didn't I put that on the application?"

Turner rechecked. "Ah . . . yes," he said thoughtfully. "As a matter of fact, you did."

"I was sports editor of the *Daily Press,*" Kemp said. "I have clippings to prove it."

Turner eyed him warily. "Now don't get upset, Kemp," he said quietly. "I'm not saying these papers don't exist. I've just never heard of them."

Kemp smiled contemptuously.

"You say you have clippings?" Turner asked.

Kemp reached into his briefcase and pulled out a pile of clippings. "I've been meaning to get these into a scrapbook," he said, "but I never seem to have the time."

Turner lifted the top clipping from the stack and read through it. He read two more, scanning them quickly and without comment.

"What kind of a job are you looking for?"

"Reporting," Kemp said. "Something I can sink my teeth into."

"Teeth?"

"Something important," Kemp explained. "I'm tired of writing tripe."

"You mean the . . . larger issues," Turner said with a smile.

"Yeah," said Kemp. "That's right . . . silly things like communism and education and national survival."

Turner continued to smile, drumming his fingers on the desk and staring at the wastebasket.

"What's so funny about that?" Kemp demanded.

"Nothing," Turner said quickly. "Nothing at all. It's just that attitude."

"What attitude?"

"Oh, it's a common thing," Turner assured him. "That old hero pose . . . that idea that you're out to change the world."

Kemp checked a sarcastic reply and remained silent.

"It's an occupational disease with young reporters," Turner said with a grin. "But you're the first case I've run into in a long time. I was beginning to think it was dying out." He grinned broadly now, leaning back in his chair with the pleased expression of a man continually amazed by his own wisdom.

Kemp felt his temper slipping; he leaned forward and spoke impatiently. "What about this job?"

Turner's mirth seemed to fade instantly. "Oh yes," he said, swiveling around in his chair. "Yes, job . . . job." He looked down at the application. "Well, let's see now. . . ."

Kemp lit a cigarette.

Turner spoke slowly, looking Kemp straight in the eye: "You have a good background, Kemp . . . you're young, you write well . . . you're bright . . . I think we can use you."

Kemp brightened.

"You know, this business has changed a lot in the past twenty years,"
Turner said. "It used to be run like a circus." He looked back at
Kemp. "Did you know that?"

Kemp nodded, and Turner went on: "What we've done, you
know . . . we've rooted out most of the irresponsibles." He swiveled
to stare out the window. "Rooted them out!" he said proudly.

"Yeah," Kemp muttered uneasily.

"Damned right!" Turner said, swiveling back to face Kemp.
"Damned right. The main thing, though, the main thing . . . we
bounced the drunks."

Kemp felt a nervous churning in his stomach.

Turner was talking again. "We have a new breed of people nowa-
days—good men, solid backgrounds." He flashed a brief smile: Backgrounds very much like yours, in fact—college graduates, good
training—*reliable* people. . . ."

"Yeah," said Kemp with a weak grin, "we live in happy times."

"The day of the prima donna is gone!" Turner exclaimed vehe-
mently. "They were hooligans, and they got what they deserved!"

Kemp tried to think who "they" were, and what they had "gotten."

Turner spun suddenly in his chair. "You don't see me running around
drunk in the streets!" he shouted. "Not *me* . . . I know what's going
on!"

Kemp nodded politely.

Now Turner was calm, intense. "It's a responsibility, Kemp, and a
damned big one! You think you can handle it?"

Handle what? Kemp thought. What the hell are you talking about?
(Pause)

"We need men like you," Turner said, "men with good backgrounds . . . steady!"

Kemp smiled modestly.

"It's a long, hard pull," Turner warned. "The road to the top is not
easy."

Kemp stared at the floor, already feeling the mantle of that terrible
responsibility settling on his shoulders.

"What do you say, Kemp, can you handle it?"

"Sure," Kemp said. "Are you offering me the job?"

"You're damned right!" Turner blurted. "We need men like you."

"I'll have to give *Business Age* two weeks' notice," Kemp said.

"Right you are," Turner replied. "You can start here in two weeks."

"What about salary?" Kemp asked.

Turner hesitated, then reached into his desk and brought out a small booklet. He flipped over a few pages, ran his finger along a column of figures, then put it face down on the desk.

"The guild minimum is fifty-five a week," he said, "but in your case we can make it sixty-five." He smiled proudly.

"My God!" Kemp shouted hoarsely. "I'm making eighty-five a week right now!"

"But look what you're doing!" Turner reminded him. "You said yourself the job was driving you crazy . . . look at the opportunity you'll have here!"

"But sixty-five a week!" Kemp protested. "How in the hell can you get reporters for that kind of money? It's hardly enough to live on!"

The blank stare returned to Turner's face. "Oh no," he said quickly. "No . . . reporters get more than that. Hell, I think the minimum is eighty-five."

"Then I should get eighty-five," Kemp said. "That would be fine."

Turner stared at him. "But we don't start our beginners as report-ers," he said quietly. "You'll have to get familiar with the operation first—there's a lot to learn around here."

Kemp's stomach tightened and his palms began to sweat. "Then what the hell kind of job is this?" he demanded.

"We'll start you as a copyboy," Turner explained. "After a few months—if you work out—we'll begin working you up to a writing spot."

The word "copyboy" hit Kemp like a blow to the genitals. He began to stammer, but caught himself and tried to calm down.

Turner rambled on, heedless of Kemp's reaction. "Hell, we've had men who got bylines inside of a year. Why, in two years, you'll be pulling down ninety or a hundred a week!"

Kemp could hardly breathe: "You mean to say you think I'm actually going to take a job as a copyboy?" he said.

Turner focused the blank look on him.

"You must be out of your damned mind!" Kemp shouted. "What the hell . . . ?"

Turner spoke soothingly, but Kemp was already on his feet, stuffing the clippings back in the briefcase. "Wait a minute, Kemp," Turner was saying, "you're getting all excited . . ."

Kemp headed for the door, his eyes blurred and his chest tight with humiliation. Turner's voice came from somewhere behind him, but it faded out in the ceaseless clatter of the city room.

The wind stung his eyes as he hurried into the street. He buttoned his coat as he walked swiftly to the subway. Gradually his brain cleared, and only a dull pain remained in his chest. It soon turned to anger, and he found himself muttering as he waited for the train. The sleazy little bastard! he thought. I should have hauled off and bashed him in the face!

CHEROKEE PARK

For several days following the country club debacle, Kemp stayed close to home. He slept as much as possible, read constantly when he wasn't sleeping, and waited nervously (so to speak) for the "heat" to lift. What a hell of a way to start a vacation, he thought despairingly. I've got to get a grip on myself or this goddamned drink will destroy me!

On Friday night Billy Porter stopped by after dinner. "I can't stay but a minute," he explained, easing himself into the big living room chair. "I have to go by for Nancy at eight-thirty."

"Where are you going?" Kemp asked.

"Just out to the Pine Room," Porter replied. "Why don't you get a date and come with us—won't be many people there."

The mere thought of a date sent Kemp into a quiet frenzy of frustration. "Hmmnnn . . ." he mused. "No, I don't really feel like it. Couldn't get a date this time of night anyway."

"Sure," said Porter, "I know of at least three girls you could call right now and get a date. Hell . . . good ones, too."

Well, Kemp thought, why not? Then his stomach tightened as he imagined the whispers that would accompany his entrance to the Pine Room: There he is! Welburn Kemp . . . Did you hear about his stunt at Betsy Stites's party the other night? Certainly! Drunk as a hoot owl . . . called her a whore . . . I don't know . . . been living in New York the past few years . . . guess he's gone to the dogs. . . .

He slumped back in a corner of the couch, staring at his bare feet. "Hell," he mumbled, "I don't really feel like it. No sense in going out, anyway."

Porter looked at him with a faint grin. "Don't tell me you're still sulking over that thing at the Club the other night," he said.

"Oh no," Kemp blurted, "hell no . . . I just don't feel like going out."

"Lord alive," Porter said with a chuckle, "everybody's forgotten about that. Why let it worry you?"

"It doesn't," said Kemp.

"Well get off your ass and get a date then," Porter exclaimed. "Call Lee Pennington; she doesn't have one. I talked to her this afternoon."

Kemp pondered. Sooner or later I'll have to go out. Why not get it over with? He wavered, feeling a mounting desire to get up and call Lee Pennington. But the whispering: Oh God, there's Welburn Kemp. . . . Let's get out of here . . . gone all to pieces, I tell you . . . New York does it every time . . . gone straight to the dogs. . . .

"Aw hell," he said gruffly, "I can't waste my nights talking to a bunch of boobs at the Pine Room. No, to hell with it."

Porter shook his head sadly and stood up. "Ah well," he said, "it's none of *my* business; if you want to sulk, go ahead and sulk. I have to go."

Kemp stood up and followed him to the door. "I'll give you a ring some time tomorrow," he said. "Thanks anyway. . . ."

Porter grinned as he started across the lawn to his car. "Have a good time," he said. "If I see Betsy I'll tell her you said hello."

"Yeah," said Kemp, "you do that."

For almost an hour he read the afternoon paper, going through it page by page. When he finished he went to the bookshelf and rummaged till he found a copy of *War and Peace*. I've been trying to get to this for years, he thought. Now would be a good time.

So he stretched out on the couch with a fresh cup of coffee, a good overhead light, and his copy of *War and Peace*.

By ten-thirty he was nearly out of his mind with restlessness. Grimly, he stuck to the book, forcing himself to concentrate. But finally it was no use; he dropped it to the floor and stared up at the ceiling. I must go somewhere, he decided. But where? Why the hell didn't I call Lee Pennington? To hell with those fools at the Pine Room; let 'em talk all they want! He searched his mind for someone to call, somewhere to go, a reason—even an excuse—to get out of the house. Finally it came to him: cigarettes, he thought happily, I'm just about out of cigarettes. I'll have to go out and get some.

He got up and put on his socks and shoes, then called to his mother in the den: "Mom, I'm taking the car for a minute. I have to get some cigarettes."

Her voice was faint behind the heavy door. "I have some," she said. "They're in here."

"No," he called, "I don't like those. I want some Kools."

"Great heavens!" came her faint reply. "What's happened to your taste?"

"See you later," he called from the doorway. "Be back in a few minutes."

He backed hastily out of the driveway and felt the cool September night blow through the car as he started up the street. Damn, he thought, it's actually cold. He rolled up his window and turned the radio on: something about a football game. Football? he wondered. Then he remembered reading in the paper that the local high schools opened their seasons tonight. Damn! he thought. That was the fastest summer I've ever spent in my life!

He turned down Iroquois Road, a dark tunnel between rows of old sycamores on either side of the street. A thick canopy of leaves waved gently in the breeze above the road; they rustled peacefully in the night, absorbing the dull yellow glow of street lights and waiting patiently for autumn (cold red-brown autumn) to sweep down from the north and rob them of their summer life. Kemp felt another chill and turned the heater on. Music, night music, sugary sounds for a teenage Friday night moaned out of the radio, and now he slowed down for the STOP sign at the entrance to the park.

I'll go through the park, he thought. They used to have a cigarette machine at the Kingston Inn out by the driving range. He stepped on the gas and pointed his headlights into the park. The road was empty, and he picked up speed as he came over the hill by the golf course. He remembered the sharp curve by the clubhouse, and slowed down as his headlights swept through a grove of silent trees behind the first tee. The road was still empty, and he heard no sound but the soft thunder of his big engine, the music on the radio, the monotonous whirling of the heater fan above his legs, and the humming of his tires on the black asphalt.

How completely different this is from Central Park, he mused, how beautifully wild and uncivilized: no buildings, no taxis, no traffic lights. . . . Just a sprawling, lonely woods, here on the edge of the city. How many times have I come over this road? he wondered. God knows; and yet it's no different now than it was the first time I saw it . . . hell, at least twenty years ago. He let his mind drift back over the years, easing his foot on the gas pedal as he watched his headlights probing into the trees.

How long have I known this park? How old was I when I first walked along this road? Two . . . ? Three . . . ? No older, certainly. A tiny boy in a red jacket and brown corduroy pants . . . walking along that same sidewalk beside my grandfather—my mother's father, who was once a tiny boy himself—stopping to feed the squirrels, leaving the sidewalk and climbing up that hill, resting at the top on a stone bench, sitting beside my grandfather in the crisp September breeze, while the autumn golfers trudged and slammed along the fairway at the bottom of the hill. . . .

More curves now, and heading away from the golf course, across the creek on a stone bridge, and leveling out beside the old football field. He peered into the darkness, trying to see if the goalposts were still there, wondering if they still chalked the lines at the beginning of every season. But it was too dark to tell, even in the cloudy moonlight.

I was ten or eleven then, he thought; my grandfather dead, me no longer feeding the squirrels . . . but riding by that time on my own bicycle, coasting with the others down that long hill to the football field, wearing my old Hutch helmet and my blue jersey over the shoulder pads—number 22—wearing my black tennis shoes and my yellow padded pants, parking my bike at the edge of the field and running out for a pass, racing along in the warm September sun—Saturday morning and no school—yelling, "Throw it, throw it," in my piercing small-boy voice that has vanished now with all the rest: the old Hutch helmet, the size-five tennis shoes, the wild-eyed excitement of a ten-yard sprint around right end . . . all gone now; for just as they have paved this road with new asphalt, they have covered our old football field with other people's children. . . .

He lit a cigarette now, leaving the football field behind and starting up the winding road to the softball diamond. He knew they would be there, parked all along the road—all together, for some reason he could never understand—for he had always parked in lonely, unfrequented spots . . . where you could be alone . . . and get out and stretch if you wanted to . . . and sometimes walk over and sit in the grass if the night was warm enough. . . .

How many nights have I parked on these dark roads, with a warm head against my shoulder, and a six-pack of beer almost as warm in the back seat. . . . Ah, but I was older then . . . no longer playing football, no more to wear my shoulder pads and yell in a small-boy voice . . . but to wear a tie, and drive a car . . . and feel small arms around my neck, soft hair against my cheek . . . and strange to have said, "I love you" only once in all those nights; all those parked cars, those trembling hours, those soft lips and six-packs. . . . So strange that I often wonder why I've never said it since; wonder first and then feel sad because I haven't wanted to . . . and rightly sad, at that. . . .

And so his mind wandered, hopping across the years, whirling along the dark roads of that huge and ageless park, pausing here and there to wipe the cobwebs from some long-forgotten face, or to stop and listen tensely for some once-enchanting voice. And, all the while, he drove on, almost to the end of the park now, the trees behind him and the driving range on his left, the lights of the highway just ahead.

The Kingston Inn was no more. The building was still there, but now it was the Hi-Dee-Ho-Club. Kemp swung into the parking lot, barely missing the giant tailfin of a parked car as he cut sharply into an empty space beside the building. Cars streamed by on the highway as he hurried through the parking lot to the front door. The sidewalk in front of the building was brightly lit, and he felt certain as he hurried toward the door that someone he knew would pass on the highway and see him going, all alone, into something called the Hi-Dee-Ho Club just before midnight. He turned his head away from the highway as he ran up the stairs and through the door.

"You have a cigarette machine?" he asked the bartender. The man pointed toward the rear of the bar.

As he approached the machine, Kemp noticed a vaguely familiar face at a nearby table. Do I know him? he wondered. He looked hard at the face, then at the pretty girl at the same table. Yes, he decided, I know him . . . but what the hell is his name? Just then the face swung toward him; he looked quickly away and fumbled in his pocket for some change as he came to the machine. As he was putting the coins in the slot, the name came to him: I'll be damned! he said to himself. That's Dave Briscoe, my old playmaker! Dave Briscoe, the all-city guard, his teammate for two years . . . frantic stomping in the academy student section as Briscoe brings the ball across mid-court, looks intently at the defense, then dribbles over cross-court to set up the play. Kemp breathing heavily, draws his man into the corner, sees the play, now jumps around his man and takes a quick pass. Briscoe right behind the ball, whirling by on the outside, brushes his man off on Kemp, takes the hand-off, now driving hard for a lay-up. Kemp's man drops off on Briscoe, Kemp spins to the inside, all alone, takes Briscoe's underhand flip . . . jumps, shoots . . . no good . . . goddamnit!

He pulled the lever and picked his cigarettes out of the tray. I'll be damned, Dave Briscoe! I wonder if he remembers me. . . . Maybe I should say hello. . . .

He turned, intending to speak, and found Briscoe watching him. He looked quickly away as Kemp started for the door. Damn, I don't think he remembers me. What the hell could I say to him anyway? He hurried along the bar, passed within five feet of Briscoe's table, felt eyes on his back as he crossed to the door, and then forgot Briscoe instantly as he saw a face watching him from a car stopped at the red light. He jerked his head in the other direction and broke into a run. Good God! he thought. Who was that? He sprinted across the parking lot and scrambled into the welcome darkness of his car.

Damn, he thought as he started the motor, I should have spoken to Briscoe. He used to be a hell of a good guy. I wonder if he knew who I was. . . . Probably. . . . Why the hell didn't I speak? Now he'll figure I've turned into a bastard . . . a snob . . . and damn, people watching me from that car, too. . . . Wonder who it was. . . .

He relaxed slightly as he sped along the road beside the airport. "Goddamn," he muttered to the steering wheel, "my nerves are driving me crazy."

Now he was back in the park again, headlights sweeping through the darkness as his tires squealed softly on a curve, heading for the big lake and the tennis courts on the other side. . . . And there they were again, long rows of taillights on either side of the road beside the lake. He drove between them, looking straight ahead and feeling horribly alone in this little cluster of intense togetherness.

Good lord, there must be a hundred cars here, he thought. Prices must have gone up at the drive-ins.

Now he left the lake behind and the road was empty. He thought again of his six-pack days, remembering how he used to take his shoes off and drive in his socks, a can of beer resting on the seat between his legs.

He wondered if anyone had found his old parking spot, far down at the end of a gravel road behind the archery range. I'll drive down there, he decided, just for the hell of it.

On the way he passed another cluster; anonymous, sinful-looking taillights, gleaming red along the peaceful roads, dotting the midnight landscape from one end of the park to the other. But there was no one at the archery range, thank God, and as he turned down the familiar gravel road he thought immediately of Elaine Holland. That one time. . . . "I love you." He hadn't seen her since high school, not one time during four years of college vacations. How long? Eight years? Impossible, for now on this gravel road it seems like only yesterday. But it is, by God, eight years! He could almost feel her in the car beside him as he listened to the familiar crunching of his tires on the gravel. Where is she now? he wondered. He remembered asking, several years ago, and hearing someone say she'd dropped out of college and gotten married. That's right, some guy in the navy at Pensacola, a pilot or something.

But where is she now? Here in the city? If I knew, I'd go throw rocks at her window like I used to. . . . Bring her over here and park, husband be damned. . . . Wonder if she has any children, or maybe she's pregnant right now. . . . God, how awful. . . .

He was right on top of the car before he saw it. One second he was floating along in his peaceful dream, remembering her soft voice and her arms around his neck . . . and the next instant he saw the car. Great Jesus! he thought, slamming on the brakes. There it was, black and almost invisible with all the lights turned out, but now framed in the terrible glare of his headlights as he sat there, unable to move. Oh God, he thought as his mind whirled in panic, what a ghastly goddamn thing! Still he was unable to move, and now a head jerked up in the front seat of the black car. A face, with one hand trying to shade the eyes, squinting into Kemp's headlights. Then a scream of anger: "Turn out those lights, you son of a bitch!" Suddenly the door opened, and a figure leaped into the light, running toward Kemp's car.

The sight of the man running toward him jolted Kemp into action; he jerked the car into reverse and stomped on the accelerator. The car leaped backward, and he heard himself cursed again as he gripped the wheel desperately to keep the car from weaving into the trees on either side of the road. His heart was thumping with terror as he felt his wheels grip the asphalt of the main road. He screeched to a stop, jammed the car into first, and roared away.

God almighty lord! he muttered as he fled along the winding road. I should have *known* there'd be somebody there!

Now he was on the golf course road, only a little way from the entrance. I've got to get home! he thought wildly; my nerves are going all to pieces!

New York City, 1959

FLEEING NEW YORK

I WENT TO UPSTATE New York and got a job as a reporter on a paper called the Middletown Daily Record. I was there about two months. I was fired after I got in a vicious fight with an advertiser over lasagna.

The guy's place was right across the street from the paper where they all ate. He made rotten lasagna. I sent it back to the kitchen about five times. His name was Gallo, Joe Gallo, or Joey Gallo, something like that, I really don't know. Sounded like Joey Gallo. And nobody sent his lasagna back.

So finally he came out one day, after I'd sent it back again, and attacked me with a wooden kitchen fork. Then we got in a fist fight in the restaurant. I was perfectly justified. It was stinking lasagna.

The next day I went to work and the publisher called me in. Here was this bastard standing there in his apron. They were complaining that first I'd fucked his food over and then I'd beaten him up. I tried to explain myself—all I'd done was send the rotten food back to the kitchen. I thought that the publisher, naturally, would support me. I was writing good stories. Typical things—Lion's Club luncheons, you know, the typical cub reporter's beat, City Hall.

But the publisher warned me that one more thing and I would be fired. I was very surprised. And the advertiser felt vindicated. I had to apologize, I think, for calling his lasagna bad.

About four or five days later I went out of the newsroom to a candy machine back behind the composing room. I wanted a candy bar.

I put a nickel in the machine and nothing happened. I pulled the thing—nothing came out. I put another nickel in, pulled the handle—nothing came out.

I stepped back to give it a boot. You know, you smack things and coins drop. Instead, the whole bottom of the machine gave way. The bottom was where they kept all the storage stuff underneath. You know, the guy doesn't just come around and fill the candy machines with a sack. When he comes in he replaces the stock, moves the candy bars up into the rack from underneath.

So I couldn't get the damn metal panel back into the machine. I had kicked it very hard and sprung it out. I couldn't get it back in, so I propped it up and thought nothing more of it. I just took two candy bars out of the bottom, which I had paid for, and put the tin piece back in there. It looked almost right. Somehow someone figured out that it wasn't quite right and the people in the composing room stole the candy bars and ate them, naturally, free. I didn't think that anybody else knew that the whole bottom was full of candy bars.

So I go in the next day and I get fired. And they docked my pay for all those candy bars. I had to pay something like $17.85 for 350 candy bars, something like that. That was when I gave up on journalism completely.

They hadn't hassled me at all about my copy but they hassled me a lot about my personal attitude, the fact that I would take my shoes off in the winter. Wet shoes, of course you take them off. No, I never got into trouble about the work I did, it was always about personal relations with people.

So I moved into a cabin deep in the hills about twenty miles out of Middletown. I couldn't afford heat so I would turn the heat way down until my hands got too cold to work and then I'd go to sleep. The next day I'd work again and I'd get in about three hours work at night.

I was just living off unemployment and driving a huge black Jaguar Mark VII and was writing short stories. Seems like I have a long history of constantly retreating from journalism to fiction, which is the exact opposite of the traditional American writer, where the noble novelist is continually forced by rejection and ignorance and money pressure to resort to journalism.

I saw an ad in Editor and Publisher *for a new sports magazine starting in Puerto Rico. They needed staff writers. The guy said it was going to be the* Sports Illustrated *of the Caribbean. I thought this thing was made for me. I got the job and went down to Puerto Rico.*

It turned out that the bastard was running a bowling magazine.

He was using the magazine as a vehicle to promote bowling. They were introducing bowling to Puerto Rico. I had to go out and cover bowling every night in San Juan. Bowling was going big. Bowling alleys were popping up everywhere. What could you say about bowling? Bowlers just wanted to see their names in the paper. That was the essential thing. I also had one-angle assignments, like I did a lot of research and a big piece on cockfighting. But about half my work was making sure every bowler in San Juan got his name in the magazine called Sportivo. *And ever since then I've hated the word* bowling.

At almost precisely the same time, for some reason, they were starting San Juan's first English newspaper. I had sent the editor, Bill Kennedy, what I thought was a really elegant letter of application. I had cited the bronze plaque on the side of The New York Times *building in New York— a thing about truth in journalism and dignity of man.*

The tone of my letter was that I'll accept employment with you under certain circumstances. I had said I won't be kept fucked over like I have in the past with these pigs in journalism. I told him it was time for me to get serious, that I wasn't going to come and cover City Hall, that kind of crap. I said I didn't want to be just any reporter.

I was rejected, I thought somewhat brutally. I had put a lot of idealism and effort into this letter of application. Meanwhile a friend of mine was hired as a photographer, a guy from the Middletown Record, *Bob Bone.*

So I had written the editor back saying, "You worthless hack motherfucker," having no idea that Sportivo *would open up like a month later. I said, "You filthy cheap hack, I'm going to come down there sometime—it might be next week, or next year or ten years—but when I see you I'm going to ram a bronze plaque far into your small intestine and kick your teeth out." All this kind of thing.*

So by some weird twist of luck about a month later I showed up in San Juan with a job at Sportivo, *knowing Bone was then working for the* Star, *which had attracted all manner of geeks, a whole colony of floating expatriate journalists, people who worked for English-language newspapers in other countries.*

Kennedy was advised at once of my presence on the island by Bone. Finally I met Kennedy, and we became instant good friends.

So I hung on down there, mounting various wars and diatribes in a constant fight with the publisher of the Star, *who hated me. I had an apartment on the beach. I had a motor scooter, a Lambretta. The beach house rent was like $50 a month and another friend of mine came down, an artist, and shared the rent with me, and Sandy came down.*

Meanwhile, to augment my income I would pick up jobs doing tourist and brochure folders for a thing called Puerto Rican News Service, the official government propaganda, and I became a sort of part-time Caribbean stringer for the Herald Tribune. *It was a prestigious gig and of course the News Service loved it because it was publicity for Puerto Rico. Everything I wrote was selling. I was clearly the preeminent writer or journalist on the island and I didn't even work at the* Star.

Woody Creek, March 1990

The SIXTIES

WHAT THE HELL?
IT'S ONLY ROCK AND ROLL . . .

LETTER TO ANGUS CAMERON

March 22, '60
c/o Semonin
San Juan Star
San Juan, P.R.

Angus Cameron
Knopf Inc.
501 Madison Ave.
NYC

Dear Mr. Cameron:

I want to thank you for your meaningful and perceptive comments on my manuscript. Few editors, I'm sure, would have taken the time to compose such an informative rejection slip, and few indeed could have put down their thoughts with such style and mastery of tone. It's been said, I know, that most editors are boobs, cretins, and witless crayfish who have edged into their jobs through some devious means made possible by the slothful and incestuous nature of the World of Publishing. Ha! Let me say now, Mr. Cameron, that if more editors write letters like yours, the people who say these wretched things will certainly be laughing out of the other side of their mouths. Just where do they get the gall to talk like that?

But be all that as it may, we still have to dispose of *Prince Jellyfish*, don't we? I tried like hell to finish it. Since September, however, the people who sheltered me have applied for divorce, I was beaten by hoodlums in New York, put in jail in Virginia Beach, arrested for drunken driving in Louisville; then I was taken by plane to San Juan where the man who hired me to write sports copy proved to be an insolvent liar. All this has somewhat hindered the progress of the book. But now I am ready to roll again; the typewriter is rusty and full of sand, but I have stolen a ribbon from the *San Juan Star* and now feel ready to complete this wretched thing I began in what seems like another world. Suppose we send it to an agent named Elisabeth McKee. It would take me two or three months to find her address, because I left it in a box of paper somewhere in the Catskills. I feel, however, that it's somewhere in the East Sixties (enviable, eh?) and I feel, also, that one of your people can locate it in the Manhattan Telephone Directory. I am enclosing a note to her, and if you find that your facilities are insufficient to the task of getting both note and manuscript sent to the McKee address, please send all back to me and I will take care of it myself. If this happens, of course, you will soon find in your mailbox a packet of sea urchins: to derive full enjoyment from them, take one in each hand and squeeze.

With fondness and admiration, I remain,

quite gratefully,

Hunter S. Thompson

THE RUM DIARY

I

THE ATMOSPHERE AT the paper was more tense than ever. On Wednesday, Lotterman got a summons from the Department of Labor, inviting him to a hearing on the question of Yeamon's severance pay. He cursed about it all afternoon, saying it would be a cold day in hell before he'd give that nut a dime. Sala began taking bets on the outcome, giving three-to-one odds that Yeamon would collect.

To make things worse, Tyrrell's departure had forced Lotterman to take over as city editor. This meant he did most of the work. It was only temporary, he said, but so far his ad in *Editor and Publisher* had drawn a blank.

I was not surprised. "Editor," it said. "*San Juan Daily*. Begin immediately. Drifters and drinkers need not apply."

At one point he offered the job to me. I came in one day and found a note in my typewriter, saying Lotterman wanted to see me. When I opened the door to his office he was fumbling idly with his baseball. He smiled shrewdly and tossed it up in the air. "I've been thinking," he said. "You seem pretty sharp. Ever handled a city desk?"

"No," I replied.

"Like to give it a whirl?" he asked, tossing the ball again. I wanted no part of it. There would be a good raise, but there would also be a hell of a lot of extra work. "I haven't been here long enough," I said. "I don't know the city."

He tossed the baseball up in the air and let it bounce on the floor. "I know," he said. "I was just thinking."

"What about Sala?" I said, knowing Sala would turn it down. He had so many free-lance assignments that I wondered why he bothered to keep his job at all.

"Not a chance," he replied. "He doesn't give a damn about the paper—he doesn't give a damn about anything." He leaned forward and dropped the ball on the desk. "Who else is there? Moberg's a drunk, Vanderwitz is a psycho, Noonan's a fool, Benetiz can't speak English . . . Christ! Where do I get these people?" He fell back in his chair with a groan. "I've got to have somebody!" he shouted. "I'll go crazy if I have to do the whole paper myself!"

"What about the ad?" I said. "No replies?"

He groaned again. "Sure—wineheads! One guy claimed he was the son of Oliver Wendell Holmes—as if I gave a goddamn!" He bounced the ball violently on the floor. "Who keeps sending these wineheads down here?" he shouted. "Where do they come from?"

He shook the ball at me and spoke as if he were uttering his last words. "Somebody has to fight it, Kemp—they're taking over. These wineheads are taking over the world. If the press goes under, we're sunk—you understand that?"

I nodded.

"By Jesus!" he went on, "we have a responsibility! A free press is vital! If a pack of deadbeats get hold of this newspaper it's the beginning of the end. First they'll get this one, then they'll get a few more, and one day they'll get hold of the *Times*—can you imagine it?"

I said I couldn't.

"They'll get us all!" he exclaimed. "They're dangerous—insidious! That guy claiming he was the son of Justice Holmes—I could pick him out of a crowd—he'd be the one with hair on his neck and a crazy look in his eye!"

Just then, as if on cue, Moberg came through the door, carrying a clipping from *El Diario*.

Lotterman's eyes became wild. "Moberg!" he screamed. "Oh Jesus—where do you get the nerve to come in here without knocking! By God I'll have you locked up! Get out!"

Moberg retreated quickly, giving me a puzzled look as he darted out.

Lotterman glared after him. "The nerve of that goddamn sot," he said. "Christ, a sot like that should be put to sleep."

Moberg had been in San Juan only a few months, but Lotterman seemed to loathe him with a passion that would take most men years to cultivate. Moberg was a degenerate. He was small, with thin blond hair and a face that was pale and flabby. I have never seen a man so bent on self-destruction—not only self, but destruction of everything he could get his hands on. He was lewd and corrupt in every way. He hated the taste of rum, yet he would finish a bottle in ten minutes, then vomit and fall down. He ate nothing but sweet rolls and spaghetti, which he would vomit the moment he got drunk. He spent all his money on whores and when that got dull he would take on an occasional queer, just for the strangeness of it. He would do anything for money, and this was the man we had on the police beat. Often he disappeared for days at a time. Then someone would have to track him down through the dirtiest bars in La Perla, a slum so foul that on maps of San Juan it appeared as a blank space. La Perla was Moberg's headquarters; he felt at home there, he said, and in the rest of the city—except for a few horrible bars—he was a lost soul.

He told me that he'd spent the first twenty years of his life in Sweden, and often I tried to picture him against a crisp Scandinavian landscape. I tried to see him on skis, or living peacefully with his family in some cold mountain village. From the little he said of Sweden I gathered that he'd lived in a small town and that his parents had been comfortable people with enough money to send him to college in America.

He spent two years at NYU, living in the Village at one of those residence hotels that cater to foreigners. This apparently unhinged him. Once he was arrested on Sixth Avenue, he said, for pissing on a fireplug like a dog. It cost him ten days in the Tombs, and when he got out he left immediately for New Orleans. He floundered there for a while, then got a job on a freighter headed for the Orient. He worked on boats for several years before drifting into journalism. Now, thirty-three years old and looking fifty, his spirit broken and his body swollen with drink, he bounced from one country to another, hiring himself out as a reporter and hanging on until he was fired.

Disgusting as he usually was, on rare occasions he showed flashes of a stagnant intelligence. But his brain was so rotted with drink and dissolute living that whenever he put it to work it behaved like an old engine that had gone haywire from being dipped in lard.

"Lotterman thinks I'm a Demogorgon," he would say. "You know what that is? Look it up—no wonder he doesn't like me."

One night at Al's he told me he was writing a book, called *The Inevitability of a Strange World.* He took it very seriously. "It's the kind of book a Demogorgon would write," he said. "Full of shit and terror—I've selected the most horrible things I could imagine. The hero is a flesheater disguised as a priest—cannibalism fascinates me. Once down at the jail they beat a drunk until he almost died—I asked one of the cops if I could eat a chunk of his leg before they killed him. . . ." He laughed. "The swine threw me out—hit me with a club." He laughed again. "I'd have eaten it—why shouldn't I? There's nothing sacred about human flesh—it's meat like everything else—would you deny that?"

"No," I said. "Why should I deny it?"

It was one of the few times I talked to him that I could understand what he said. Most of the time he was incoherent with drink. Lotterman was forever threatening to fire him, but we were so understaffed that he couldn't afford to let anyone go. When Moberg spent a few days in the hospital after his beating at the hands of the strikers, Lotterman had hopes that he might straighten out. But when he came back to work he was more hopeless than before.

At times I wondered which would be the first to go—Moberg or the *News*. The paper gave every appearance of being on its last legs. Circulation was falling off and we were losing advertising so steadily that I didn't see how Lotterman could hold out. He had borrowed heavily to get the paper going, and according to Sanerson, it had never made a nickel.

I kept hoping for an influx of new blood, but Lotterman had become so wary of "wineheads" that he rejected every reply to his ads. "I've got to be careful," he explained. "One more pervert and we're finished."

I suspected that he couldn't afford to pay any more salaries, but one day a man named Schwartz appeared in the office, saying he had just been thrown out of Venezuela for some reason, and Lotterman hired him immediately. To everyone's surprise he turned out to be competent. After a few weeks he was doing all the work that Tyrrell had done.

This took a lot of the strain off Lotterman, but it didn't do much for the paper. We went from twenty-four pages down to sixteen, and finally to twelve. The outlook was so bleak that people began saying *El Diario* had the *News'* obituary set in type and ready to go.

I had no feeling for the paper, but it was good to have a salary while I fished for something bigger. The idea that the *News* might fold began to worry me and I wondered why San Juan, with all its new prosperity, couldn't support such a small thing as an English-language newspaper. The *News* was no prizewinner, but it was at least readable.

A large part of the trouble was Lotterman. He was capable enough, in a purely mechanical way, but he had put himself in an untenable position. As an admitted ex-Communist, he was under constant pressure to prove how much he'd reformed. At that time the U.S. State Department was calling Puerto Rico "America's advertisement in the Caribbean—living proof that capitalism can work in Latin America." The people who had come there to do the proving saw themselves as heroes and missionaries, bringing the holy message of Free Enterprise to the downtrodden *jibaros*. They hated Commies like they hated sin, and the fact that an ex-Red was publishing a paper in their town did not make them happy.

Lotterman simply couldn't cope with it. He went out of his way to attack anything that smelled even faintly of the political Left, because he knew he'd be crucified if he didn't. On the other hand, he had the free-wheeling Commonwealth government, whose subsidies were not only supporting half the new industry on the island but were paying for most of the *News* advertising as well. It was quite a bind—not just for Lotterman, but for a good many others. In order to make money they had to deal with the government, but to deal with the government was to condone "creeping Socialism"—which was not exactly compatible with their missionary work.

It was amusing to see how they handled it, because if they thought about it at all there was only one way out—to praise the ends and ignore the means, a time-honored custom that justifies almost anything except shrinking profits.

To go to a cocktail party in San Juan was to see all that was cheap and greedy in human nature. What passed for society was a loud, giddy whirl of thieves and pretentious hustlers, a dull sideshow full of quacks and clowns and Philistines with gimp mentalities. It was a new wave of Okies, heading south instead of west, and in San Juan they were kingfish because they had literally taken over.

They formed clubs and staged huge social events, and finally one of them started a gossip sheet that terrified and intimidated everyone whose past was not an open book. This took in half the gang, including poor Lotterman, who suffered some vicious libel almost every week.

There was no shortage of free liquor for the press, because all hustlers crave publicity. No occasion was too small for them to give what they called a "press party" in its honor. Each time Woolworth's or the Chase Manhattan Bank opened a new branch, they celebrated with an orgy of rum. Not a month went by without the opening of a new bowling alley; they were building them on every vacant lot, so many bowling alleys that it was horrible to ponder the meaning of it.

From the new San Juan Chamber of Commerce came a stream of statements and proclamations that made Jehovah's Witnesses seem pale and pessimistic—long breast-beating screeds, announcing one victory after another in the crusade for The Big Money. And on top of all this there was a never-ending round of private parties for visiting celebrities. Here again, no half-wit Kiwanian was too insignificant for a blowout in his honor.

I usually went to these things with Sala. At the sight of his camera the guests would turn to jelly. Some of them would act like trained pigs and others would mill around like sheep, all waiting for "the man from the paper" to push his magic button and make their lavish hospitality pay off.

We tried to go early, and while Sala was herding them around for a series of meaningless photos that would probably never even be developed, I would steal as many bottles of rum as I could carry. If there was a bartender I would tell him I wanted a bit of drink for the press, and if he protested I would take them anyway. No matter what kind of outrage I committed, I knew they would never complain.

Then we would head for Al's, dropping the rum at the apartment on the way. We put all the bottles on an empty bookshelf and sometimes there were as many as twenty or thirty. In a good week we would hit three parties and average three or four bottles for each half-hour of painful socializing. It was a good feeling to have a stock of rum that would never run out, but after a while I could no longer stand even a few minutes at each party and I had to give it up.

II

One Saturday in late March, when the tourist season was almost over and the merchants were bracing themselves for the muggy low-profit summer, Sala had an assignment to go down to Fajardo on the eastern tip of the island and take some pictures of a new hotel that was going up on a hill overlooking the harbor. Lotterman thought the *News* could strike a cheerful note by pointing out that things were going to be even better next season.

I decided to go along for the ride. Ever since I'd come to San Juan I'd been meaning to get out on the island, but without a car it was impossible. My rurthest penetration had been to Yeamon's, about twenty miles out, and Fajardo was twice as far in the same direction. We decided to get some rum and stop by his place on the way back, hoping to get there just as he paddled in from the reef with a bulging sack of lobsters. "He's probably damn good at it by now," I said. "God knows what he's living on—they must have a steady diet of lobster and chicken."

"Hell," Sala remarked, "chicken's expensive."

I laughed. "Not out there. The niggers let them run wild. He shoots them with a spear gun."

"God almighty!" Sala exclaimed. "That's voodoo country—they'll croak him, sure as hell!"

I shrugged. I'd assumed from the very beginning that Yeamon would sooner or later be croaked—by somebody or some faceless mob, for some reason or other, it seemed inevitable. Ten years before—even five—I had been the same way. I wanted it all and I wanted it fast and no obstacle was big enough to put me off. Since then I had learned that some things were bigger than they looked from a distance, and now I was not so sure anymore just what I was going to get or even what I deserved. At the most, I was five years older than Yeamon, but I had come a long way in that time, and if I was not proud of what I had learned I never doubted it was worth knowing. Yeamon would either learn the same things, or he would certainly be croaked. This is what I told myself on those hot afternoons in San Juan when I was thirty-one years old and my shirt stuck damply to my back and I felt myself on that big and only hump, with my hardnose years behind me and all the rest downhill. They were eerie days, and my fatalistic view of Yeamon was not so much conviction as necessity, because if I granted him even the slightest optimism I would have to admit a lot of unhappy things about myself.

We came to Fajardo after an hour's drive in the hot sun and immediately stopped for a drink at the first bar. Then we drove up a hill on the outskirts of town, where Sala puttered around for almost an hour, getting his shots. He was a grudging perfectionist, no matter how much contempt he had for his assignment. As the only pro on the island, he felt he had a certain reputation to uphold.

When he finished we bought two bottles of rum and a bag of ice. Then we drove back to the turnoff that would take us to Yeamon's. The road was paved all the way to the river, where two natives operated a ferry. They charged us a dollar for the car, then poled us across to the other side, not saying a word the whole time. I felt like a pilgrim crossing the Ganges, standing there in the sun beside the car and staring down at the water while the ferrymen leaned on their poles and shoved us toward the palm grove on the other side. We bumped against the dock and they secured the barge to an upright log while Sala drove the car to solid ground.

We still had five miles of sand road before we got to Yeamon's place. Sala cursed the whole way, swearing he would turn back except that he'd be hit for another dollar to go back across the river. The little car thumped and bounced in the ruts and I thought it would come to pieces at any moment. Once we passed a pack of native children, stoning a dog beside the road. Sala stopped, took several pictures, then shouted for them to let the dog alone, but they paid no attention.

"Jesus," he muttered, "look at those vicious bastards! We'll be lucky to get out of here alive."

When we finally got to Yeamon's we found him on the patio, wearing the same black trunks and building a bookshelf out of driftwood. The place looked a little better now; part of the patio was covered with an awning made of palm fronds, and beneath it were two canvas deck chairs that looked like they belonged in one of the better beach clubs.

"Man," I said, "where did you get those?"

"The nigger," he replied. "Sold 'em to me for five dollars. I think he stole 'em in town."

"Where's Chenault?" Sala asked.

Yeamon pointed down at the beach. "Probably sunning herself down by that log. She puts on a show for the natives—they love her."

Sala brought the rum and the bag of ice from the car. Yeamon chuckled happily and poured the ice in a tub beside the door. "Damn fine," he said. "This poverty is driving me nuts—we can't even afford rum."

"Man," I said. "You'll have to get some work. You'll turn into a nigger out here."

He laughed and filled three glasses with ice. "I'm still after Lotterman," he said. "It looks like I might get it."

"You will," said Sala. "Things are slow here, but they'll nail him."

"I hope so," Yeamon replied. "We're getting pretty low."

Just then Chenault came up from the beach, wearing the same white bikini and carrying a big beach towel. She smiled at Yeamon. "They came again. I heard them talking."

"Goddamnit," Yeamon snapped. "Why do you keep going down there? What the hell is wrong with you?"

She smiled and sat down on the towel. "It's my favorite place. Why should I leave just because of them?"

Yeamon turned to me. "She goes down to the beach and takes off her clothes—the niggers hide back in the palms and watch her."

"Not always," Chenault said quickly. "Usually it's just on weekends."

Yeamon leaned forward and shouted at her. "Well goddamn you, don't go there anymore! From now on you stay up here if you want to lie around naked! I'll be goddamned if I'll spend all my time worrying about a bunch of niggers raping you down there on the beach!" He shook his head with disgust. "One of these days they'll get you, by God, and if you keep on teasing the poor bastards I'll damn well let them have you!"

She stared down at the concrete. I felt sorry for her and stood up to make her a drink. When I handed it to her she looked up gratefully and took a long swallow.

"Drink up," said Yeamon. "We'll invite some of your friends and have a real party!" Then he fell back in the chair. "Ah, the good life," he muttered. "Might as well try to share it with a wild boar as with a woman."

We sat there drinking for a while, Chenault saying nothing, Yeamon doing most of the talking and finally he got up and picked a coconut off the sand beside the patio. "Come on," he said, "let's have a little football."

I was glad for anything that would clear the air so I put down my drink and ran awkwardly out for a pass. He spiraled it perfectly, but it smacked my fingers like lead and I dropped it.

"Let's get down on the beach," he called. "Plenty of room to run."

I nodded and waved to Sala. He shook his head. "Go play," he muttered. "Me and Chenault have serious things to discuss." Chenault smiled half-heartedly and waved us down to the beach. "Go on," she said.

I slid down the bluff to the hard-packed sand on the beach. Yeamon threw up his arm and ran at an angle toward the surf. I tossed the nut high and long, watching it fall just beyond him in the water and make a quick splash. He fell on it and went under, bringing it up in his hands.

I turned and sprinted away, watching it float down at me out of the hot blue sky. It hurt my hands again, but this time I hung on. It was a good feeling to snag a long pass again, even if it was a coconut. We played for several hours, running up and down the beach and falling in the water when the nut fell out of reach. My hands grew red and tender but it was a good clean feeling and I didn't mind. We ran short over-the-middle passes and long floaters down the sideline, and after a while I couldn't help but think we were engaged in some kind of holy ritual, the reenactment of all our young Saturdays—expatriated now, lost and cut off from those games and those drunken stadiums, beyond the noise and blind to the false color of those happy spectacles—after years of jeering at football and all that football means, here I was on an empty Caribbean beach, running these silly pass plays with all the zeal of a regular sandlot fanatic.

But there is no getting away from football. Americans are cursed with it. The quarterback is God, and to stand back there with the ball—or the nut—resting easily in your hand, your arm cocked and hell breaking loose all around you, is to know the real essence of the mythical American; a foolish game with no foundation in reality, and yet a childish faith that a man can be a good sport and a winner on the same day.

As we raced back and forth on that sandy beach, falling and plunging in the surf, I recalled my Saturdays at Vanderbilt and the precision beauty of a Georgia Tech backfield, pushing us back and back with that awful belly series, a lean figure in a gold jersey, slashing over a hole that should never have been there, now loose on the crisp grass of that secondary and the unholy shout from the stands across the way; and finally to bring the bastard down, escape those blockers coming at you like cannonballs, then line up again and face that terrible machinery. It was a tortuous thing, but beautiful in its way; here were men who would never again function or even understand how they were supposed to function as well as they did today. They were dolts and thugs for the most part, huge pieces of meat, trained to a fine edge—but somehow they mastered those complex plays and patterns, and in rare moments they were artists.

Finally I got too tired to run anymore and we went back up to the patio, where Sala and Chenault were still talking. They both seemed a little drunk, and after a few minutes of conversation I realized that Chenault was fairly out of her head. She kept chuckling to herself and mocking Yeamon's southern accent, which was so faint that I'd never noticed it.

We drank for another hour or so, laughing indulgently at Chenault and watching the sun slant off toward Jamaica and the Gulf of Mexico. It's still light in Mexico City, I thought. I had never been there and suddenly I was overcome by a tremendous curiosity about the place. Several hours of rum, combined with my mounting distaste for Puerto Rico, had me right on the verge of going into town, packing my clothes, and leaving on the first westbound plane. Why not? I thought. I hadn't cashed this week's paycheck yet; a few hundred in the bank, nothing to tie me down—why not, indeed? It was bound to be better than this place, where my only foothold was a cheap job that looked ready to collapse any day.

I turned to Sala. "How much is it from here to Mexico City?"

He shrugged and sipped his drink. "Too much," he replied. "Why—you moving on?"

I nodded. "I'm pondering it."

Chenault looked up at me, her face serious for a change. "You'd love Mexico City, Paul."

"What the hell do you know about it?" Yeamon snapped.

She glared up at him, then took a long drink from her glass.

"That's it," he said. "Keep sucking it down—you're not drunk enough yet."

"Shut up!" she screamed, jumping to her feet. "Leave me alone, you goddamn pompous fool!"

His arm shot out so quickly that I barely saw the movement; there was the sound of a smack as the back of his hand hit her cheek. It was almost a casual gesture, no anger, no effort, and by the time I realized what had happened he was leaning back in the chair again, watching impassively as she staggered back a few feet and burst into tears. No one spoke for a moment, then Yeamon told her to go inside. "Go on," he snapped. "Go to bed."

She stopped crying and took her hand away from her cheek. "Damn you," she sobbed.

"Get in there," he said sternly.

She glared at him a moment longer, then turned and went inside. We could hear the squeak of the springs as she fell on the bed, then the sobbing continued.

Yeamon stood up. "Well," he said quietly, "sorry to subject you people to that sort of thing." He nodded thoughtfully, glancing at the hut. "I think I'll go on into town with you—anything happening tonight?"

Sala shrugged. I could tell he was upset. "Nothing," he said. "All I want is food, anyway. The rest can wait."

Yeamon turned toward the door. "Hang on," he said. "I'll get dressed."

After he went inside, Sala turned to me and shook his head sadly. "He treats her like a slave," he whispered. "She'll crack up pretty soon."

I stared out to sea, watching the sun as it slowly approached the horizon. I felt sorry for Chenault, but a drunken woman is something I've never liked and her witless chatter had been getting on my nerves. If that was the only way to stop her, then he had done a quick and painless job, and the only thing I disliked about it was having to sit there and watch.

We could hear him moving around inside, but there was no talk. When he came out he was dressed in his tan suit, with a tie flung loosely around his neck. He pulled the door shut and locked it from the outside. "Keep her from wandering around," he explained. "She'll probably pass out pretty soon, anyway."

There was a sudden burst of sobbing from inside the hut. Yeamon gave a hopeless shrug and tossed his coat in Sala's car. "I'll take the scooter," he said, "so I won't have to stay in town."

We backed out to the road and let him go ahead. His scooter looked like one of those things they used to parachute behind the lines in World War II—a skeleton chassis, showing signs of a red paint job far gone with rust, and beneath the seat was a little engine that made a sound like a Gatling gun. There was no muffler and the tires were completely bald.

We followed him along the road, nearly hitting him several times when he slid in the sand. He set an awful pace and we were hard pressed to keep up without tearing the car to pieces. As we passed the native shacks little children came running out to the road to wave at us. Yeamon waved back, grinning broadly and giving a tall, straight-armed salute as he sped along, trailing a cloud of dust and noise and weaving now and then to avoid the chuckholes.

We stopped where the paved road began, and Yeamon suggested we go to a place just a mile or so farther on. "Pretty good food and cheap drink," he said, "and, besides, they'll give me credit." He nodded. "It's a native place, but they know me."

We followed him down the road until we came to a sign that said "Casa Cabrones." An arrow pointed to a dirt road that branched off toward the beach. It went through a grove of palms and ended in a small parking lot, next to a small and ratty restaurant with tables on the patio and a jukebox beside the bar. Except for the palms and the Puerto Rican clientele, it reminded me of a third-rate tavern in the American Midwest. A string of blue bulbs hung from two poles on either side of the patio, and every thirty seconds or so the sky above us was sliced by a yellow beam from the airport tower, no more than a mile away.

As we sat down and ordered our drinks I realized we were the only white men in the place. The others were not blacks but tan little men with thin mustaches and greasy hair. They made a great deal of noise, singing and shouting with the jukebox, but they all seemed tired and depressed. It was not the rhythmic sadness of Mexican music but the howling emptiness of a sound I have never heard anywhere but in Puerto Rico—a combination of groaning and whining, backed up by a dreary thumping and the sound of voices bogged down in despair.

It was terribly sad—not the music itself, but the fact that it was the best they could do. Most of the tunes were translated versions of American rock-and-roll, with all the energy gone. I recognized one as "Long Fat Lover." The original version had been a hit when I was in high school. I recalled it as a wild and racy tune, but the Puerto Ricans had made it a repetitious dirge, as hollow and hopeless as the faces of the men who sang it now in this lonely wreck of a roadhouse. They were not hired musicians, but I had a feeling they were putting on a performance, and any moment I expected them to fall silent and pass the hat. Then they would finish their drinks and file quietly into the night, like a troupe of clowns at the end of a laughless day.

I had seen enough of this kind of dreariness to take it for granted. The myth of Latin virility goes all to pieces in Puerto Rico. This was one of Yeamon's earliest observations. "These people have no balls," he said. "They've been gibbed—like cats."

As a brutal generalization, it was pretty apt. At times I felt like a spectator at a worldwide convention of fugitive eunuchs. Queers who had thought New York was a pretty good deal came to San Juan and called it Valhalla. One of them, a massive fellow with a full beard, told me the boys were "the sweetest little buggers in the world."

"Not a bit of fuss," he assured me. "Touch 'em once and they melt like butter."

All manner of fearful deviations thrived in that muggy air. A legion of pederasts wandered the narrow sidewalks of the Old City, giggling at every crotch. The bars, the beaches, and even the best sections of town literally crawled with rapists and dykes and muggers and people with no sex or sanity at all. They lurked in the shadows and foamed through the streets, grasping and grabbing like crazed shoplifters, driven mad by the Tropic Rot.

And here I was in the midst of it, pausing now and then to wonder what the hell I was doing, what it all meant, then chuckling like an ass and sitting back with a fresh drink. Now, slaking my thirst in a dirty roadhouse, I slumped in my chair and watched the light sweep through the trees above the patio.

Suddenly the music stopped and several men rushed for the jukebox. A quarrel broke out, a flurry of insults—and then, from somewhere far in the distance, like a national anthem played to calm a frenzied crowd, came the slow tinkling of Brahms's "Lullaby." The quarrel ceased, there was a moment of silence, several coins fell into the bowels of the jukebox, and then it broke into a whimpering yell. The men returned to the bar, laughing and slapping each other on the back.

We ordered three more rums and the waiter brought them over. We'd decided to drink a while, putting off dinner till later, and by the time we got around to ordering food the waiter told us the kitchen was closed.

"Never in hell!" Yeamon exclaimed. "That sign says midnight." He pointed to a sign above the bar.

The waiter shook his head.

Sala looked up at him. "Let's cut the crap, fella. I'm too hungry to fuck around—bring us three steaks and some french fries."

The waiter shook his head again, staring at the green order pad in his hand.

Suddenly Yeamon banged his fist on the table. The waiter looked fearful, then scurried behind the bar. Everyone in the place turned to look at us.

"Let's have some meat!" Yeamon shouted. "And more rum!"

A fat little man wearing a white short-sleeve shirt came running out of the kitchen. He patted Yeamon on the shoulder. "Good fellows," he said with a nervous smile. "Good customers—no trouble, okay?"

Yeamon looked at him. "All we want is some food," he said pleasantly. "A simple thing, just three steaks and another round of drinks."

The little man shook his head. "No dinner after ten," he said. "See?" He jabbed his finger at the clock. It was ten-twenty.

"That sign says midnight," Yeamon replied.

The man shook his head.

"What's the problem?" Sala asked. "The steaks won't take five minutes. Hell, forget the potatoes."

Yeamon held up his glass. "Let's get these drinks," he said, waving three fingers at the bartender.

The bartender looked at our man, who seemed to be the manager. He nodded quickly, then walked away. I thought the crisis had passed.

In a moment he was back, bringing a little green check that said $11.50. He put it on the table in front of Yeamon.

"Don't worry about that," Yeamon told him.

The manager clapped his hands. "Okay," he said angrily. "You pay." He held out his hand.

Yeamon brushed the check off the table. "I said don't worry about it."

The manager snatched the check off the floor. "You pay!" he screamed. "Pay now!"

Yeamon's face turned red and he rose half out of his chair. "I'll pay it like I paid the others," he yelled. "Now get the hell away from here and bring us some food."

The manager hesitated, then leaped forward and slapped the check on the .able. "Pay now!" he shouted. "Pay now and get out—or I call police."

He had barely got the words out of his mouth when Yeamon grabbed him by the front of his shirt. "You cheap little bastard!" he snarled. "You keep yelling and you'll never get paid."

I watched the men at the bar. They were bug-eyed and tense as dogs. The bartender stood poised at the door, ready to either flee or run outside and get a machete—I wasn't sure.

The manager, out of control by this time, shook his fist at us and screeched. "Pay, you damn, damn Yankees! Pay and get out!" He glared at us, then ran over to the bartender and whispered something in his ear.

Yeamon got up and put on his coat. "Let's go," he said. "I'll deal with this bastard later."

The manager seemed terrified at the prospect of welshers walking out on him. He followed us into the parking lot, cursing and pleading by turns. "Pay now!" he howled. "When will you pay? . . . you'll see, the police will come . . . no police, just pay!"

I thought the man was crazy and my only desire was to get him off our backs. "Christ," I said. "Let's pay it."

"Yeah," said Sala, bringing out his wallet. "This place is a looney bin."

"Don't worry," said Yeamon. "He knows I'll pay." He tossed his coat in the car, then turned to the manager. "Get a grip on yourself, you fat little punk."

We got in the car. As soon as Yeamon started his scooter the manager ran back and began shouting to the men inside the bar. His screams filled the air as we pulled off, following Yeamon out the long driveway. He refused to hurry, idling along like a man intrigued with the scenery, and in a matter of seconds two carloads of screaming Puerto Ricans were right behind us. I thought they might run us down; they were driving big American cars and could have squashed the Fiat like a roach.

"Holy shit," Sala kept saying, "this may be the end of us."

When we came to the paved road, Yeamon pulled over and let us pass. We stopped a few yards ahead of him and I called back. "Come on, damnit! Let's get out of here."

The other cars came up beside him and I saw him throw up his hands as if he'd been hit. He jumped off the scooter, letting it fall, and grabbed at a man whose head was outside the window. Almost at the same moment I saw the police drive up. Four of them leaped out of a little blue Volkswagen, waving their billyclubs. The Puerto Ricans cheered wildly and scrambled out of their cars. I was tempted to run, but we were instantly surrounded. One of the cops ran up to Yeamon and pushed him backward. "What is it?" he shouted. "What are you trying to do?"

At the same time, both doors of the Fiat were jerked open and Sala and I were pulled out. I tried to break loose, but several people were holding my arms. Somewhere beside me I could hear Yeamon saying over and over: "Well the man spit on me, well the man spit on me. . . ."

Suddenly everybody stopped shouting and the scene boiled down to an argument between Yeamon, the manager, and what appeared to be the cop in charge. Nobody was holding me now, so I moved up to hear what was going on.

"Look," Yeamon was saying. "I paid the other bills—what makes him think I won't pay this one?"

The manager said something about drunk, arrogant Yankees.

Before Yeamon could reply, one of the cops stepped up behind him and slammed him on the shoulder with his billy. He shouted with pain and lurched to one side, onto one of the men who had come after us in the cars. The man swung wildly with a beer bottle, hitting him in the ribs. The last thing I saw before I went down was Yeamon's savage rush on the man with the bottle. I heard several swacks of bone against bone, and then, out of the corner of my eye, I saw something coming at my head. I ducked just in time to take the main force of the blow on my back. It knocked the wind out of me and I lost my balance.

Sala was screaming somewhere above me and I was thrashing around on my back, trying to avoid the feet that were pounding me like hammers. I covered my head with my arms and lashed out with my feet, but the awful hammering continued. There was not much pain, but even through the numbness I knew they were hurting me and I was suddenly sure I was going to die. I was still conscious, and the knowledge that I was being kicked to death in a Puerto Rican jungle for no reason at all filled me with such terror that I began to scream like an animal. Finally, just as I thought I was passing out, I felt myself being shoved into a car.

III

I was half-unconscious during the ride, and when the car finally stopped I looked out and saw ten or fifteen Puerto Ricans gathered on the sidewalk. I knew I couldn't stand another beating; when they tried to haul me out I clung desperately to the back of the seat until one of the cops hit me on the arm with a billy.

To my surprise, the crowd made no move to attack us. We were pushed up the steps, past a group of sullen cops at the door, and led into a small windowless room where they told us to sit on a bench. They then closed the door and left us alone.

"Jesus Christ," said Yeamon. "This is incredible. We have to get hold of somebody."

"We're headed for *La Princessa*," Sala groaned. "The bastards have us now—this is the end."

"They have to let us use the phone," I said. "I'll call Lotterman."

Yeamon snorted. "He won't do a damn thing for me. Hell, he wants me locked up."

"He won't have any choice," I replied. "He can't afford to abandon me and Sala."

Yeamon looked doubtful. "Well . . . I can't think of anybody else to call."

Sala groaned again and rubbed his head. "Christ, we'll be lucky to get out of here alive."

"We got off easy," said Yeamon, gently feeling his teeth. "I thought we were done for when it started."

Sala shook his head sadly. "These people are vicious," he muttered.

"I was dodging that cop and somebody hit me from behind with a coconut—nearly broke my neck."

The door opened and the boss cop appeared, smiling as if nothing had happened. "Okay?" he said, watching us curiously.

Yeamon looked up at him. "We'd like to use the phone," he said.

The cop shook his head. "Your names?" he said, pulling out a small notebook.

"If you don't mind," said Yeamon. "I think we have a right to make a phone call."

The cop made a menacing gesture with his fist. "I said NO!" he shouted. "Give me your names!"

We gave our names.

"Where are you staying?" he asked.

"Goddamnit, we live here!" Sala snapped. "I work for the *Daily News* and I've lived on this stinking rock for more than a year!" He was trembling with rage and the cop looked startled. My address is 409 Calle Tetuan," Sala continued, "and if I don't get an attorney down here pretty quick I'm going to cause you some trouble."

The cop thought for a moment. "You all work for the *Daily News?*"

"You're damn right," Sala replied.

The cop looked down at us and smiled wickedly. "Tough guys," he said. "Tough Yankee journalists."

No one said anything for a moment, then Yeamon asked again to use the phone. "Look," he said. "Nobody's trying to be tough. You just beat the hell out of us and now we want a lawyer—is that too much to ask?"

The cop smiled again. "Okay, tough guys."

"What the hell is this 'tough guy' business?" Sala exclaimed. "Where the Christ is a phone?"

He started to get up and he was still in a crouch, halfway off the bench, when the cop stepped forward and gave him a savage rabbit punch on the neck. Sala dropped to his knees and the cop kicked him in the ribs. Three more cops burst into the room as if they'd been waiting for the signal. Two of them grabbed Yeamon, twisting his arm behind his back, and the other one knocked me off the bench and stood over me with his billy. I knew he wanted to hit me and I didn't move, trying not to give him an excuse. After a long moment, the boss cop yelled, "Okay, tough guys, let's go." I was jerked off the floor and we were forced down the hall at a half-trot, our arms twisted painfully behind our backs.

At the end of the hall we came into a big room, full of people and cops and a lot of desks—and there, sitting on a table in the middle of the room, was Moberg. He was writing in a notebook.

"Moberg!" I yelled, not caring if I was hit as long as I attracted his attention. "Call Lotterman! Get a lawyer!"

At the sound of Moberg's name, Sala looked up and screamed with rage and pain: "Swede! For Christ's sake call somebody! We're being killed!"

We were pushed through the room at high speed and I had no more than a glimpse of Moberg before we were in another hallway. The cops paid no attention to our shouts; apparently they were used to people screaming desperately as they were led away to wherever we were being taken. My only hope was that Moberg had not been too drunk to recognize us.

We spent the next six hours in a tiny concrete cell with about twenty Puerto Ricans. We couldn't sit down because they had pissed all over the floor, so we stood in the middle of the room, giving out cigarettes like representatives of the Red Cross. They were a dangerous-looking lot. Some were drunk and others seemed crazy. I felt safe as long as we could supply them with cigarettes, but I wondered what would happen when we ran out.

The guard solved this problem for us, at a nickel a cigarette. Each time we wanted one for ourselves we had to buy twenty—one for every man in the cell. After two rounds, the guard sent out for a new carton. We figured out later that our stay in the cell cost us more than fifteen dollars, which Sala and I paid, since Yeamon had no money.

It seemed like we had been there for six years when the guard finally opened the door and beckoned us out. Sala could hardly walk and Yeamon and I were so tired that we had trouble supporting him. I had no idea where we were going. Probably to the dungeon, I thought. This is the way people disappear.

We went back through the building, along several hallways, and finally into a large courtroom. As we were shoved through the door, looking as dirty and disheveled as the most horrible bums in the cell we had just left, I looked around anxiously for some familiar face.

The place was jammed and I looked for several minutes before I saw Moberg and Sanerson standing solemnly in one corner. I nodded to them and Moberg held up his fingers in a circle.

"Thank God," said Sala. "We've made contact."

"Is that Sanerson?" Yeamon asked.

"Looks like it," I said, not having the faintest idea what it meant.

"What's that prick doing here?" Sala mumbled.

"We could do a hell of a lot worse," I said. "We're damn lucky anybody's here."

It was almost an hour before they called our case. The boss cop was the first to speak and his testimony was delivered in Spanish. Sala, who understood parts of what he was saying, kept muttering: "That lying bastard . . . claims we threatened to tear the place up . . . attacked the manager . . . ran out on our bill . . . hit a cop . . . Christ Jesus . . . started a fight when we got to headquarters . . . God, this is too much! We're done for!"

When the boss cop had finished, Yeamon asked for a translation of the testimony, but the judge ignored him.

The manager testified next, sweating and gesturing with excitement, his voice rising to a hysterical pitch as he swung his arms and shook his fists and pointed at us as if we had killed his entire family.

We understood nothing of what he said, but it was obvious that things were going against us. When it finally came our turn to speak, Yeamon got up and demanded a translation of all the testimony against us.

"You heard it," said the judge in perfect English.

Yeamon explained that none of us spoke Spanish well enough to understand what had been said. "These people spoke English before," he said, pointing at the cop and the manager. "Why can't they speak it now?"

The judge smiled contemptuously. "You forget where you are," he said. "What right do you have to come here and cause trouble, then tell us to speak your langauge?"

I could see that Yeamon was losing his temper and I motioned to Sanerson to do something. Just then I heard Yeamon say he "would expect fairer treatment under Trujillo."

A dead silence fell on the courtroom. The judge stared at Yeamon, his eyes bright with anger. I could almost feel the ax descending.

Sanerson called from the back of the room: "Your honor, could I have a word?"

The judge looked up. "Who are you?"

"My name is Sanerson. I'm with Adelante.."

A man I had never seen stepped quickly up to the judge and whispered in his ear. The judge nodded, then looked back at Sanerson. "Go ahead," he said.

Sanerson's voice seemed out of place after the wild denunciations of the cop and the manager. "These men are American journalists," he said. "Mr. Kemp is with *The New York Times,* Mr. Yeamon represents the American Travel Writers' Association, and Mr. Sala works for *Life* magazine." He paused and I wondered just how much good this kind of thing was going to do. Our earlier identification as Yankee journalists had been disastrous.

"Perhaps I'm wrong," Sanerson continued, "but I think this testimony has been a little confusing, and I'd hate to see it result in any unnecessary embarrassment." He glanced at the boss cop, then back to the judge.

"Jesus," Yeamon whispered. "I hope he knows what he's doing."

I nodded, watching the judge's face. Sanerson's last comment had been delivered in a tone of definite warning and it crossed my mind that he might be drunk. For all I knew, he had come straight from some party where he'd been drinking steadily since early afternoon.

"Well, Mr. Sanerson," said the judge in an even voice. "What do you suggest?"

Sanerson smiled politely. "I think it might be wise to continue this hearing when the atmosphere is a little less strained."

The same man who had spoken to the judge earlier was back at the bench. There was a quick exchange of words, then the judge spoke to Sanerson.

"You have a point," he said, "but these men have behaved in an arrogant way—they have no respect for our laws."

Sanerson's face darkened. "Well, your honor, if the case is going to be tried tonight, I'll have to ask for a recess until I can contact Adolfo Quinones." He nodded. "I'll have to get him out of bed, of course, but I don't feel qualified to act any further as an attorney."

There was another hurried conference at the bench. I could see that the name Quinones had given the court some pause. He was the *News'* attorney, an ex-senator, and one of the most prominent men on the island.

We all watched nervously as the conference continued. Finally the judge looked over and told us to stand. "You will be released on bail," he said. "Or you may wait in jail—as you like." He jotted something down on a piece of paper.

"Robert Sala," he said. Sala looked up. "You are charged with public drunkenness, disorderly conduct, and resisting arrest. Bail is set at one thousand dollars."

Sala grumbled and looked away.

"Addison Yeamon," said the judge. "You are charged with public drunkenness, disorderly conduct, and resisting arrest. Bail is set at one thousand dollars."

Yeamon said nothing.

"Paul Kemp," said the judge. "You are charged with public drunkenness and disorderly conduct. Bail is set at three hundred dollars."

This was almost as much of a shock as anything that had happened all night. I felt as if I'd committed a treachery of some kind. It seemed to me that I'd resisted well enough—had it been my screaming? Was the judge taking pity on me because he knew I'd been stomped? I was still pondering it as we were led out of the courtroom and into the hall.

"What now?" said Yeamon. "Can Sanerson afford this kind of bail?"

"Don't worry," I said. "He'll handle it." As I said it I felt like a fool. If worse came to worst, I could cover my bail out of my own pocket. And I knew somebody would post Sala's, but Yeamon was a different matter. Nobody was going to make sure he came to work on Monday. The more I thought about it, the more certain I was that in a few minutes we were going to go free and he would go back to that cell, because there wasn't a soul on the island with a thousand dollars who had even the slightest interest in keeping Yeamon out of jail.

Suddenly Moberg appeared, followed by Sanerson and the man who'd been huddling with the judge. Moberg laughed drunkenly as he approached us. "I thought they were going to kill you," he said.

"They almost did," I replied. "What about this bail? Can we get that much money?"

He laughed again. "It's paid. Segarra told me to sign a check." He lowered his voice. "He said to pay the fines if they weren't more than a hundred dollars. He's lucky—there weren't any fines."

"You mean we're out?" said Sala.

Moberg grinned. "Of course. I signed for it."

"Me too?" said Yeamon.

"Certainly," Moberg replied. "The deed is done—we're all free men."

As we started for the door, Sanerson shook hands with the man he'd been talking with and hurried after us. It was almost dawn and the sky was a light gray. Except for a few people around the police station, the streets were calm and empty. A few big freighters stood at anchor in the bay, waiting for morning and the tugboats that would bring them in.

By the time we got to the street I could see the first rays of the sun, a cool pink glow in the eastern sky. The fact that I'd spent all night in a cell and a courtroom made that morning one of the most beautiful I've ever seen. There was a peace and a brightness about it, a chilly Caribbean dawn after a night in a filthy jail. I looked out at the ships and the sea beyond them and I felt a real excitement at being free with a whole day ahead of me.

Then I realized I would sleep most of the day, and my excitement disappeared. Sanerson agreed to drop us at the apartment and we said goodnight to Moberg, who was going off to look for his car. He'd forgotten where he'd left it, but he assured us it was no problem. "I'll find it by the smell," he said. "I can smell it for blocks." And he shuffled off down the street, a small figure in a dirty gray suit, sniffing for his car.

Sanerson explained that Moberg had first called Lotterman, who was not home, then Quinones, who was in Miami. Then he had called Segarra, who told him to sign a check for what he presumed would be small fines. Sanerson had been at Segarra's house, just ready to leave when Moberg called, and he had stopped by the court on his way home.

"Damn good you did," I said. "We'd be back in that goddamn dungeon if you hadn't come."

Yeamon and Sala mumbled agreement.

"That's probably what you deserve," Sanerson replied. "What got into you, anyway?" Then he smiled and held up his hand. "Never mind. I'm too tired for an argument—we'll talk about it later."

We rode the rest of the way in silence. As we passed the Plaza Colon, I heard the first sounds of morning—a bus beginning its run, the shouts of early fruit peddlers, and from somewhere up on the hill came the rhythmic jangling of Brahms's "Lullaby."

IV

"I loved you once, but now you belong with the dead."
HEROINE, *THE MUMMY*

At times I think that any one of a hundred simple things could have brought that day to a different end. If we had lingered ten minutes longer over dinner, for instance, we'd have joined that awful dancing parade at a different point. Or if we'd turned right, instead of left, when we came down the stairs from the restaurant. Or even if I had run out of cigarettes, and we had stopped for two minutes to buy another pack. If any of those things had happened, we would not have found ourselves in that procession next to the same people we found ourselves next to when we grabbed the first waists we saw and started that maddening shuffle.

Yet at other times I think the events of that night were so inevitably predictable that nothing we might have done would have taken us in any other direction. I think of the day before, and the week before, and the month before that; I can even go back in the years and see the chain of apparently haphazard circumstances that brought me into that yelling, drunken parade at that certain spot at that certain time, next to those people I would never have met if I'd been a minute early or late. I remember decisions made in Europe and New York, at times when I never dreamed of going to any carnival on St. Thomas, at times when I felt I could go anywhere and do anything, holding myriad life patterns in my hand like cards, and feeling free to choose—yet if I look at all that from a certain angle, I see that I never had a choice at all but was only submitting to a fate that had long since been chosen for me.

I have thought this way several times in my life but only when circumstances have led me to a bad pass. No man who has chosen well and wisely will ever credit it to fate; the only real fatalist is a man on his way down the pipe. There is no solace in fatalism. A believer is robbed even of the pleasure of shouting, "Fuck you, I quit," because he knows he was born a quitter and it would be only a matter of time before he threw in the towel, surprising no one, not even himself.

As it happened we joined the dance at a certain point on a street that ends at the waterfront and fell in next to some blacks who seemed to know each other. Somehow we got mixed up so that I was between a thin black girl with a long braid and a squatty black girl with a wide grin; Chenault was between the thin girl and a small man with a spade beard who spoke English with a Harlem accent and kept shouting, "Big noise up there, you Hell Riders! Suck 'em up and GO!" He kept yelling this and it took me a while to understand that the particular band we were following was called the Hell Riders. After each hoot of encouragement, the little man would turn to Yeamon and talk very rapidly.

After an hour or so of this locked-in dancing, we were all old friends. When I finally had to drop out, the two girls acted as if they were losing a vital member of the team. The rhythm of the dance meant quite a bit to them, and to alter it was not a good thing.

Yeamon was happy to quit, but he had to drag Chenault out bodily. We went back to Oliver's and ordered three cups of ice, then sat there for a while and rested our legs. I was half-dead, but Chenault seemed hardly winded. Yeamon was soaked with sweat and after a while he announced that we would go swimming in the harbor to cool off.

We left Oliver's, which was crowded now with all manner of sweaty, half-naked people, and walked across the street to where the boats were tied up. There were people on most of them, but a few were deserted, and we boarded one that looked like a converted native sloop. We took off our clothes on the stern and dove in, much to the amusement of the people on the boat in the next slip. They yelled encouragement and offered drinks, warning us constantly about barracuda.

We finally ended up on their boat, a sleek power cruiser from San Juan. They were wealthy Puerto Ricans, and decent people in a way, but we were all so drunk that we ended up insulting each other and parting company on very ugly terms. One man claimed to be the president of Banco Popular, and I recall Yeamon telling him that when he saw him in San Juan he would kick his ass till his nose bled.

The man came back with what must have been some very elegant threats, but they were in Spanish and all I understood was something about "cutting out the heart."

We stood on the pier and listened to the sounds of the dance. It was moving through the streets a few blocks across town and I marveled at the endurance of those who had managed to hang in. Chenault wanted to join it again, but Yeamon refused and I was glad. I told myself I wouldn't have done it anyway, but I probably would have, rather than be left alone in that drunken chaos of a town.

We went to the balcony of the Grand and made fresh drinks. Sitting there in the wicker chair, with my foot on the wrought-iron railing, I thought I would like to come here sometime when the town was quiet and the natives were not howling through the streets in a great snake dance. Just for the simple luxury of sitting there with a cold gin and tonic, a faint breeze from the slow propeller of the ceiling fan, staring down at the peaceful palm-ringed plaza with the white man's burden on my shoulders and a lazy smile in my heart.

Sometimes after midnight we found ourselves in front of a place called the Blue Grotto. It was jammed, and the noise inside was unholy. We were just about to go in when we were surrounded with happy, friendly shouts. It was our friends from the dance. They were headed for the "real party" and insisted we come along. The squatty girl with the wide grin took hold of my arm, and many times in the next few days did I wish that I might have fallen drunk and helpless on the street at that moment. If my liver had suddenly been split asunder by drink it would have been good luck compared to what followed.

The small, shouting fellow was slapping Yeamon on the back and telling some tale of what we had missed just a few moments before—something about a whip fight and some spicks with a case of gin. We went down the street to where they had a car, and about six more people piled in with us, laughing happily about all the things that had happened.

The car was so crowded I could barely breathe, and all the while I was in it some voice in my gut kept saying, "Get the hell out of here and call a cab for St. Louis. Get out and go back, back, back. . . ." And I remember thinking that I'd read somewhere how experience makes the man, how he should push on into unknown worlds and plumb their meaning.

At the end of the main street we turned up toward the hills above the town, climbing and twisting on a dark little road through what appeared to be the residential section. The houses at the bottom of the hill were wooden, with peeling paint, but as we went higher, more and more houses were made of concrete blocks. Finally they became almost elaborate, with screen porches and lawns and here and there a car parked in a gravel driveway. I couldn't see too well because the squatty girl was sitting on my lap.

We stopped at a house full of lights and music. The street in front of it was jammed with cars and there was no place to park. The driver let us out and said he'd join us when he found a place for the car. The squatty girl gave a loud whoop and ran up the steps to the front door. I followed, very reluctantly, and saw her talking to a fat black woman in a bright blue dress. Then she pointed back at me. Yeamon and Chenault and the others caught up with me as I stopped at the door.

"Six dollars, please," said the woman, holding out her hand.

"Christ!" I said. "How many does that pay for?"

"Two," she said curtly. "You and the young lady." She nodded at the girl who had ridden out from town on my lap.

I cursed silently and gave up six dollars. My date repaid me with a coy smile and took my hand as we entered the house. My God, I thought, this pig is after me.

Yeamon was right behind us, muttering about the six-dollar fee. "This better be good," he told Chenault. "You might as well figure on getting a job when we get back to San Juan."

She laughed, a happy little shriek that had nothing to do with Yeamon's remark. I glanced at her and saw the excitement in her eyes. That dip in the harbor had sobered me up a bit, and Yeamon seemed pretty steady, but Chenault had the look of a hophead, ready to turn on.

We went down a dark hall toward a room full of music and noise. Halfway down the hall was a closet that served as a bar. A huge black man in a blue button-down shirt was mixing drinks and handing them over the makeshift counter to dozens of grasping hands. I stopped and bought one, a rum on ice, for a quarter. It was the ice I wanted—ice, and a cup to drink from.

At the end of the hall we came into the main room. It was jammed from wall to wall, and over in one corner a band was playing. Not the steel band I expected to see but three horns and a drum. The sound was familiar, but I couldn't place it. Then, looking up at the ceiling where the light bulbs were wrapped in blue gelatin, I knew the sound. It was the music of a Midwestern high school dance in some rented club. And not just the music; the crowded, high-ceilinged room, the makeshift bar, doors opening onto a terrace, giggling and shouting and drinking out of paper cups—it was all exactly the same, except that every head in the room was black.

Seeing this made me a bit self-conscious and I began looking around for a dark corner where I could drink without being seen. My date still had me by the arm, but I shook her off and moved toward one corner of the room. No one paid any attention to me as I eased through the mob, bumping dancers here and there, keeping my head lowered and moving cautiously toward what looked like a vacant spot.

A few feet to my left was a door and I edged toward it, bumping more dancers. When I finally got outside I felt like I'd escaped from a jail. The air was cool and the terrace was almost empty. I walked out to the edge and looked down on Charlotte Amalie, the whole town in a cluster of lights at the bottom of the hill. I could hear music floating up from the waterfront, probably from the bars along Queen Street. It sounded like several steel bands, but I was so far away that I couldn't tell. Off to my right and left, in a half-moon of twinkling lights, I could see more houses and a few small hotels where red and blue lights marked something more than a simple residence. Maybe another party, another dance, another blue gelatin orgy full of swaying dancers and syrupy saxophones. I tried to remember the other places we'd been told to go for the "real fun" and wondered if they were any better than this one. I finished my drink and poured another from the bottle.

I thought of Vieques, and for a moment I wanted to be there. I remembered sitting on the hotel balcony and hearing the hoofbeats in the street below. Then I remembered Zimburger, and Martin, and the Marines—the empire builders, setting up frozen-food stores and aerial bombing ranges, spreading out like a piss-puddle to every corner of the world.

There was no peace in Vieques, and certainly none here—only moments snatched out of time, pure little pauses between one madness and the next. I turned to watch the dancers, thinking that since I'd paid six dollars to get into this place, I might as well try to enjoy it. A black fellow appeared at the door and grinned at me. I nodded back, never doubting the wisdom of maintaining an amiable appearance. He came over and talked for a while, and after he'd mentioned the car once or twice I realized he was one of the people who had come up from town with us. I felt bad for not remembering him and tried to make up for it by being overly sociable. I offered him a drink out of my bottle and made some decent comments about the decor of the place, the relaxed atmosphere and the fine view—but all the while I was talking I had an awful suspicion that I wouldn't recognize him again, even if he appeared a few minutes later, smiling in exactly the same way. I remembered that old saying that "all niggers look the same," a foul and callous outlook generally attributed to white trash. But when I looked into that room full of black dancers I saw that it was true—they all looked the same. And this man in front of me looked like all the others. He might as well have been the president of Ghana, without his fancy hat. I had a feeling that it couldn't be true, that there was something terribly wrong with me because the only black face that stood out in my mind was the face of Patrice Lumumba. What is it? I wondered. And I tried to tell myself that all car salesmen looked the same, and all bank tellers. That's it, I thought, it's an occupational thing, not ethnic at all. Then I remembered that not all Jews looked the same, nor all Danes. I got extremely nervous, standing there on the terrace and trying to deny to myself that "all niggers look the same." The one beside me kept up a pleasant chatter, and the idea that I could not recognize him in ten minutes made me feel inadequate and guilty. I felt like beating my breast and cursing God for putting this terrible mote in my eye. I wanted to confess, to grab this well-meaning black fellow by the collar and ram my frightful secret into his ear.

Instead, I said I was going back for more ice and left him standing there on the terrace, blissfully ignorant of all that had gone through my mind while he talked. Or maybe not, I thought. Maybe he knows. This made me feel worse than ever, and I tried not to look at any faces as I made my way across the room toward the bar.

The dancing was getting wilder now. No more of the swaying fox-trot business. There was a driving rhythm to the music; the movements on the floor were jerky and full of lust, a swinging and thrusting of hips, accompanied by sudden cries and groans. I felt a temptation to join it, if only for laughs. But first I would have to get drunker.

On the other side of the room I found Yeamon, standing by the entrance to the hall. "I'm ready to do the dinga," I said with a laugh. "It's finally getting hold of me."

He glared at me, taking a long slug of his drink.

I shrugged and moved on toward the hall closet, where the button-down bartender was still laboring over the drinks. "Rum and ice," I shouted, holding my cup aloft. "Heavy on the ice."

He seized it mechanically, dropped in a few lumps of ice, a flash of rum, then handed it back. I stabbed a quarter into his palm and went back to the doorway. Yeamon was staring at the dancers, looking very morose.

I stopped beside him and he nodded toward the floor. "Look at that bitch," he said.

I looked, and saw Chenault, dancing with the small, spade-bearded black we had met at the beginning of the All-Out Tramp, and who had later brought us to the party. It occurred to me that he looked like Lumumba, but he was a good dancer, and whatever step he was doing was pretty involved. Chenault was holding her arms out like a hula charmer, a look of tense concentration on her face, while her body jerked back and forth with the rhythm of the dance. Now and then she would spin, swirling her plaid skirt around her like a fan.

"Yeah," I said. "She's hell on this dancing."

"She's part nigger," he replied, in a tone that was not soft enough to make me feel at ease.

"Careful," I said quickly. "Watch what you say in this place."

"Balls," he said loudly.

Great Jesus, I thought. Here we go. I put my hand on his arm. "Take it easy," I said. "Why don't we head back to town?"

"Fine with me," he replied. "Try talking to her." He nodded at Chenault, dancing feverishly just a few feet away.

"Hell," I said. "Just grab her. Let's go."

He shook his head. "I did. She screamed like I was killing her."

There was something in his voice that I'd never heard before, an odd wavering that suddenly made me very nervous. "Jesus," I muttered, looking around at the crowd.

"I'll just have to bat her in the head," he said.

Just then I felt a hand on my arm. It was the pig, my squatty date. "Let's go, big boy!" she whooped, dragging me onto the floor. "Let's do it!" She laughed wildly and began to stomp her feet.

Good God, I thought. What now? I watched her, holding my drink in one hand and a cigarette in the other. "Come on!" she shouted. "Give me some business!" She hunched up toward me, pulling her skirt up around her thighs as she wiggled back and forth. I began to stomp and weave; my dancing was shaky at first, then I leveled out to a sort of distracted abandon. Somebody bumped me and I dropped my drink on the floor. It made no difference to the frenzied couples that hemmed us in. Nothing seemed to make any difference; I had a feeling that the dance would go on forever, that they'd forgotten everything else and didn't care to remember.

Suddenly I was next to Chenault. I shrugged helplessly and kept up the stomp. She laughed and bumped me with her hips. Then she and Lumumba drifted away in the crowd, leaving me with my pig.

Finally I shook my head and quit, making gestures to indicate I was too tired to go on. The pig gave me a contemptuous glance and danced away. I went back to the bar for a fresh drink. Yeamon was nowhere in sight and I presumed he'd been sucked into the dance. I made my way through the bodies and out to the terrace, hoping for a place to sit down. Yeamon was sitting on the railing, talking to a black girl of about fifteen. He looked up with a smile. "This is Ginny," he said. "She's going to teach me the dance."

I nodded and said hello. Behind us the music was growing wilder, and at times it was almost drowned out by the yelling of the crowd. I tried to ignore it, looking out over the town, seeing the peace below us and wanting to be down there.

Soon the music from the house grew wilder. There was a new urgency about it, and the shouts of the mob took on a different tone. Yeamon and Ginny went in to see what was happening. I could see the crowd moving back to make room for something, and I walked over to see what it was.

They had made a big circle, and in the middle of it Chenault and the small, waspish black man were doing the dance. Chenault had dropped her skirt and was dancing in her panties and her white sleeveless blouse. The black man had taken off his shirt and wore nothing but a pair of tight, red toreador pants. Both of them were barefoot.

I looked at Yeamon. His face was tense as he stood on tipotoe to watch. Suddenly he called her name. "Chenault!" But the crowd was making so much noise that I could barely hear him three feet away.

She seemed oblivous to everything but the music and the waspish black man who led her around the floor. Yeamon called again, but nobody heard.

Now, as if in some kind of trance, Chenault began to unbutton her blouse. She popped the buttons slowly, like a practiced stripper, then flung the blouse aside and pranced there in nothing but her bra and panties. I thought the crowd would go crazy. They screamed encouragement, stomping and yelling as they shoved and climbed on each other to get a better view. The music never varied except in loudness, but it was already so frenzied that any variation would have been a letdown. The horns screamed madly and the drum thundered on with a harrowing Congo rhythm. I thought the house would cave in from the noise and the terrible stomping on the floor.

I looked again at Yeamon. He was shouting at the top of his lungs, waving his hands in the air now, trying to get Chenault's attention. But he looked like just another spectator, carried away with the spectacle.

Now they were close together, and I saw the black man reach around Chenault and unhook the strap of her bra. He did it quickly, expertly, and she seemed unaware that now she wore nothing but her thin silk panties. The bra slid down her arms and fell to the floor. Her breasts bounced violently with the jerk and thrust of the dance. Full, pink-nippled balls of flesh, suddenly cut loose from the cotton modesty of a New York bra.

I watched, half fascinated and half terrified, and then heard Yeamon beside me as he lunged toward the floor. There was a commotion and then I saw the big bartender move up behind him and grab his arms. Several others pushed him back, treating him like a harmless drunk as they made room for the dance to go on.

Yeamon was screaming hysterically, struggling to free himself from the maze of black arms. "Chenault!" he shouted. "What the hell are you doing?" He sounded so desperate that I wanted to do something, but I felt paralyzed.

They were coming together again, weaving slowly toward the middle of the circle. The noise was unbelievable, an overpowering roar from two hundred black throats. Chenault still wore that dazed, ecstatic expression as the one they call Hugo reached out and eased her panties over her hips and down to her knees. She let them drop silently to the floor, then stepped away, breaking into the dance again, moving against him, freezing there for a moment—even the music paused— then dancing away, opening her eyes and flinging her hair from side to side on her shoulders.

Suddenly Yeamon broke loose. He leaped into the circle and they were on him immediately, but this time he was harder to pin. I saw him whack the big bartender in the face, using his arms and elbows to keep them off, screaming with such a fury that the sound of it sent chills up my spine, and finally going down under a wave of black bodies.

The melee stopped the dance. For an instant I saw Chenault standing alone; she looked surprised and bewildered, with that little muff of brown hair standing out against the white skin and her blonde hair falling around her shoulders. She looked small and naked and helpless, and then I saw Hugo grab her arm and start pulling her toward the door.

I bulled through the crowd, cursing, shoving, trying to get to the hall before they disappeared. Behind me I could hear Yeamon, still yelling, but I knew they had him now and my only thought was to find Chenault. Several people hit me before I got to the door, but I paid no attention. Once I thought I heard her scream, but it could have been anyone. When I finally got through to the hall it was so crowded that I couldn't get through. It seemed like hours before I was able to get to the door.

When I finally got outside I saw a crowd at the bottom of the stairs. I hurried down and found Yeamon lying there on the ground, bleeding from the mouth and groaning. Apparently they had got him out a back door. The big, button-down black was leaning over him, holding his head in his hand and wiping his mouth with a handkerchief.

I forgot about Chenault and shoved through the ring of people, mumbling apologies as I made my way to where Yeamon was stretched out. When I got there the bartender looked up and said, "Is this your friend?"

I nodded, bending down to see if he was hurt.

"He's okay," somebody said. "We tried to be easy with him but he kept swinging."

"Yeah," I said. Yeamon was sitting up now, holding his head in his hands. "Chenault," he mumbled. "What the hell are you doing?"

I put my hand on his shoulder. "Okay," I said. "Take it easy."

"That weasel of a nigger," he said loudly.

The bartender tapped me on the arm. "You better get him out," he said. "He's not hurt now, but he will be if he stays around."

"Can we get a cab?" I asked.

He nodded. "I'll get you a car." He stepped back and yelled across the crowd. Somebody answered and he pointed at me.

"Chenault!" Yeamon shouted, trying to get up off the ground. I shoved him back down, knowing that the moment he got up we'd have another fight. I looked up at the bartender. "Where's the girl?" I said. "What happened to her?"

He smiled faintly. "She enjoyed herself."

I realized then that we were going to be sent off without Chenault. "Where is she?" I said too loudly, trying to keep the panic out of my voice.

A black man I had never seen, or at least didn't recognize, stepped up to me and snarled, "Man, you better get out."

I shuffled nervously in the dirt, looking back at the bartender who seemed to be in charge. He smiled maliciously, pointing behind me. I turned and saw a car, coming slowly through the crowd. "Here's your cab," he said. "I'll get your friend." He stepped over to Yeamon and jerked him to his feet. "Big man go to town," he said with a grin. "Leave little girl here."

Yeamon stiffened and began to shout. "You bastards!" He swung savagely at the bartender, who dodged easily and laughed while several blacks shoved Yeamon into the car. They shoved me in after him, and I leaned out the window to yell at the bartender: "I'll be back with the police—that girl better be all right." Suddenly I felt an awful jolt on the side of my face, and I drew back just in time to let the second punch go flying past my nose. Without quite knowing what I was doing, I rolled up the window and fell back on the seat. I heard them all laughing as we started down the hill.

San Juan, 1962

REVISITED: THE PUERTO RICAN PROBLEM

TWO YEARS AGO Alfred Kazin, the hard-nosed literary critic, published a searing appraisal of Puerto Rico in the magazine *Commentary*.

It did not create much of a stir in the States, but when it was reprinted front page in the *San Juan Star,* all hell broke loose.

Letters poured in, calling Kazin everything from a "crazy Jew" to a "stupid provincial Americano." A few people agreed with him, but to do so in public was to provoke a wild and woolly argument. The dialogue lasted for months—in the press, in bars, in private homes, until eventually the name Kazin evolved into a sort of dirty word from one end of the island to the other.

I was living in San Juan at the time and each day I would sally forth to the fray, defending Kazin more out of sport than any real conviction, and happy in the knowledge that I had a surefire antidote to any dull conversation.

Now all that is changed. If Kazin came back now and wrote the same article it would fall flat. Puerto Rico has made it. The one-time "poorhouse of the Caribbean" is now a blue-chip tourist attraction, and what Alfred Kazin happens to think about it does not make much difference except as a literary curiosity.

This is too bad, in a way, because Puerto Rico, and especially San Juan, is a much duller place than it was two years ago. About the only way to rouse a good argument these days is to gripe about the sky-rocketing prices, and of course that's a waste of time. Success has not gone so much to the Puerto Rican's head as to his belly, and a satisfied man is not nearly so quick to take insult as a scrambling neurotic.

There is no longer that defensiveness that marked the Puerto Rico of the formative years. As recently as 1960, the vested interests and even the would-be vested interests were so insecure that most people would fly off the handle at the slightest inference that this island was anything less than a noble experiment and a budding Valhalla. Now the beachhead has been won. The pattern is no longer Boom or Bust, but more along the lines of Organize and Solidify.

For several years the Commonwealth promoted itself with an ad that said: SUDDENLY, EVERYBODY'S GOING TO PUERTO RICO. And as one wag put it, "Suddenly everybody went to Puerto Rico." Which is one of the reasons why the place has gone dull.

All during the fifties San Juan was literally brimming with geeks and hustlers and gung-ho promoters. Absolute incompetents were getting rich overnight, simply because they had stumbled on a good thing at a ripe time. You would meet a man in a bar and he might have $200 to his name: two months later you would meet him again and he'd have more money than he knew what to do with.

Gimmicks were paying off with a lunatic consistency. A whole tribe of hustlers got rich selling bowling balls to the natives. Another tribe sold Formica-top tables, and still another pushed transistor radios. Now they are all captains of commerce—and the ones who had the wrong gimmicks went broke and disappeared.

The small operator was often a big wheel in the fifties, but now the Big Boys are moving in—people like Clint Murchison of Texas and Gardner Cowles of *Look* magazine—and the methods are changing. Things are not so rough-edged, so crude as they were before. Everybody has a public-relations man and ready cash is no longer so all-important. They are even giving credit to the natives, which pretty well tells the story.

One of the surest signs of the new status level is that the people who once felt they had a mission here are getting apathetic. Most of those missions are accomplished, and a lot of people who grew up with the island are talking about shoving off to seek what might be called "the challenge of the uncertain."

Chuck New, a columnist for the *San Juan Star,* says he has a feeling that "Puerto Rico doesn't need me anymore." This may or may not be true, but what is beyond any question is the fact that New doesn't need Puerto Rico anymore, either. He came here on a shoestring, started doing a gossip column for the newspaper, and one day found he was sole owner of La Botalla, San Juan's most popular bistro. New is not particularly cunning and offers no explanation for his success except that he claims to lead a Christian life—and that he happened to be in San Juan when things were up for grabs.

Another ex-missionary is Bill Kennedy, managing editor of the *Star* since its beginning in the fall of 1959, who several months ago gave up his job and turned to the writing of fiction. "There was no more challenge on the paper," he says. "The excitement went out of it."

Another man, a promoter who worked for more than five years to make Puerto Rico what it is today, put it a little differently. "You know," he said, "San Juan is getting bourgeois—that's why I'm leaving."

One of the best examples of how Puerto Rico has changed can be seen in the *San Juan Star*. On its first anniversary it had a circulation of 5,000 or so. Now, two years and one Pulitzer Prize later, the figure is 17,000 and climbing steadily. The fact that Gardner Cowles owns it may or may not explain anything, but it is worth noting.

In the beginning the *Star* was staffed largely by drifters, transients who showed up out of nowhere and disappeared with a baffling and unexplained regularity. Some of them left vast debts behind, and others went to jail. On any given night the city editor was just as likely to pick up the phone and get a routine story as he was to hear that half his staff had been locked up for creating a riot.

Nothing like that is very likely to happen now. The wild boys have moved on, and the English-speaking press is pretty staid. This is also what happened to the rest of San Juan—the nuts and the cranks and the oddballs have either fled or stayed long enough to become respectable.

Now the streets of the Old City are full of people who look like New Yorkers wearing ManTan—and most of them are. The streets are also full of American homosexuals—so many that the government has begun an official investigation to find out why this is. The Old City itself is getting very quaint; whole blocks of slums are being "reconstructed" and knick-knack shops are sprouting everywhere.

In a phrase, San Juan is over the hump, and the rest of Puerto Rico will not be far behind. After ten years of toil and trouble, millions of dollars spent to attract industry and tourists, savage debates and dialogues as to whether all that money and effort was worthwhile—all that is history now, and whatever happens from here on in will very definitely be a second stage. There are still problems, but they are of a different sort, and dealing with them will require different methods and even different men. For better or for worse, it is the end of an era.

San Juan, 1964

THE KENNEDY ASSASSINATION

"If you want your dreams to come true, don't sleep."
OLD YIDDISH PROVERB

I was in Woody Creek when Kennedy was killed. I had no radio or telephone. Some rancher from up the road knocked on the door and said some Cuban shot Kennedy and he's dying in Dallas.

I was extremely jolted and angry and distraught. I immediately went into town and started doing a piece on the reaction. Just a journalist's instinct. It was so heavy the Observer refused to run it. It was never printed anywhere.

I had just returned from South America, and I had regained that sort of beat generation attitude about the country. I sort of liked the great American West, and a sense of renewing, and I was feeling good about the country.

But all of a sudden that day the country looked different to me, and I felt very bad about it.

Woody Creek, March 1990

BACK TO THE U.S.A.

WHEN I CAME back from South America to the National Observer, *I came as a man who'd been a star—off the plane, all the editors met me and treated me as such. There I was wild drunk in fatigues and a Panama hat. . . . I said I wouldn't work in Washington. National Observer is a Dow Jones company so I continued to write good stories— just without political context. I drifted west. National Observer became my road gig out of San Francisco. I was too much for them. I would wander in on off hours drunk and obviously on drugs, asking for my messages. Essentially, they were working for me. They liked me, but I was the Bull in the China Shop—The more I wrote about politics the more they realized who they had on their hands. They knew I wouldn't change and neither would they.*

The Free Speech Movement was virtually nonexistent at the time, but I saw it coming. There was a great rumbling—you could feel it everywhere. It was wild, but Dow Jones was just too far away. I wanted to cover the Free Speech Movement, but they didn't want me to.

Berkeley, Hell's Angels, Kesey, blacks, hippies . . . I had these con-nections. Rock and roll. I was a crossroads for everything and they weren't making use of it. I was withdrawn from my news position and began writing book reviews—mainly for money.

My final reason for leaving was that I wrote this strongly positive review of Wolfe's Kandy-Kolored Tangerine Flake Streamline Baby. The feature editor of the Washington Post killed it because of a grudge. I took Observer's letter and a copy of the review with a brutal letter about it all to Wolfe. I then copied that letter and sent it to the Observer. I had told Wolfe that the review had been killed for bitchy, personal reasons. The final blow was the Wolfe review. I left to write Hell's Angels in 1965.

Woody Creek, March 1990

HELL'S ANGELS: LONG NIGHTS, UGLY DAYS, ORGY OF THE DOOMED . . .

IN '64 THIS EX-HELL'S Angel, Bernie Jarvis, a reporter for the Chronicle, took me out to a transmission shop in South San Francisco, and introduced me to them.

I was a little edgy in the box shop . . . I was surrounded by clearly vicious hoodlums who were getting kind of a kick out of me being brought in there, wing-tipped shoes and a Madras sports coat and tie.

Jarvis really helped. I would have gotten to know them eventually, but he made it much easier. I got to know the San Francisco Angels, then through them I got to know the Oakland Angels, and then when the Nation piece came out, the word got around that I was all right. Not all of them read it, but enough of them did so they were okay. That was my credential for going back to write the book.

They said it was the only honest thing ever written about them. They didn't mind the brutality or the ugliness of it, they were mainly concerned with the fact that they could identify with the reality of what they were reading. They knew it was a straight, honest account of what the hell they were up to. That's why it was a credential. They weren't worried about what I would write in the book.

I wrote the Nation piece in about a month. I didn't intend to put that much into it. I just got kind of fascinated by the weirdness of it. When it finally came out, I was just sitting there, doing nothing. I paid the rent with the check for the piece, but I was still stuck with having quit journalism and trying to get back into fiction.

I went down to the lineup for the longshoremen there at the docks, where they pick people to work. The regulars all have jobs, but if they need a hand, they sort of say, you, you, you. . . . It didn't work. It was politics: the dock bosses knew whom to pick. I was a stranger.

I ended up lining up about four or five in the morning with winos down at Fifth and Folsom. A truck would pull up and they would say, "We need twelve men to deliver circulars." Out in the Sunset district for a dollar an hour . . . those things you find on your doorstep: SPECIAL AT SAFEWAY TODAY, MEAT, PRODUCE, 14 cents.

But I couldn't even get wino's work. They wouldn't choose me there either. Hell, I was the healthiest person there . . . these were serious winos. Nobody gets up and stands on the street corner in the darkness waiting for a truck to come by and pick maybe six of twenty-five men, unless he's pretty damned desperate.

But all of a sudden when the Nation piece came out, I got about six book offers all at once, in the mail. (My phone had been taken out because I hadn't paid the bill.) I was astounded. I didn't know what the hell had happened. And one of them was an offer from Ballantine, the paperback house, that said they would give me $1,500 just for signing. The Nation piece was the equivalent of an outline for a book, so they said, "Can you write a book on this?" And only a fool would have said no.

The other offers were kind of interesting, a little more prestigious. But the Ballantine thing was a firm offer. It was a $6,000 advance and I could get $1,500 just by signing. I would have signed anything at the time. I'd have signed a contract to write a book about hammerhead sharks, go out in the bay, and swim with the bastards.

Of course, I had already written two novels. . . . I'd always regarded journalism as a lower form of work, a left-handed thing to make money. But of course I'd never seen any journalism that struck me as being special. It was all the same, newspaper writing.

But this subject was so strange that for the first time in any kind of journalism, I could have the kind of fun with writing that I had had in the past with fiction. I could bring the same kind of intensity and have the same kind of involvement with what I was writing about, because there were characters so weird that I couldn't even make them up. I had never seen people this strange. In a way it was like having a novel handed to you with the characters already developed.

That happened to me again eight years later when I got into national politics. But until the Angels I had always been writing in the same mold as other newspaper hacks and I thought that was the way to do it. With the Angels, however, there was a freedom to use words. I'm a word freak. I like words. I've always compared writing to music. That's the way I feel about good paragraphs. When it really works, it's like music. In sportswriting, you have the freedom to use really aggressive words. There's a whole breadth of vocabulary. The Angels gave me that same feeling, like hot damn, the thing was rolling right in front of you. You could touch them on their cycles, you could hear them, and you could see the fear and fright in the citizens' faces. And so I took that first $1,500 and went out and bought a motorcycle. At that point it was the fastest bike ever tested in Hot Rod magazine. And then I destroyed the son of a bitch.

I found out then that writing is a kind of therapy. One of the few ways I can almost be certain I'll understand something is by sitting down and writing about it. Because by forcing yourself to write about it and putting it down in words, you can't avoid having to come to grips with it. You might be wrong, but you have to think about it very intensely to write about it. So I use writing as a learning tool.

Later on I can look back at something like that thing about "the edge," which I wrote about twenty minutes after coming back from doing it. My face was still almost frozen, dark red and crusted with tears, not from crying but tears that start coming to your eyes just from the wind. I was so high on that—from coming back—that I sat and wrote the whole thing, right through, and never changed a word of it. It's one of my favorite pieces of writing.

Woody Creek, March 1990

MIDNIGHT ON THE COAST
HIGHWAY

All my life my heart has sought a thing I cannot name.
—Remembered line from a long-forgotten poem

Months later, when I rarely saw the Angels, I still had the legacy
of the big machine—four hundred pounds of chrome and deep red
noise to take out on the Coast Highway and cut loose at three in the
morning, when all the cops were lurking over on 101. My first crash
had wrecked the bike completely and it took several months to have
it rebuilt. After that I decided to ride it differently: I would stop pushing
my luck on curves, always wear a helmet, and try to keep within range
of the nearest speed limit . . . my insurance had already been canceled
and my driver's license was hanging by a thread.

So it was always at night, like a werewolf, that I would take the
thing out for an honest run down the coast. I would start in Golden
Gate Park, thinking only to run a few long curves to clear my head,
but in a matter of minutes I'd be out at the beach with the sound of
the engine in my ears, the surf booming up on the sea wall and a fine
empty road stretching all the way down to Santa Cruz . . . not even
a gas station in the whole seventy miles; the only public light along
the way is an all-night diner down around Rockaway Beach.

There was no helmet on those nights, no speed limit, and no cooling
it down on the curves. The momentary freedom of the park was like
the one unlucky drink that shoves a wavering alcoholic off the wagon.
I would come out of the park near the soccer field and pause for a
moment at the stop sign, wondering if I knew anyone parked out there
on the midnight humping strip.

Then into first gear, forgetting the cars and letting the beast
wind out . . . thirty-five, forty-five . . . then into second and wailing
through the light at Lincoln Way, not worried about green or red
signals but only some other werewolf loony who might be pulling out,
too slowly, to start his own run. Not many of these—and with three
lanes on a wide curve, a bike coming hard has plenty of room to get

around almost anything—then into third, the boomer gear, pushing seventy-five and the beginning of a windscream in the ears, a pressure on the eyeballs like diving into water off a high board.

Bent forward, far back on the seat, and a rigid grip on the handlebars as the bike starts jumping and wavering in the wind. Taillights far up ahead coming closer, faster, and suddenly—zaaapppp—going past and leaning down for a curve near the zoo, where the road swings out to sea.

The dunes are flatter here, and on windy days sand blows across the highway, piling up in thick drifts as deadly as any oil slick . . . instant loss of control, a crashing, cartwheeling slide and maybe one of those two-inch notices in the paper the next day: "An unidentified motorcyclist was killed last night when he failed to negotiate a turn on Highway I."

Indeed . . . but no sand this time, so the lever goes up into fourth, and now there's no sound except wind. Screw it all the way over, reach through the handlebars to raise the headlight beam, the needle leans down on a hundred, and wind-burned eyeballs strain to see down the centerline, trying to provide a margin for the reflexes.

But with the throttle screwed on there is only the barest margin, and no room at all for mistakes. It has to be done right . . . and that's when the strange music starts, when you stretch your luck so far that fear becomes exhilaration and vibrates along your arms. You can barely see at a hundred; the tears blow back so fast that they vaporize before they get to your ears. The only sounds are wind and a dull roar floating back from the mufflers. You watch the white line and try to lean with it . . . howling through a turn to the right, then to the left and down the long hill to Pacifica . . . letting off now, watching for cops, but only until the next dark stretch and another few seconds on the edge. . . . The Edge. . . . There is no honest way to explain it because the only people who really know where it is are the ones who have gone over. The others—the living—are those who pushed their control as far as they felt they could handle it, and then pulled back, or slowed down, or did whatever they had to when it came time to choose between Now and Later.

But the edge is still Out there. Or maybe it's In. The association of motorcycles with LSD is no accident of publicity. They are both a means to an end, to the place of definitions.

San Francisco, 1965

KEN KESEY: WALKING WITH THE KING

TWENTY FIVE YEARS ago. That's incredible. It seems like at the most twenty-five months. It was a wild time, folks—the good old days for sure. We stomped on the terra. San Francisco in 1965 was the best place in the world to be. Anything was possible. The crazies were seizing the reins, craziness hummed in the air, and the heavyweight king of the crazies was a rustic boy from La Honda named Ken Kesey.

He had the craziest gang in the West. LSD-25 was legal in those days, and Kesey's people were seriously whooping it up. It was a whole new world. "Do it now" was the motto, and anything not naked was wrong. The best minds of our generation somehow converged on La Honda, and Kesey had room for them all. His hillside ranch in the canyon became the world capital of madness. There were no rules, fear was unknown, and sleep was out of the question.

How I became involved with these people is a long, queer story. I'd done an article on the Hell's Angels for The Nation, *and once that was out I had my entree. After that, as far as the Angels were concerned, I was "good people."*

As for Kesey, I always liked his work and believed then, as I still do, that he is one of the really good writers of our time. Earlier, I'd been to one of the Prankster things at Kesey's La Honda place and I liked it.

I happened to have a foot in both camps, and what I did basically was act as a social director mixing a little Hell's Angel with a little Prankster to see what you came up with—for fun, of course, but I was also acting in my own interest because I wanted to have something interesting to write about. To do this safely, well, you must have control—my control ran out early on.

To the credit of Kesey and the pranksters, they were too crazy to be scared. Kesey invited the boys down to La Honda for a full scale set-to with scores of Angels converging for rapine, LSD, and fried chicken. I told Kesey that he would deserve to be shot as a war criminal if he went through with this. I remember thinking, "What the fuck have I wrought here? I have destroyed all kinds of things I've been entrusted to at least be careful with." I was opposed, but there wasn't time to be opposed, there was only time to turn on my tape recorder.

I remember the hordes snarling down the road and amassing near the big welcome banner the Pranksters had stretched across the gate. At the entrance stood the young innocents eager to extend their tribal hospitality.

It was quite a scene. People were bursting into flame everywhere you looked. There were speakers everywhere—all around the trees— there were other big delay speakers on the cliff across the road with wires. And there were about six cop cars parked in the road, flashing lights, cops everywhere, they could see right across the creek. And all the while more Angels were coming down the road and being welcomed with great happiness and friendliness. The simple fact that carnage was averted was impressive, but this was incredible.

Yep. That was Uncle Ken. He couldn't laugh unless he was going fast, and then you couldn't hear him at all because the wind made his lips flap like rubber.

One thing he never knew, though, was what it felt like to get from his house back to mine in thirty-three minutes on a 650BSA Lightning. . . . It was fifty-five miles: which is very, very fast. But there was no speed limit on Highway 1, back then: and on most nights there was no traffic. All you had to do was screw it all the way over and hang on. Everything after that was like being shot through the looking glass. It was faster than a brain full of DMT—one of the most powerful psychedelics ever made. As Grace Slick observed one day, "Acid is like being sucked up a tube, but DMT is like being shot out of a cannon."

Maybe I have gone faster, since then, but somehow it's always felt slow.

Woody Creek, March 1990

LSD-25: *RES IPSA LOQUITOR*

I FIRST GOT INTO acid when I lived in Big Sur in the early '60s. Mike Murphy and Joanna, a Stanford research psychiatrist, were experimenting with it. The idea fascinated me, but they said, wait a minute, there are some people who cannot take acid, and you are one of them. You're the most violent son of a bitch that's ever walked the earth. We both like you, and we probably understand you. It's just too dangerous for you to take acid. You might kill us all, or kill yourself.

Mike had been into weird Indian drugs for a long time, and I gathered that he had to be locked up himself when he took it. He was a pretty peaceful guy, but he had run amuck in Palo Alto, so I took their word for it. I stayed away from it then, and I didn't have any for a long time after that.

Even later, when I was around Kesey's place, I refused to take it, because I figured I might go crazy and do something violent. But then finally I took it down there, in a fit of despair, the night that the Angels showed up. Kesey had invited them down after I'd introduced him to them, and I felt responsible for whatever was going to happen. I thought the Angels were going to beat people up and rape them.

So I figured, why not just get it on, and I asked somebody to give me a hit of acid. I thought, whatever I do can't be worse than what's already going on around me, so I may as well do it. I can't stand it straight.

I took it and it was quite a ride. I went completely out of my head and I had a wonderful time, didn't bother a soul. Not a hint of violence. I thought, aha, I've gone to the bottom of the well here and the animal's not down there, the one they said was there.

I had a lot of confidence, and you need a lot. You have to give yourself over to your instinct because with a head full of acid you can't pull back. You're going to do whatever you feel like doing. You can't repress anything. If you're going to jump out the window, you're going to jump out the window. If you're going to get violent, you're going to get violent. But I didn't.

Instead, I usually get very calm. I get into music, and talking, and laughing, and heavy thinking, images coming, connections. But they come so fast it's very hard to come back from the trip and still keep them intact. Nobody's really described an acid experience properly because it's impossible to come back to one and you can't really describe it.

That's why it's hard to write on mescaline, too, because your mind is going four times as fast as your hands can go, and you get disorganized and you can't keep your mind in phase with your fingers. That's why I have to get increasingly faster typewriters.

Whatever they make, if it's faster, I'll buy it.

Woody Creek, March 1990

CHICAGO 1968: DEATH TO THE WEIRD

BEFORE CHICAGO

NOBODY SENT ME to Chicago.

I had a contract to write a book. I got an advance on it. The working title was The Death of the American Dream. I had no idea what it meant. I didn't care what it meant. I just wanted money from a publisher and I wanted to write something else. I'd tried to sell Random House on a book that Tom Wolfe eventually wrote, on the whole psychedelic thing, the next uprising.

I called Silberman collect one morning from Dick Alpert's house in Palo Alto. Crazed on acid. I spent about half an hour with the phone in my hand, holding it out so Silberman could hear the sound of a bee buzzing in a lilac bush. Meanwhile, I was trying to sell him on sending me $10,000 for an advance on the book. He took it in a good-humored way, but he rejected the idea.

So what came up was this Death of the American Dream thing, and I thought, well, the best way to do that is to take a look at politics. The first thing I did after I signed the contract was to go up to the New Hampshire Primary in '68 to do an article on Nixon. That was just an excuse. I wanted to see politics working.

A presidential campaign would be a good place, I thought, to look for the Death of the American Dream. And by the time I went up to write the piece on Nixon in New Hampshire I got to know all the McCarthy people because he was running at the same time. Johnson was still president and hadn't quit yet. McCarthy had no chance, supposedly, and I just happened to get mixed up with his people because they were sort of my kind of people. Like Sy Hersh, who was McCarthy's press secretary at the time.

So when Chicago came around, my head had gotten into politics, and I thought, well, if we're going to have a real bastard up there I may as well go. I went totally prepared. You don't take a motorcycle helmet to Chicago, normally, without a motorcycle. . . . And I still got the shit beaten out of me by the police.

AFTER CHICAGO

I figured, if this is the way you bastards want to play, okay, and I went back and shook up politics in Aspen pretty seriously. I persuaded a person I didn't know at all, never even talked to, to run for mayor. The current mayor was running unopposed, and I thought, when the system is as rotten as I saw in Chicago, nobody should run unopposed, particularly a bad candidate. I just got angry that the mayor of Aspen, an old Republican lady, could run unopposed.

The McCarthy movement had floundered, and Bobby Kennedy had been killed, and it was a very low time for involvement in national politics. It was a crushing defeat for this kind of political notion that had been building for three or four years, that began out in Berkeley.

So it was time to do something else. We'd been beaten in Chicago. The lesson was very clear.

I figured that first, you change a small town. Politics in a small town is very apparent. You can get hold of things much more easily. Joe Edwards, the guy I persuaded to run for mayor, lost by six votes. I'd seen the ignorant hate vote come out and beat us, so I thought next year we'll fool the bastards, we'll run somebody else for county commissioner, and I'll run for sheriff and give the bastards a real scare. We all lost by a very small margin.

Later, of course, in '72 when I was covering the national campaign, Joe Edwards and his law partner both ran for county commissioner. There were only three seats and if you control two, you control the county.

So while I was off covering McGovern, Sandy organized Joe's campaign, and he won. Hell, he won easily, but by that time we'd managed to make Aspen politics pretty interesting. It was no longer fashionable to refuse to register, to get deliberately stoned on election day and refuse to vote. But that process took about two years.

Hell, we had the votes to win the mayor's race in '69, but we couldn't convince them to register. Aspen was a really apolitical place. We were dealing with refugees from California, refugees from the East, real dropouts from everything. The last thing they wanted to do was get involved with regular politics.

So I wrote this article, "The Battle of Aspen," and I thought, now where should I publish this? I was writing for Scanlan's at the time. But rather than give it to them, I thought, no, this one belongs in Rolling Stone. I figured the people I wanted to get to, the dropouts, would read Rolling Stone. I thought of it more as an ad than an article. And it worked—the vote tripled in one year.

Another reason we had lost in '69 was that the Aspen Times, the only paper of any influence in town at the time, refused to back Joe Edwards. We just had no way to reach people in town. So I thought, what we have to have is a newspaper. And you can't just go starting newspapers. But we could start a wall poster.

With the posters on one side they became something people would put on a wall. And I could write my gibberish on the back. Tom Benton and Joe Edwards and I became partners in the Meat Possum Corporation. I figured if there are going to be any libel suits, they should sue the fucking Meat Possum Press and not me. Edwards was a lawyer so I made him a partner. That way we had a lawyer, and a judgment-proof corporation. I could run completely amok on the back of Benton's posters.

The Wall Posters were a booming success for a while, but then we pushed it a little too far. We doubled the size, made it four pages, selling ads on the back to pay for it. That meant that I had the middle, Benton had the front, and we had the ads on the back. It worked for one issue, but what I put in the middle scared the hell out of a lot of people.

I threatened the sheriff. That was sort of my announcement for running for sheriff, a long article mocking him—mocking his fear of being shot by a hired freak gunman, a hippie-Mafia type. He was always muttering about how he wouldn't do this or couldn't do that because the hippies would shoot him. He was always mumbling that there was an emergency condition in the town because he had heard from "unnamed sources" that three freaks had come in there to kill him. So I mocked him, which in effect read like I was threatening to kill him.

Also I insisted, since I had the middle two pages, on running a large picture of a Japanese girl masturbating. It really freaked people out, but I thought it was one of the most erotic shots I'd ever seen. We called her "Jilly."

And then Oscar came out.

He'd been coming out to Aspen off and on for years. But he came up and did our ad for us on the radio. We've always used the radio as our television, or the equivalent of television, in Aspen. There was no local television then.

And Oscar read this grisly ad about his wife being taken from him in L.A., his wife named "Jilly," who'd run off with some editor from the Wall Poster, and he'd come to Aspen to look for her. He was pleading with the people of the town to help him find his wife, who had run off with these terrible dope addicts and drunkards. He had a breakdown on the radio. It was one of the funniest and weirdest tapes *you'll ever hear, by anybody. I wrote the script for the thing and we ran it four or five times. Of course, everybody in town took it seriously.*

We had to take it off the air because people were calling from Denver and the AP office about some "kidnapping" and "extortion," something going on in Aspen. Some Chicano lawyer had come looking for his wife who had been kidnapped and taken to Aspen. So it got too serious.

Oscar came back out later in the campaign to be a bodyguard. That scared a lot of people, too. They accused me of bringing in Communists, foreigners, strangers, outside agitators.

But people were threatening to kill me. The Colorado Bureau of Investigation sent a man over with a list of twelve names that they had already identified as having uttered serious assassination threats. Now, looking back on it, I really think it was an attempt by the sheriff to use the CBI to scare me out of the campaign.

Dave Meggessy, this huge brute of a linebacker with hair all the way down to his waist, came out to be a bodyguard, too. It got very violent toward the end. We were all armed. It was ironic, because one of the planks of my platform was that the police shouldn't be armed.

Meanwhile, I'd shaved my head. It was sort of a strange accident. I was going up to cover an American Legion convention in Portland, Oregon, for Scanlan's early that summer, and in order to do that I thought I should get a bit of a trim in order to look like an American Legionnaire. So I went to a friend's house. He was sort of my personal barber. Anyway, we smoked about four joints, and he started with this goddamned electric razor and just went right over one side of my head, completely down to the bone. Once a person has done that there's no choice, of course. Once you're half bald you'd look insane if the other side had hair on it. So I had no choice but to shave my head completely . . . which went over pretty well at the convention, but there wasn't enough time between the convention and the Aspen campaign to let the hair grow out to the point where it would look half normal. When that little fuzz comes up you look like a psychotic Nazi prison guard. So I had to keep it shaved.

But we brought out a massive backlash vote. They couldn't handle a mescaline-eating sheriff who shaved his head and looked like the devil.

Woody Creek, March 1990

FIRST VISIT WITH MESCALITO

February 16, 1969

AGAIN IN L.A., again at the Continental Hotel . . . full of pills and club sandwiches and Old Crow and now a fifth of Louis Martini Barbera, looking down from the eleventh floor balcony at a police ambulance screaming down toward the Whiskey A Go-Go on the Strip, where I used to sit in the afternoon with Lionel and talk with off-duty hookers . . . and while I was standing there, watching four flower children in bell-bottom pants, two couples, hitch-hiking toward Hollywood proper, a mile or so up the road . . . they noticed me looking down and waved. I waved, and moments later, after pointing me out to each other, they hoisted the "V" signal—and I returned that. And one of them yelled, "What are you doing up there?" And I said, "I'm writing about all you freaks down there on the street." We talked back and forth for a while, not communicating much, and I felt like Hubert Humphrey looking down at Grant Park. Maybe if Humphrey had had a balcony in that twenty-fifth-floor Hilton suite he might have behaved differently. Looking out a window is not quite the same. A balcony puts you out in the dark, which is more neutral—like walking out on a diving board. Anyway, I was struck by the distance between me and those street freaks; to them, I was just another fat cat, hanging off a balcony over the strip . . . and it reminded me of James Farmer on TV today, telling "Face the Nation" how he'd maintained his contacts with the Black Community, talking with fat jowls and a nervous hustler style, blundering along in the wake of George Herman's and Daniel Schorr's condescension . . . and then McGarr talking later, at the Luau, a Beverly Hills flesh pit, about how he could remember when Farmer was a radical and it scared him to see how far he'd drifted from the front lines . . . it scared him, he said, because he wondered if the same thing could happen to him . . . which gets back to my scene on the balcony—Hubert Humphrey looking down at Grant Park on Tuesday night, when he still had options (then, moments later, the four flower children hailed a cab—yes, cab, taxi—and I walked down to the King's Cellar liquor store where the clerk looked at my Diners

Club card and said "Aren't you the guy who did that *Hell's Angels* thing?" And I felt redeemed. . . . Selah).

February 18

L.A. notes, again . . . one-thirty now and pill-fear grips the brain, staring down at this half-finished article . . . test pilots, after a week (no, three days) at Edwards AFB in the desert . . . but trying to mix writing and fucking around with old friends don't work no more, this maddening, time-killing late-work syndrome, never getting down to the real machine action until two or three at night, won't make it . . . especially half drunk full of pills and grass with deadlines past and people howling in New York . . . the pressure piles up like a hang-fire lightning ball in the brain. Tired and wiggy from no sleep or at least not enough. Living on pills, phone calls unmade, people unseen, pages unwritten, money unmade, pressure piling up all around to make some kind of breakthrough and get moving again. Get the gum off the rails, finish something, croak this awful habit of not ever getting to the end—of anything.

And now the fire alarm goes off in the hall . . . terrible ringing of bells . . . but the hall is empty. Is the hotel on fire? Nobody answers the phone at the desk; the operator doesn't answer . . . the bell screams on. You read about hotel fires: 75 KILLED IN HOLOCAUST: LEAPING OFF BALCONIES (I am on the eleventh floor) . . . but apparently there is no fire. The operator finally answers and says a "wire got crossed." But nobody else is in the hall; this happened in Washington too, at the Nixon gig. False alarms and a man screaming down the airshaft, "Does anybody want to fuck?" The foundations are crumbling.

Yesterday a dope freak tried to steal the Goodyear blimp and take it to Aspen for the Rock and Roll festival . . . carrying a guitar and a toothbrush and a transistor radio he said was a bomb. . . . "Kept authorities at bay," said the L.A. *Times,* "for more than an hour, claiming to be George Harrison of the Beatles." They took him to jail but couldn't figure out what to charge him with . . . so they put him in a looney bin.

Meanwhile the hills keep crumbling, dropping houses down on streets and highways. Yesterday they closed two lanes of the Pacific Coast highway between Sunset and Topanga . . . passing the scene in McGarr's little British-souvenir car on the way to Gover's house in Malibu . . . we looked up and saw two houses perched out in space, and dirt actually sliding down the cliff. It was only a matter of time, and no cure, no way to prevent these two houses from dropping on the highway. They keep undercutting the hills to make more house sites, and the hills keep falling. Fires burn the vegetation off in summer, rains make mudslides in the winter . . . massive erosion, fire and mud, with The Earthquake scheduled for April. Nobody seems to give a fuck.

Today I found marijuana seeds all over the rug in my room . . . leaning down to tie my shoes I focused low and suddenly the rug was alive with seeds. Reminds me of the time I littered a hotel room in Missoula, Montana, with crab lice . . . picking them off, one by one, and hurling them around the room. . . . I was checking out for Butte. And also the last time I was in this hotel I had a shoe full of grass, and John Wilcock's package . . . awful scene at the Canadian border in Toronto, carrying all that grass and unable to say where I lived when they asked me. . . . I thought the end had come, but they let me through.

And now, by total accident, I find "Property of Fat City" (necessary cop-out change self-preservation—Oscar—looting) painted on the side of this borrowed typewriter. Is it stolen? God only knows . . . seeds on the rug and a hot typewriter on the desk, we live in a jungle of pending disasters, walking constantly across a minefield . . . will my plane crash tomorrow? What if I miss it? Will the next one crash? Will my house burn down? Gover's friend's house in Topanga burned yesterday, nothing saved except an original Cezanne. Where will it all end?

February 18/19

Getting toward dawn now, very foggy in the head . . . and no Dexedrine left. For the first time in at least five years I am out of my little energy bombs. Nothing in the bottle but five Ritalin tablets and a big spansule of mescaline and "speed." I don't know the ratio of the mixture, or what kind of speed is in there with the mescaline. I have no idea what it will do to my head, my heart, or my body. But the Ritalin is useless at this point—not strong enough—so I'll have to risk the other. Oscar is coming by at ten, to take me out to the airport for the flight to Denver and Aspen . . . so if I sink into madness and weird hallucinations, at least he can get me checked out of the hotel. The plane ride itself might be another matter. How can a man know? (Well, I just swallowed the bugger . . . soon it will take hold; I have no idea what to expect, and in this dead-tired, run-down condition almost anything can happen. My resistance is gone, so any reaction will be extreme. I've never had mescaline.)

Meanwhile, outside on the Strip the zoo action never stops. For a while I watched four L.A. sheriffs beat up two teenagers, then handcuff them and haul them away. Terrible howls and screams floated up to my balcony. "I'm sorry, sir. . . . Oh God, please, I'm sorry." WHACK. One cop picked him up by the feet while he was hanging onto a hurricane fence; the other one kicked him loose, then kneeled on his back and whacked him on the head a few times. I was tempted to hurl a wine bottle down on the cops but refrained. Later, more noise . . . this time a dope freak, bopping along and singing at the top of his lungs—some kind of medieval chant. Oblivious to everything, just bopping along the strip.

And remember that shooting scene in Alfie's . . . also the film opening with a man reeling into a plastic house, vomiting, cursing the news, picking up a pistol, and firing into the ceiling . . . driven mad by the news and the pressures of upward mobility . . . then, perhaps, to the Classic Cat on amateur night, his neighbor's wife . . . and from there to the shooting at Alfie's . . . yes, it begins to jell.

Jesus, 6:45 now and the pill has taken hold for real. The metal on the typewriter has turned from dull green to a sort of high-gloss blue, the keys sparkle, glitter with highlights. . . . I sort of levitated in the chair, hovering in front of the typewriter, not sitting. Fantastic brightness on everything, polished and waxed with special lighting . . . and the physical end of the thing is like the first half-hour on acid, a sort of buzzing all over, a sense of being gripped by something, vibrating internally but with no outward sign or movement. I'm amazed that I can keep typing. I feel like both me and the typewriter have become weightless; it floats in front of me like a bright toy. Weird, I can still spell . . . but I had to think about that last one. . . . "Weird." Christ, I wonder how much worse this is going to get. It's seven now, and I have to check out in an hour or so. If this is the beginning of an acid-style trip I might just as well give up on the idea of flying anywhere. Taking off in an airplane right now would be an unbearable experience, it would blow the top right off my head. The physical sensations of lifting off the ground would be unbearable in this condition; I feel like I could step off the balcony right now and float gently down to the sidewalk. Yes, and getting worse, a muscle in my thigh is seized by spasms, quivering like something disembodied. . . . I can watch it, feel it, but not be connected. There is not much connection between my head and my body . . . but I can still type and very fast too, much faster than normal. Yes, the goddamn drug is definitely taking hold, very much like acid, a sense of very pleasant physical paralysis (wow, that spelling) while the brain copes with something never coped with before. The brain is doing all the work right now, adjusting to this new stimulus like an old soldier ambushed and panicked for a moment, getting a grip but not in command, hanging on, waiting for a break but expecting something worse . . . and yes, it's coming on. I couldn't possibly get out of this chair right now, I couldn't walk, all I can do is type . . . it feels like the blood is racing through me, all around my body, at fantastic speeds. I don't feel any pumping, just a sense of increased flow. . . . Speed. Interior speed . . . and a buzzing without noise, high speed vibrations and more brightness. The little red indicator that moves along with the ball on this typewriter now appears to be made of arterial blood. It throbs and jumps along like a living thing.

I feel like vomiting, but the pressure is too great. My feet are cold, hands cold, head in a vise . . . fantastic effort to lift the bottle of Budweiser and take a sip, I drink like breathing it in, feeling it all the way cold into my stomach . . . very thirsty, but only a half a beer left and too early to call for more. Christ, there's the catch. I am going to have to deal with all manner of complicated shit like packing, paying, all that shit any moment now. If the thing bites down much harder I might wig out and demand beer . . . stay away from the phone, watch the red arrow . . . this typewriter is keeping me on my rails, without it I'd be completely adrift and weird. Maybe I should call Oscar and get him down here with some beer, to keep me away from that balcony. Ah shit, this is very weird, my legs are half frozen and a slow panic in my stomach, wondering how much stranger it will get . . . turn the radio on, focus on something but don't listen to the words, the vicious bullshit. . . . Jesus, the sun is coming up, the room is unbearably bright, then a cloud across the sun, I can see the cloud in the sudden loss of light in the room, now getting brighter as the cloud passes or moves . . . out there somewhere, much harder to type now, but it must be done, this is my handle, keep the brain tethered, hold it down. Any slippage now could be a landslide, losing the grip, falling or flipping around, Christ, can't blow my nose, can't find it but I can see it and my hand too, but they can't get together, ice in my nose, trembling with the radio on now, some kind of flute music, cold and fantastic vibration so fast I can't move . . . the ball just flipped back, a space capsule floating across the page, some kind of rotten phony soul music on the radio, Melvin Laird singing "The Weight" "O yes we get wear-

ahe, weeri, wearih?" Some fuckawful accent. Hairjelly music. Anthony
Hatch in Jerusalem, great God, the stinking news is on, get rid of it,
no mention of Nixon, too much for a tortured head. . . . Christ, what
a beastly job to look for a new station on this radio dial, up and down
the bright blue line and all these numbers, quick switch to FM, get
rid of the fucking news, find something in a foreign language . . . the
news is already on the TV screen, but I won't turn it on, won't even
look at it . . . . Nixon's face. . . . GODDAMN, I just called Oscar,
fantastic effort to dial, and the fucking line is busy . . . hang on now,
no slippage, ignore this weird trembling . . . laugh, yes, that sense of
humor, snag it down from somewhere, the skyhook. . . . Jesus, I have
to lock that door, get the DO NOT DISTURB sign out before a maid
blunders in. I can't stand it, and I just heard one out there, creeping
along the hallway, jiggling doorknobs . . . ho ho, yes, that famous
smile . . . yes, I just got hold of Oscar . . . he's coming with some
beer . . . that is the problem now, I can't start fucking around with
the management, shouting for beer at this hour of dawn . . . disaster
area that way, don't fuck with the management, not now in this wiggy
condition . . . conserve this inch of beer until Oscar arrives with more,
get a human buffer zone in here, something to hide behind . . . the
fucking news is on again, on FM this time. Singer Sewing time is fifteen
minutes until eight o'clock, Washington's birthday sale we cannot tell
a lie, our machines will sew you into a bag so fast you'll think you
went blind . . . goddamn is there no human peaceful sound on the
radio . . . yes, I had one for an instant, but now more ads and
bullshit . . . now, right there, a violin sound, hold that, stay with it,
focus on that violin sound, ride it out . . . ah, this beer won't last, the
thirst will doom me to fucking with the management . . . no, I have
some ice left—on the balcony—but careful out there, don't look over
the edge . . . go out backward, feel around for the paper ice bucket,
seize it carefully between thumb and forefinger, then walk slowly back
to this chair . . . try it now. . . . DONE, but my legs have turned to
jelly, impossible to move around except like a rolling ball, don't
bounce, get away from that phone, keep typing, the grip, the handle . . . Jesus, my hands are vibrating now, I don't see how they can
type. The keys feel like huge plastic mounds, very mushy and that
bright red arrow jumping along like a pill in one of those singalong
movie shorts, bouncing from word to word with the music. . . . Thank
God for the *Sonata in F Major for Oboe and Guitar* by Charles Stark-
weather . . . no ads, listener-sponsored radio, not even news . . .
salvation has many faces, remind me to send a check to this station
when I get well. . . . KPFA? Sounds right. The beer crisis is building,

I am down to saliva in this last brown bottle . . . goddamn, half my brain is already pondering how to get more beer, but it won't work . . . no way. No beer is available here. No way. Nao tem. Think about something else, thank God for this music; if I could get to the bathroom I'd like to get a towel and hang it over the face of this stinking TV set, the news is on there, I can smell it. My eyes feel bigger than grapefruits. Where are the sunglasses, I see them over there, creep across, that cloud is off the sun again, for real this time, incredible light in the room, white blaze on the walls, glittering type-writer keys . . . and down there under the balcony traffic moves stead-ily along the Sunset Strip in Hollywood, California zip code unknown . . . we just came back from a tour of the Soviet Union and Denmark, careful now, don't stray into the news, keep it pure, yes, I hear a flute now, music starting again. What about cigarettes, another problem area . . . and I hear that wily old charwoman sucking on the doorknob again, goddamn her sneaky ass what does she want? I have no money. If she comes in here the rest of her days will be spent in a fear-coma. I am not in the mood to fuck around with charwomen, keep them out of here, they prowl this hotel like crippled wolves . . . smile again, yes, gain a step, tighten the grip, ho ho. . . . When will this thing peak? It seems to be boring deeper. I know it can't be worse than acid, but that's what it feels like now. I have to catch a plane in two hours. Can it be done? Jesus, I couldn't fly now. . . . I couldn't walk to the plane . . . oh Jesus, the crunch is on, my throat and mouth are like hot gravel and even the saliva is gone . . . can I get to the bottle of Old Crow and mix it up with the remains of these ice fragments . . . a cool drink for the freak? Give the gentleman something cool, dear, can't you see he's wired his brain to the water pump and his ears to the generator . . . stand back, those sparks! Back off, maybe he's too far gone . . . coil a snake around him . . . get that drink, boy, you are slipping, we need CONCEN-TRATION . . . yes, the music, some kind of German flower song. Martin Bormann sings WHITE RABBIT . . . ambushed in the jungle by a legion of naked gooks . . . whiskey uber alles, get that drink, get up, move.

DONE . . . but my knees are locked and my head is about twenty feet higher than my feet . . . in this room with an eight-foot roof, making travel very difficult. The light again, get those sunglasses, unlock the knees and creep over there . . . not far . . . yes, I'm wear-ing the glasses now, but the glare is still all around. Getting out of this hotel and catching this plane is going to be weird. . . . I see not much hope, but that's not the way to think. . . . I have managed to do everything else I've had to do so far. Twenty-three minutes past eight on this brain-saving station, I hear echoes of the news, leaking out the back of the TV set. . . . Nixon has ordered the Condor Legion into Berkeley . . . smile . . . relax a bit, sip that drink. Bagpipes now on the radio, but it's really violins . . . they're fucking around with these instruments, sounds like a tractor in the hall, the charwomen are going to cave my door in with a fucking webbed vehicle, a crane in the hall, snapping doors off their hinges like so many cob-webs . . . creaking and clanking along, this hotel has gone all to hell since the chain took it over, no more grapefruit in the light sockets, the lamp sockets . . . put some lampblack on these walls, take off the glare. We need more hair on these walls, and crab-lice in the rug to give it life. There are marijuana seeds in this rug, the place is full of them. The rug crackles like popcorn when I walk, who planted these seeds in this rug, and why aren't they watered? Now . . . yes . . . there is a project, tend the crops, soak this rug like a drenching rain, some kind of tropical downpour . . . good for the crops, keep the ground damp and prune the leaves every other day. Be careful about renting the room, special people, nature freaks, tillers of the soil . . . let them in, but for Christ's sake keep the charwomen out. They don't like things growing in the rug, most of them seem like third generation Finns, old muscles turned to lard and hanging like wasps nests. . . .

Wasps nests? Slipping again, beware, Oscar just came in, bringing beer. I seem to have leveled out, like after the first rush of acid. If this is as deep as it's going to bore I think we can make that plane, but I dread it. Getting in a steel tube and shot across the sky, strapped down . . . yes, I sense a peak, just now, a hint of letdown, but still vibrating and hovering around with the typewriter. The cloud is over the sun again, or maybe it's smog . . . but the glare is gone from the walls, no highlights on the buildings down below, no sparkle on the rooftops, no water, just gray air. I see a concrete mixer moving, red and gray, down on that other street a long way off. It looks like a matchbox toy; they sell them in airports. Get one for Juan. I think we will catch that plane. Someday when things are right and like they should be we can do all this again by putting a quarter in the Holiday Inn vibrator bed and taking a special madness pill . . . but wait, hold over there, we can do *that* now. We can do almost anything now . . . and why not?

Xerox copy with author's notes of yesterday's program for today's Continental Airlines tape concert—private earphones for all passengers and six-channel selector dials, along with individual volume controls, built into each seat. The "program" being twenty-four hours old plays hell with a head full of cactus madness—like watching an NFL football game with an AFL roster.

11:32—hovering again. Weightless—weird—L.A. down below—earphones and knobs—switching around Jesus, Leon Blum—the Canadian Legion Hailie Selassie speech.

Cheap rental cars at the airport—seize Batrollers and zang up to Big Sur—have Michael Murphy arrested for restraint of trade, killing the last true hillbilly-music cabal on the West Coast. Who can blame me for whipping on that paraplegic in the baths? Anyone would have done it—Selah.

Who are these pigs—as a validated addict I demand to be left alone—drink the eucalyptus oil—with dials and knobs still high as a freak male locked into the vibrations of the jet engines—get a bag of acid and a credit card for airlines—evaluate the pitch, roll and yaw—no sense of movement in this plane—just humming—the phones—acid-style high tingling and strange, intense vibrations. Get that dead animal off the seat—put it under—where is the drink? These pigs are taking us for a ride—put it on the card. Strange feedback echoes on the headset. Gabriel Heatter screaming in the background—telephone conversations—fantastic people talking. This is yesterday's program—new songs today. A dingbat across the aisle and Kitty Wells on the headphones. This channel is hag-ridden with echoes—telephone conversations. See no wings on this plane—good God the lock on my whiskey bag is frozen—a lifting body, tends to destroy itself, very wormy. I seem to be getting higher. (12:15.) Warn the pilot—this plane feels very wormy at this altitude. An ominous sense of yaw . . . sliding off edge—fire in the ashtray. Weird things in this channel.

Further notes in the Denver airport—coming down but can't relax, looking for a plane ride to Aspen with all legitimate flights canceled due to snowstorm—if not to Aspen, then back to L.A.—last chance to get straight—final effort—and half-wanting the abyss. One of you pigs will find me a plane—sweating obscenely, hair plastered down and dripping from the cheekbones—the drug is gone now, no more zang, failing energy, disconnected thoughts—the Goodyear blimp as a last resort but no driving. Beware of (unreadable) hawks in the company of straight people—get that charter, leaving in five minutes—fiery stomach, running through the airport screaming for Bromo-Seltzer—coming down again in the Denver airport. Now, sitting in the copilot's seat of an Aero Commander—weirdness feeds on itself—with a wheel in my lap and pedals on the floor at my feet—forty-one round dials in front of me, blinking lights, jabbering radio noise—smoking, waiting for the oxygen—sick, feeling deranged—two Ritalins don't help much—sliding—no hope of pulling out—air bubbles in the brain—open this window beside me, a rush of air and crisis sounds from the others. Smelling of booze in this tiny cabin, nobody speaks—fear and loathing, dizzy, flying and bouncing through clouds. No more hole-cards, drained. Back to L.A., rather than Grand Junction—why go there? Chaos in the Denver airport—soaking sweats and all flights canceled—charwomen working—lying swine at the counters—"here boy, rent this car." Sorry, as a certified addict I cannot drive on snow—I must fly!

Los Angeles, 1969

The SEVENTIES

REAPING THE WHIRLWIND,
RIDING THE TIGER

IGUANA PROJECT

THE IGUANA PROJECT is as good a name as any other for this volatile thing that we're into. Why not? And so much for labels. The potential of the thing is so vast that we can't possibly define the ends—so all we can talk about for now is the "potential," the "goals," the possibility of massive "leverage," and the entirely reasonable idea that any body or bloc who can speak for 20 million voters will emerge—by mathematical definition—as a primary force in American politics.

The original discussions—in Aspen, during late June and early July of 1971—have all been agreeably resolved to the same ends: one, that the ugly realities of 1971 America leave us no choice but to involve ourselves in basic politics on the national level—beginning with the presidential campaign of 1972, then to the congressional campaigns of 1974, and *finally* the presidential campaign of 1976. This scenario should be kept in mind by everybody involved with this project.

The likelihood of mounting an Aspen-style "Freak Power" campaign on the national level is a far-fetched joke for 1972—at least that's what it looks like, for now. We should keep in mind, however, that in July of 1970 we all (in Aspen) considerd it a "far-fetched joke" that I might run for sheriff three months later. Yet in November of 1970 I got something like 44 percent of the total vote in a three-way race with two establishment candidates—the incumbent sheriff and the under-sheriff—backed by the local Democratic and Republican parties. Even with my head shaved completely bald and running full-bore on the "Mescaline Ticket," I *forced* a coalition of the establishment parties that resulted in total humiliation for the GOP candidate. He got about 250 votes, compared to my 1,065 or so, and the incumbent's 1,500. (These figures and percentages are approximate; but no matter how they're cut or interpreted, a bald-headed "dope fiend" (admitted) got at least 40 percent of the vote in a three-way race . . . which suggest to me that I was right (in *Rolling Stone* 10/1/70) when I said that the electorate here was far more (potentially) radical than anyone knew.

Whether this is true on a national level is another question. I think not. At least not until somebody runs a genuinely Weird campaign on a national level—to put the Freak Vote together and let them see their strength. This is what the "Joe Edwards for Mayor" campaign accomplished in Aspen in the fall of '69. We came out of nowhere and lost that one by only six votes. And it was easy, a year later, to mount a heavy Freak Power registration campaign.

There is a *possibility* that the McCarthy campaign of '68—which formed the death-aborted RFK effort—could provide us with the frustrated momentum and unfocused power base for a full-bore power move in 1972. If so, this would be a disastrous thing to ignore—because it might not exist in 1976.

This is a crucial and perhaps fatal question. Can we *afford* to nurse our momentum along for another four years? Personally, I can't be sure—but I tend to think we have to establish a national equivalent of Freak Power in '72, before we can work off a genuine power base in '74 and especially '76. Everything in the history of political base-building points in this direction—especially with regard to *getting on the ballot.*

On the other hand, I remember that month I spent covering the Nixon campaign in New Hampshire in '68: I spent a lot of time around McCarthy headquarters, but only because they were in the same motor inn as George Romney's hq . . . and Romney, at the time, was considered the Main Challenger.

I also remember that we began the "Thompson for Sheriff" campaign in Aspen as a joke and a smokescreen—only to find, too late, that we'd tapped a latent firestorm of political energy that none of us had ever anticipated . . . and in the final analysis, this failure to take ourselves seriously, soon enough, was what cost us the whole campaign.

We can afford this kind of loss on a local level, but we can't afford it nationally. If the momentum exists in '72, it should be used in '72. (According to Carl Oglesby's analysis of American politics and the prevailing winds in the Pentagon "H ring," there will be no elections in 1976.)

But Oglesby is a fool—an SDS refugee who got hired by MIT to explain "radical politics" to old liberals. He makes a good living doing this, but as far as we're concerned he's absolutely useless.

And so much for all that. In the first three pages of this memo I have tried to define the Main Question we're faced with—whether to mount a flat-out Alternative Campaign/Candidate in 1972, or use this coming year to build a base for a total shot in 1976. We should also consider the notion that if we mount anything serious in 1972—and if Nixon wins, which is likely—anybody identified with our '72 campaign will be living in a fishbowl for the next four years. There will be IRS harassment, phone taps, drug surveillance, all the normal bullshit that comes with menacing a high-stakes establishment.

So, where do we go from here? Mike is finally convinced that realpolitic is inevitable, even for Essalen. John agrees with a vengeance—to the point that he feels only a Freak Power-type *candidate* (a "Free" Democrat, entering Democratic primaries) will accomplish what we're after. Jann, from a journalistic viewpoint, is opposed to running a Freak Power or Free Democratic candidate; he favors the original idea/mechanics of a "summit conference," out of which will come a Platform/Statement that will speak for the 20 to 30 million *potential* voters who will *not go to the polls* unless they're convinced that at least one of the candidates (in November or even the primaries) is representing *them*. In other words, if we can put together a platform that speaks not only for the new eighteen-to-twenty-one vote but also the 11 million or so who turned twenty-one since '68, and also the Rock vote, the Drug vote, the Vet vote, the Hippie Vote, the Beatnik Vote, the Angry Liberal Vote—if we can do all this, we can force at least one candidate for the Democratic nomination to endorse our position and sink or swim with it.

My own point of view (somewhat reluctantly) is basically in tune with Jann's. I think the best we can hope for in '72 is the creation of a general platform and a cohesive voting bloc for 1976. (Jesus, this is such an obviously dull and foredoomed notion that I don't have much stomach for it, myself . . . and frankly I doubt if we could generate much stomach for it in anybody else, once the word got out that we were only greasing the rails for a run in '76.) This visceral reaction just occurred to me, about eighteen seconds ago. And now, after eighty more seconds of further reflection, I can see where I couldn't possibly involve myself in any kind of political effort, next year, that wouldn't focus on total victory or defeat in *November 1972*. Anything less than that would deprive us, I think, of that energy edge that comes with running an honest, full-bore campaign . . . and the loss of that edge would be fatal to the only advantage we have.

What we have to decide, then, is what exactly would constitute a flat-out run for a "victory" in '72. Would we have to run a *candidate*?

Or could we win by constructing a platform that would speak for a minimum of 20 million potential voters . . . and then use this platform as a bargaining vehicle for that massive voting bloc?

What would McGovern, for instance, say to a platform that included (1) Total amnesty for *all* draft dodgers, deserters, etc. (2) Legalization of *all* drugs (without dropping the "by Rx only" concept, which would place the responsibility on doctors, where it should be, instead of cops) . . . and (3) a mandatory cut of 25 percent in the Pentagon budget in fiscal '73, followed by a mandatory cut of 50 percent in fiscal '74. Then another cut of 25 percent in '75, and back to 50 percent in '76.

My own feeling is that if we could force this sort of a radical position on *any* serious candidate in '72, it would constitute the sort of victory we could work from in '76 . . . but this could work only (according to the scenario that Jann and I worked out) if the Demo nomination were still up for grabs by June of '72, with Lindsay and Kennedy (or Bayh and McGovern) going into the California primary head to head.

At this point—and especially in California—a dramatic bid for the Youth/Freak vote might make the crucial difference. But, as John has pointed out, you can't just *wander* into the California primary like an acid freak with a manifesto in his hand. To have any leverage in California, we will need the exposure that can come only from a skill-fully orchestrated participation in at least a few other primar-ies . . . and this, unfortunately, would require at least a dummy candidate.

But the idea of a "dummy" is sick. If we entered Ken Kesey in the Alaska primary, for instance, we'd play hell dumping Kesey for Nick Johnson if our gig looked good by the time California came around. The idea that almost anybody can run on our Platform is a nice, idealistic sort of notion—but the savage realities of running *any* po-litical campaign would croak the idea of switching candidates in mid-stream, no matter what the rationale.

Maybe we should settle, from the start, on a Kesey/Ramsey Clark ticket. Or Nick Johnson and Jerry Garcia. Any combination of these four names would be good for 20 million votes, I think, if we could get on somebody's ballot.

We might even consider the possibility of letting George Wallace fight the battle to put the American Independent Party on the ballot in all fifty states, then suddenly forcing him into a primary race for the AIP nomination. He is, after all, a Populist—and so are we. The only difference is that Wallace hates Niggers and Radicals, but I think we could turn that shit back on him. His main trip is anti-Establishment, and we can beat him like a gong on that one.

I think we should consider this angle. It's so incredibly bizarre that it makes sense only when you remember that the polls in April/May of '68 showed that Robert Kennedy was the only candidate who also appealed to the Wallace voters. A lot of people called this "weird," but it wasn't. Both RFK and Wallace appealed to the "Fuck the Bosses" vote—and Wallace will be going the same racist/populist route in '72. His people are already working twenty-five hours a day to get the AIP on the ballot—on the assumption that Wallace is that party's *only* candidate.

This is admittedly a lunatic idea, but if we let Wallace get the AIP party on the ballot in all fifty states—then took the nomination away from him—we'd be in a hell-heavy position by November of '72. And even if we lost, we'd have generated enough national publicity to consolidate that vote-bloc we're talking about—which means we could wield it as honest leverage between Nixon and the Demo candidate.

The other way to go, of course, is to run a traditional race against all comers in the Democratic primaries. But this would require a hell of a lot of money—and with our prospects of victory almost nil, big money would be a hard thing to come by.

On the other hand, I suspect it might be cheap—at least in terms of dollars—to beat Wallace out of the AIP nomination. This would, after all, be a sudden/savage return to the Power Coalition that led to the breakup of SDS . . . and beyond that, it's so crazy, so intolerably weird, that the very idea would probably attract a laughing, wild-eyed swarm of dropout SDS organizers.

The only serious problem with this plan . . . provided it's mechanically feasible—is that it would require the full-time salaried services of at least a dozen Kennedy-style, state-level political operatives. The first moves would have to be made *quietly* . . . or we would lose the advantage of total surprise. But once we got the basic organizing machinery working, I think the excitement and crazy adrenalin of the thing would take care of the rest.

For the first steps, however, we need somebody who *understands* that kind of local machinery, and who is also *not committed right now to any other candidate*. I think we can get the mechanics/type information we need for this move by brain-picking Radical/Lib Demos on the pretense that we want to "take over" the New Party—or maybe Peace and Freedom; whatever's on the ballot. The idea is to learn all the local A B C steps (that's A-B-C) of taking over the state-level machinery of a party that's getting on the statewide ballot for the first (or second) time. Then, once we get this information, I think we could move in and grab the AIP nomination just about the time they get themselves on the ballot.

Woody Creek, 1971

NEVER APOLOGIZE, NEVER EXPLAIN

I WAS SITTING IN Aspen about a week before the Derby. I hadn't done anything in a long time.

I was having dinner with a writer named Jim Salter, a good writer—he did the screenplay for Downhill Racer. *I think it was the first time we met; they invited Sandy and me over for dinner. I guess the question of where I was from came up. I said Kentucky, Louisville. And just joking they said, well, my God, what are you doing here? You should be back there writing about the Derby.*

It was late at night and I was drunk. At first I laughed, and then I thought, Mother of God, what a wonderful idea. I called Hinckle at about three in the morning and said, look, don't ask me why, but this is very important, I got to go to Louisville and cover the Derby and I want Pat Oliphant to go with me. It seemed to me that Oliphant would catch the madness of things, and the weird humor, better than any photographer.

Hinckle said wonderful. Call Oliphant, set it up. Go. Do it. Hinckle's a terrible editor for touching copy, but he's my idea of a really good editor as a guy who never touches your copy but makes your life easier when you're working.

I called Oliphant the next day, and he couldn't do it because he was under contract somehow that wouldn't let him draw for anyone else. So I called Hinckle back—by this time I was really wired on the idea— and said, Oliphant can't do it. I'm trying to think of somebody else.

A few hours later he called back and said I have an idea, just the guy I think, this weird person in London who works for Private Eye, reminds me very much of Oliphant, same kind of humor. I think you might like him.

So I said, good, then we'll try him. I had never seen his work. So I went to Louisville and Hinckle got Ralph Steadman over and I met him at the Browns and Bourbon Hotel in Louisville. It was his first trip to this country. Imagine that, being plunged into the Derby.

Of course, it became the Gonzo breakthrough piece, but at the time I thought I was finished as a writer. I remember lying in a tub in New York in some hotel where Hinckle had locked me up with nothing but a wide-open room-service account and four quarts of Johnny Walker Scotch. I was there for days. At first I was typing, then I was just ripping the pages out of my notebook, because I'd worn myself down to the point where I couldn't even think, much less write. The magazine was holding the presses . . . I thought it was a disaster.

But then just days after it came out, I began to get calls and letters from all over the country saying what a fantastic breakthrough format in journalism. I thought, Jesus Christ . . . I guess I shouldn't say anything. In a way it was an almost accidental breakthrough—a whole new style of journalism which now passes for whatever Gonzo is . . . accident and desperation.

Woody Creek, January 1990

VEGAS WITCHCRAFT

MY ATTORNEY WAS downstairs talking to a sporty-looking cop about forty whose plastic name tag said he was the D.A. from someplace in Georgia. "I'm a whiskey man, myself," he was saying. "We don't have much problem with drugs down where I come from."

"You will," said my attorney. "One of these nights you'll wake up and find a junkie tearing your bedroom apart."

"Naw!" said the Georgia man. "Not down in *my* parts."

I joined them and ordered a tall glass of rum, with ice.

"You're another one of these California boys," he said. "Your friend here's been tellin' me about dope fiends."

"They're everywhere," I said. "Nobody's safe. And sure as hell not in the South. They like the warm weather."

"They work in pairs," said my attorney. "Sometimes in gangs. They'll climb right into your bedroom and sit on your chest, with big Bowie knives." He nodded solemnly. "They might even sit on your *wife's chest*—put the blade right down on her throat."

"Jesus God almighty," said the Southerner. "What the hell's *goin' on* in this country?"

"You'd never believe it," said my attorney. "In L.A. it's out of control. First it was drugs, now it's witchcraft."

"Witchcraft? Shit, you can't mean it!"

"Read the newspapers," I said. "Man, you don't know trouble until you have to face down a bunch of these addicts gone crazy for human sacrifice!"

"Naw!" he said. "That's science fiction stuff!"

"Not where *we* operate," said my attorney. "Hell, in Malibu alone, these goddamn Satan-worshippers kill six or eight people *every day*." He paused to sip his drink. "And all they want is the blood," he continued. "They'll take people right off the street if they have to." He nodded. "Hell, yes. Just the other day we had a case where they grabbed a girl right out of a McDonald's hamburger stand. She was a waitress. About sixteen years old . . . with a lot of people watching, too!"

"What happened?" said our friend. "What did they *do* to her?" He seemed very agitated by what he was hearing.

"*Do?*" said my attorney. "Jesus Christ man. They chopped her goddamn head off right there in the parking lot! Then they cut all kinds of holes in her and sucked out the blood!"

"God *almighty!*" the Georgia man exclaimed. . . . "And nobody *did* anything?"

"What *could* they do?" I said. "The guy that took the head was about six-seven and maybe three hundred pounds. He was packing two Lugers, and the others had M-16s. They were all veterans. . . ."

"The big guy used to be a major in the Marines," said my attorney. "We know where he lives, but we can't get near the house."

"Naw!" our friend shouted. "Not a major!"

"He wanted the pineal gland," I said. "That's how he got so big. When he quit the Marines he was just a *little guy*."

"O my god!" said our friend. "That's horrible!"

"It happens every day," said my attorney. "Usually it's whole families. During the night. Most of them don't even wake up until they feel their heads going—and then, of course, it's too late."

The bartender had stopped to listen. I'd been watching him. His expression was not calm.

"Three more rums," I said. "With plenty of ice, and maybe a handful of lime chunks."

He nodded, but I could see that his mind was not on his work. He was staring at our name tags. "Are you guys with that police convention upstairs?" he said finally.

"We sure are, my friend," said the Georgia man with a big smile.

The bartender shook his head sadly. "I thought so," he said. "I never heard that kind of talk at this bar before. Jesus Christ! How do you guys *stand* that kind of work?"

My attorney smiled at him. "We *like* it," he said. "It's groovy."

The bartender drew back; his face was a mask of repugnance.

"What's wrong with you?" I said. "Hell, *somebody* has to do it."

He stared at me for a moment, then turned away.

"Hurry up with those drinks," said my attorney. "We're thirsty." He laughed and rolled his eyes as the bartender glanced back at him. "Only *two* rums," he said. "Make mine a Bloody Mary."

The bartender seemed to stiffen, but our Georgia friend didn't notice. His mind was somewhere else. "Hell, I really hate to hear this," he said quietly. "Because everything that happens in California seems to get down our way, sooner or later. Mostly Atlanta, but I guess that was back when the goddamn bastards were *peaceful*. It used to be that all we had to do was keep 'em under surveillance. They didn't roam around much. . . ." He shrugged. "But now, Jesus, *nobody's* safe. They could turn up anywhere."

"You're right," said my attorney. "We learned that in California. You remember where Manson turned up, don't you? Right out in the middle of Death Valley. He had a whole *army* of sex fiends out there. We only got our hands on a few. Most of the crew got away; just ran off across the sand dunes, like big lizards . . . and every one of them stark naked, except for the weapons."

"They'll turn up somewhere, pretty soon," I said. "And let's hope we'll be ready for them."

The Georgia man whacked his fist on the bar. "But we can't just lock ourselves in the house and be prisoners!" he exclaimed. "We don't even know who these people are! How do you *recognize* them?"

"You can't," my attorney replied. "The only way to do it is to take the bull by the horns—go to the mat with this scum!"

"What do you mean by that?" he asked.

"You *know* what I mean," said my attorney. "We've done it before, and we can damn well do it again."

"Cut their goddamn heads off," I said. "Every one of them. That's what we're doing in California."

"What?"

"Sure," said my attorney. "It's all on the Q.T., but everybody who *matters* is with us all the way down the line."

"God! I had no idea it was that bad out there!" said our friend.

"We keep it quiet," I said. "It's not the kind of thing you'd want to talk about upstairs, for instance. Not with the press around."

Our man agreed. "Hell no!" he said. "We'd never hear the goddamn end of it."

"Dobermans don't talk," I said.

"What?"

"Sometimes it's easier to just rip out the backstraps," said my attorney. "They'll fight like hell if you try to take their head without dogs."

"God almighty!"

We left him at the bar, swirling the ice in his drink and not smiling. He was worried about whether or not to tell his wife about it. "She'd never understand," he muttered. "You know how women are."

I nodded. My attorney was already gone, scurrying through a maze of slot machines toward the front door. I said goodbye to our friend, warning him not to say anything about what we'd told him.

Las Vegas, 1971

HIGH-WATER MARK

STRANGE MEMORIES ON this nervous night in Las Vegas. Five years later? Six? It seems like a lifetime, or at least a Main Era—the kind of peak that never comes again. San Francisco in the middle sixties was a very special time and place to be a part of. Maybe it meant something. Maybe not, in the long run . . . but no explanation, no mix of words or music or memories can touch that sense of knowing that you were there and alive in that corner of time and the world. Whatever it meant. . . .

History is hard to know, because of all the hired bullshit, but even without being sure of "history" it seems entirely reasonable to think that every now and then the energy of a whole generation comes to a head in a long fine flash, for reasons that nobody really understands at the time—and which never explain, in retrospect, what actually happened.

My central memory of that time seems to hang on one or five or maybe forty nights—or very early mornings—when I left the Fillmore half crazy and, instead of going home, aimed the big 650 Lightning across the Bay Bridge at a hundred miles an hour wearing L. L. Bean shorts and a Butte sheepherder's jacket . . . booming through the Treasure Island tunnel at the lights of Oakland and Berkeley and Richmond, not quite sure which turn-off to take when I got to the other end (always stalling at the tollgate, too twisted to find neutral while I fumbled for change) . . . but being absolutely certain that no matter which way I went I would come to a place where people were just as high and wild as I was: no doubt at all about that. . . .

There was madness in any direction, at any hour. If not across the Bay, then up the Golden Gate or down 101 to Los Altos or La Honda. . . . You could strike sparks anywhere. There was a fantastic universal sense that whatever we were doing was right, that we were winning. . . .

And that, I think, was the handle—that sense of inevitable victory over the forces of Old and Evil. Not in any mean or military sense; we didn't need that. Our energy would simply prevail. There was no point in fighting—on our side or theirs. We had all the momentum; we were riding the crest of a high and beautiful wave. . . .

So now, less than five years later, you can go up on a steep hill in Las Vegas and look west, and with the right kind of eyes you can almost see the high-water mark—that place where the wave finally broke and rolled back.

The whole concept of decades is wrong. That is why people have trouble with it. A decade is ten years, which some people will tell you is about as long as a dime. The only people who still talk in terms of decades are Australians and possibly some New Zealanders, but the Aussies will tell you that the New Zealanders think more in terms of twenty years, like us. In politics, a "generation" is twenty years: ten is not enough. Time flies when you do most of your real work after midnight—five months can go by and it feels like one sleepless night.

Las Vegas, 1976

FEAR AND LOATHING

THE PHRASE WORKED. *It was like Gonzo. All of a sudden I had my own standing head.*

It started when I left Vegas that first time, skipping the hotel bill, driving off in that red convertible all alone, drunk and crazy, back to L.A. That's exactly what I felt. Fear and loathing.

I was afraid of cops, mainly, extremely afraid. I figured that by noon they were bound to find out that I wasn't there anymore. And it was a long run, from Vegas to L.A. There are no side roads you can take. You can go only two directions from Route 83 out of Vegas. If you go west you can go only one. And I thought they'd catch me and bring me back and put me in the Clark County Jail. There was a guy in the Clark County Jail then who had been there for thirty years for robbing a gas station. Imagine what they'd have done to me for jumping a hotel bill.

Anyway, coming off that it worked as a standing head for the portable pieces on the 1972 campaign.

Woody Creek, January 1990

LIES—IT WAS ALL LIES—I COULDN'T HELP MYSELF

I NEVER SAID that Muskie was taking Ibogaine.

I said there was a rumor in Milwaukee that a strange Brazilian doctor had been showing up at his suite to administer heavy shots of some strange drug called Ibogaine.

Of course it wasn't true. I never said it was true. I said there was a rumor to that effect. I made up the rumor.

And the reason I made it up was that I was sitting in my working room in Washington, writing this piece and going through my mail. Here was a report from the Pharm Chem Labs in Palo Alto, which does drug testing, and it was then issuing a monthly newsletter on the latest in drug information. I like to subscribe to these weird things, and that month it happend to be on Ibogaine.

They described the effects of it, what would happen to people who took it. I read it because I was curious—I'm curious about any new drug—and I got halfway through it and I thought, My God, I've seen these symptoms, these manifestations. These are very familiar; this is not some African syndrome.

Of course, I thought, it's that bastard Muskie. They talked about stupors, and rages, uncontrollable rages, sitting mute for three days at a time. . . .

I never said that John Chancellor ate acid either, except to those people in that waiting room at the convention in Miami. These Nixon youth followers were about ready to rush out there and give a demonstration. I was putting them on.

Chancellor is still angry about that.

See, I didn't realize until about halfway through the campaign that people believed this stuff. I assumed that like the people I was around, and like myself, they were getting their primary coverage of the campaign from newspapers, television, radio, the traditional media.

When the mail started pouring into Rolling Stone and I started to get all the questions from people in the press, I thought, My God, these bastards believe these things.

I think that people took it seriously because politics, particularly *presidential campaigns and the president and the White House, have always been sacred cows in this country, almost as if the president ruled by divine right. Especially since the start of the age of television.*

Some people have that kind of respect for these people. I don't, any more than I have respect for police and chambers of commerce. I have respect for quite a few things, quite a few people. Politicians just don't happen to be among them. Just because a person can subject himself to the degradations of a lifetime in politics and finally end up in the White House is certainly no reason to respect him, as Nixon has recently given us elegant evidence to confirm.

Almost all political writers cover campaigns on the basis of what they learned from the last one. I came into the '72 campaign knowing very little about the last one. I hadn't covered a campaign before. I was in and out of it in '68, so I didn't have any real preconceived strictures in my head. I just wrote what I saw, what I thought, and what I felt on instinct. I really have great faith in my instincts.

Some of the things I called Nixon obviously were not accurate. Nixon does not, as far as I know, fuck pigs and sell used cars with cracked blocks. Nor is he corrupt beyond the ability of modern man to describe it. Those are exaggerations to make a point. My concern with accuracy is on a higher level than nickels and dimes, in a word, line by line.

Woody Creek, January 1990

ED MUSKIE DOOMED BY IBOGAINE: BIZARRE DRUG PLOT REVEALED

The most common known source of Ibogaine is from the roots of Tabernanthe Iboga, a shrub indigenous to West Africa. As early as 1869, roots of T.I. were reported effective in combating sleep or fatigue and in maintaining alertness when ingested by African natives. Extracts of T.I. are used by natives while stalking game; it enables them to remain motionless for as long as two days while retaining mental alertness. It has been used for centuries by natives of Africa, Asia, and South America in conjunction with fetishistic and mythical ceremonies. In 1905 the gross effects of chewing large quantities of T.I. were described: "Soon his nerves get tense in an extraordinary way; an epileptic-like madness comes over him, during which he becomes unconscious and pronounces words which are interpreted by the older members of the group as having a prophetic meaning and to prove that the fetish has entered him."

At the turn of the century, iboga extracts were used as stimulants, aphrodisiacs, and inebriants. They have been available in European drugstores for over thirty years. Much of the research with Ibogaine has been done with animals. In the cat, for example, 2–10 mg/kg given intravenously caused marked excitation, dilated pupils, salivation, and tremors leading to a picture of rage. There was an alerting reaction; obvious apprehension and fear, and attempts to escape. . . . In human studies, at a dose of 300 mg given orally, the subject experiences visions, changes in perception of the environment, and delusions or alterations of thinking. Visual imagery becomes more vivid, with animals often appearing. Ibogaine produces a state of drowsiness in which the subject does not wish to move, open his eyes, or be aware of his environment. Since there appears to be an inverse relationship between the presence of physical symptoms and the richness of the psychological experience, the choice of environment is an important consideration. Many are disturbed by lights or noises. . . . Dr. Claudio Naranjo, a psychotherapist, is responsible for most current knowledge regarding Ibogaine effects in humans. He states: "I have been more impressed by the enduring effects resulting from Ibogaine than by those from sessions conducted with any other drug."
—From a study by PharmChem Laboratories, Palo Alto, California

NOT MUCH HAS been written about the Ibogaine Effect as a serious factor in the presidential campaign, but toward the end of the Wisconsin primary race—about a week before the vote—word leaked out that some of Muskie's top advisers had called in a Brazilian doctor who was said to be treating the candidate with "some kind of strange drug" that nobody in the press corps had ever heard of.

It had been common knowledge for many weeks that Humphrey was using an exotic brand of speed known as *Wallot* . . . and it had long been whispered that Muskie was into something very heavy, but it was hard to take the talk seriously until I heard about the appearance of a mysterious Brazilian doctor. That was the key.

I immediately recognized the Ibogaine Effect—from Muskie's tearful breakdown on the flatbed truck in New Hampshire, the delusions and altered thinking that characterized his campaign in Florida, and finally the condition of "total rage" that gripped him in Wisconsin.

There was no doubt about it: the Man from Maine had turned to massive doses of Ibogaine as a last resort. The only remaining question was, "When did he start?" But nobody could answer this one, and I was not able to press the candidate himself for an answer because I was permanently barred from the Muskie campaign after that incident on the Sunshine Special in Florida . . . and that scene makes far more sense now than it did at the time.

Muskie has always taken pride in his ability to deal with hecklers; he has frequently challenged them, calling them up to the stage in front of big crowds and then forcing the poor bastards to debate with him in a blaze of TV lights.

But there was none of that in Florida. When the Boohoo began grabbing at his legs and screaming for more gin, Big Ed went all to pieces . . . which gave rise to speculation, among reporters familiar with his campaign style in '68 and '70, that Muskie was not himself. It was noted, among other things, that he had developed a tendency to roll his eyes wildly during TV interviews, that his thought patterns had become strangely fragmented, and that not even his closest advisers could predict when he might suddenly spiral off into babbling rages or neo-comatose funks.

In retrospect, however, it is easy to see why Muskie fell apart on that caboose platform in the Miami train station. There he was—far gone in a bad Ibogaine frenzy—suddenly shoved out in a rainstorm to face a sullen crowd and some kind of snarling lunatic going for his legs while he tried to explain why he was "the only Democrat who can beat Nixon."

It is entirely conceivable—given the known effects of Ibogaine—that Muskie's brain was almost paralyzed by hallucinations at the time; that he looked out at the crowd and saw gila monsters instead of people, and that his mind snapped completely when he felt something large and apparently vicious clawing at his legs.

We can only speculate on this, because those in a position to know have flatly refused to comment on rumors concerning the Senator's disastrous experiments with Ibogaine. I tried to find the Brazilian doctor on election night in Milwaukee, but by the time the polls closed he was long gone. One of the hired bimbos in Milwaukee's Holiday Inn headquarters said a man with fresh welts on his head had been dragged out the side door and put on a bus to Chicago, but we were never able to confirm this.

Milwaukee, 1972

WASHINGTON POLITICS

I'D GO MAD if I had to live in the midst of all the weird shit I write about. I think that's why it's so easy for me to write from what seems like an original or even bizarre point of view about scenes or situations that a lot of writers tend to ignore because they live right in the middle of them. A typical Washington dinner party, for instance, is just part of the daily routine for most political writers. They do that kind of thing five nights a week, and they get very insulted when somebody calls it weird—which it is. What passes for everyday social reality in Washington strikes me as very peculiar and baroque.

Which is harmless enough, I guess, until you realize that these ata-vistic rituals are taken very seriously by the same people who have the power to plunge the whole world into a nuclear war every time they figure some boatload of uppity heathens in the South China Sea needs to be "taught a lesson" by the U.S. Marines for not showing the proper respect for God and the American Eagle.

Toward the end of '73 I got a letter from The New York Times. Charlotte Curtis was going to take over the Op Ed page as of January 1st, and they wanted to mark the changing of the guard with something very heavy, a piece that would sort of announce to everybody that the Op Ed page was no longer going to be written by a bunch of stale seventy-year-old peace-talk hacks from Washington, paid-off social butterflies, and political wizards.

This is what they told me. They were going to bring some life to it, and a new approach to journalism. And to announce this to the world they proposed that I write a long piece for January 1, for the first page Charlotte Curtis produced. Which I did, and it took up almost a whole page.

It dumbfounded them. I'd sent it in on the mojo and they didn't know they had mojos in the building. They found some in the base-ment.

It was a violent attack on Nixon. And somewhere about two-thirds down through the piece, the subject of Arab oil and Kissinger came up. I wrote then what appeared, even to me, an outlandish scenario for an American invasion of the oil fields with Russia, making a deal with the Russians, and just seizing the oil. I said this was what Kissinger would do. I was proposing it in the same kind of tongue-in-cheek style of the Ibogaine thing. I didn't say that I had heard Kissinger was planning this, or that I had some inside information. I just proposed it as a likelihood for the coming year.

Several days later the Times got a letter from one of the Arab embassies denouncing them for this incredible kind of incendiary irresponsibility, that they would allow some kind of madness like this to appear in the pages of The New York Times.

Christ, it wasn't seven months before Kissinger himself proposed this, as well as Ford, and the idea of invading the Middle East to seize the Arab oil became a definite policy option in the energy crisis.

But none of them approached Nixon. He had a classic absolute lack of any integrity or honesty or decency.

Nixon was a monument to everything rotten in the American dream—he was a monument to why it failed.

He is our monument.

Woody Creek, January 1990

SUMMIT CONFERENCE IN ELKO: SECRET GATHERING OF THE POWER ELITE

It started with me, and Adam.

Adam Walinsky is a very bright boy and has been perceived that way for a long time. I don't know what he's doing now—I think he went back to serious private law in New York—but he was the main speechwriter for Bobby Kennedy in '68.

And like a lot of the Kennedy people he'd been frozen out at the beginning of the McGovern situation.

He was out here at the house in '73. And he told me, if you run for the Senate, let me tell you about some of the things you'll be facing. There are a hell of a lot of things happening down the line here. He brought up things like baby boomers and their problem with Social Security, fewer people working to pay for more people, and the craziness in the criminal justice system, all kinds of things I hadn't had to think about.

Oddly enough, the McGovern campaign had sharpened my appetite for politics, and a lot of other people's. Looking back on it, that seems strange.

But once I'd seen how easy it was here in Aspen to grab the wheels and handles of politics, even with insane positions, and once I'd seen what McGovern had done wrong, once I'd learned national politics, I was loath to come back to Aspen and deal with local issues. By then, anyway, we'd taken over here. For the moment, that battle was won.

So I was serious about getting into national politics. It looked to me as if that could be won, too. McGovern had lost because of mistakes. If the next person running could avoid his mistakes . . .

I was teetering for a while about whether or not to run for the Senate. If Gary Hart had not decided to run, I might have. He had not announced when I started thinking about it. At that time I was thinking hard about the numbers. I thought I had a solid 20 percent. The kind of base that is unshakable and is likely to grow. But I figured Gary would come in with, maybe, 40. I talked with Gary about it.

Keep in mind, I was dead serious about politics. I had become more and more on the inside during the '72 campaign. I had gone to Washington for that, just like I said I would, pulling a trailer and driving the same fucking Volvo that's sitting outside now with a foot and a half of snow on it, eighteen years ago. As a matter of fact I drove through snow most of the way. God. Driving across goddamn Nebraska with a huge Doberman, pulling a giant U-Haul trailer, driving through a storm like this. These big 18-wheelers looming up on me suddenly out of the white. I couldn't go fast enough, couldn't see, blind in the snow, trying to pull left in the lane, put it in third, move out a little bit into the driving lane . . . ZOOOOM! Right beside you, huge blast of snow, the trailer jumps . . . they'd go by, 80 mph, barely missing me . . . but the car did well.

I went there ignorant not just about how it was run and what it all meant, but how to cover it; '68 had politicized me, and I had come back and gotten into it here, but I was really innocent. That campaign was a real education, and I think it shows through in the book.

Anyway, I decided not to run, but I still wanted to do something. And after I talked to Adam, I talked to Dick Goodwin, Doris Kearns . . . I'd met a lot of people on the campaign. I had seen what happened to the Democratic Party. I knew all the players. I had compiled a list of all the important campaign workers, cross-indexed, alliances noted. I figured if we could get the best people in the party together we could begin to create a national political machine. In essence, I was thinking, if I were running for president, whom would I want?

So, astoundingly enough, I persuaded Wenner to have a secret conference. My notion was to set the agenda, the platform for '76, bring together massive talent, heal divisions. Wenner agreed to have Rolling Stone finance the whole thing.

I picked Elko as a site because it was so far from anything that it would be safe. It was the most unlikely place I could think of. I figured that if this were known, if this group were seen together anywhere, it would fail. It had to be as secret as possible. It couldn't be here, it couldn't be New York, so I picked Elko. I liked the Commercial Hotel, with the big white polar bear in front.

The legendary White King, now a major attraction of the Monte Carlo Casino at the Commercial Hotel in Elko, Nevada. It was taken near Point Hope in 1957 by a group of native Eskimos, who accepted the challenge of finding the largest polar bear in the wide expanse of the Arctic Circle. Polars usually grow seven to eight feet in length and between 1,000 and 1,600 pounds. White King stands ten feet, four inches and weighs 2,200 pounds.

I had a bit of a romantic attachment to it.

I had to set up the conference before we talked to anybody. Adam sort of knew what I had in mind, and he helped me talk to Jann. But I didn't dare talk to too many people because the invitations themselves had to be a secret.

We couldn't invite very many. We had only eight, and I had to make the final cuts. The Kennedy wing and the McGovern wing had fought viciously with each other throughout the campaign, and I was setting out to heal that.

I started with my list . . . all the people I had picked as the best of the campaigns I had seen. I got it down to twenty people, then I asked each one of them for five names of the people they thought were the best. I made a card for each person, how often they were named. It was incredibly hard to narrow it down. Gary Hart, for instance, didn't make it . . . he was like a second-round draft pick, like Mankiewicz, Rich Johns, Bill Dixon, and Sandy Bender. We had to choose from the real intellectuals, the organizers and tacticians, the numbers junkies. . . . We just couldn't pick everybody, and the word did filter out to some of these people eventually, Dixon, Sam Jones, and it was quite hurtful to me. It was a bitch.

We'd initially talked about having some journalists there, sworn to secrecy, Greider, I.F. Stone, but we just wanted to keep it tight. There was never any hint of it in the media.

Keep in mind, it was a strategy meeting, but it was more than that. It was intended to produce a platform, and a book. The idea was to go out and have the book published, get Wenner to do it. Doris was going to edit it. I insisted that everybody bring one paper to the conference.

I was the advance man. I went out there and made reservations in the name of the National Studebaker Society. I said we were a group of Studebaker owners and enthusiasts who convened every year. I made the reservations at the Stockmen's Hotel, across from the Commercial. A little more staid. I figured I had to keep them away from the casino, or the fuckers would gamble all night. We're talking about players, gamblers by nature.

But I knew they would like Elko. No matter what they thought ahead of time, they would like it. And everybody did. . . .

Everybody who was invited came: Pat Caddell, Dick Goodwin, Dave Burke. He would later be president of CBS news. He was Kennedy's AA, and had taken some job on Wall Street; he'd signed on after the campaign to become president of Shearson Lehman, or something.

He and I were the first ones there. He came on some DC-3. Somehow to get to Elko he'd had to make about five stops, like from LaGuardia to Minneapolis to St. Louis to Denver to Salt Lake. The plane never got above, like, 5,000 feet all the way.

He and I had a night there before anyone else showed up. Jann came in the next day on a Lear jet with Goodwin, Doris, Caddell, everybody.

I'd been there about a week. I had all the rooms set up, a giant conference room, everything. I wanted to take it right up to the opening gavel, chair the first meeting, then turn it over to Wenner and the others.

We had the Kennedy axis—Walinsky, Goodwin, Kearns, Burke—and the McGovern axis—Caddell, Carl Wagner, Rick Sterns, Sandy Berger.

We were still pissed off about Chicago. We were still pissed off at being crushed twice by Nixon, who was still in control. It was not a happy time. We were on the run.

But it was exhilarating.

I stepped out for a while after chairing the opening session. I was happy to turn it over to Wenner then, although I probably should have stayed, chaired the whole thing, and rammed it through.

But that first night I ate acid and—oh, God—ran off with the Good-wins' babysitter, to a town named Wells, where I knew there was a giant truck stop.

I was pissed off at the people. They were being too contentious, and I was ready for a little break. So I went berserk and went down to this truck stop, where I bought sixteen tire checkers, big things like billy clubs that truckers use to check their tires. And I brought them back and gave one to each of them, and said, okay, you bastards, if you want to argue, here, use these.

Goodwin and Doris were mad for maybe the first twenty minutes when I got back, but no more. They understood. It was a lapse of a sort, but I had a right to a lapse. . . .

Anyway, from then on, they sat around the room with these big clubs in their hands. It helped, got the aggression out and got people to laugh. One person getting really pissed off and walking out would have killed the whole thing.

But it worked. It was one of the heaviest conferences I've ever heard about in politics. I was on a roll, of course. I had achieved a stranglehold on the political scene. I had been right for so long that nobody questioned me.

It catapulted Wenner right into the national political scene. Rolling Stone was a force, and I intended to use it.

We talked about potential candidates for '76, of course. Jimmy Carter wasn't mentioned. But for the most part it was, fuck this candidate business, we're here to talk about how to win again. We knew the arty desperately needed to win in '76, and to do that it had to be reshaped. We had to change our approach. Overcome the factional hatreds.

We really did heal the wounds of the past campaigns. It's hard to understand why we didn't come out of there with a platform. I didn't follow up on it much. My role was to make it happen, and I did. Wenner didn't really pursue it. Part of the reason may be that our collective attention soon was refocused on Watergate.

But I didn't forget about it. I figured that if we were going to do this I needed to get out on the road and start traveling with candidates . . . and that's how I met Carter.

Woody Creek, January 1990

OPENING STATEMENT: HST

A-76
Memo #Xo1
Elko, Nevada
Organizing Conference: Feb 21–24, 1974

THIS IS A FIRST-DRAFT, last-minute attempt to lash together a vague preamble, of sorts, with regard to the obvious question: What the fuck are we doing here in Elko, Nevada, in a corner of the Stockmen's Hotel about 200 feet from the Burlington Northern RR tracks on a frozen weekend in late February? Sharing the hotel with a state/sectional bridge tournament—at a time when the rest of the country seems to be teetering on the brink of an ugly, mean-spirited kind of long-term chaos that threatens, on an almost day-to-day basis, to mushroom beyond anything we can say, think, or plan out here in this atavistic sanctuary with nothing to recommend it except the world's largest dead Polar Bear and the biggest commercially available hamburger west of the Ruhr. (Both of these are in the Commercial Hotel, directly across the RR tracks from our plush HQ in the Stockmen's Motor Hotel.)

Indeed . . . This is a valid question, and in the next forty-eight hours we will not have much else to do except try to answer it. . . . Or maybe just hang weird at the gambling tables and try to ignore the whole thing.

Both the bars and casinos in Elko are open twenty-four hours a day, in addition to several nearby whorehouses staffed by middle-aged Indian ladies, so anybody who doesn't feel like getting into politics has a variety of options (the train doesn't stop here, and all departing flights are fully booked until Sunday) to while away these rude and lonesome hours until we can all flee back to our various sinecures in those bastions of liberalism where hired guns and dilletantes are still honored.

In any case, the original impulse that led to this gathering bubbled up from a conversation I had in Aspen last summer with Adam Walinsky, in which I expressed considerable reluctance vis-a-vis my long-neglected idea about running for the U.S. Senate from Colorado. I had, at that point, received several hundred letters from people who wanted to work in "my campaign," and the notion of backing off was beginning to fill me with guilt—which Adam nicely compounded by saying that, if I decided *not* to run, I'd be one of the few people in the country who could honestly say that he had "the Senator he deserved."

Which is *not* true, of course—given the gang-bang nature of the '74 Senate race in Colorado—but after brooding on that remark for many months I find it popping up in my head almost every time I start thinking about politics. And especially about the elections in 1976—which, until the unexpected demise of Spiro Agnew—I was inclined to view in very extreme and/or apocalyptic terms. Prior to Agnew's departure from the White House and (presumably) from the '76 presidential scene, I saw the 1976 elections as either a final affirmation of the Rape of the American Dream or perhaps the last chance any of *us* would ever have to avert that rape—if only temporarily—or perhaps even drive a stake of some kind into the heart of that pieced-off vampire that Agnew would have represented in '76, if "fate" had not intervened.

But things have changed now. Agnew is gone, Nixon is on the ropes, and in terms of *realpolitic* the Republican party is down in the same ditch with the Democrats—they are both looking *back* into their now loyalist ranks for names, ideas, and possibilities: the GOP has been stripped all the way back to 1964, with Goldwater/Reagan vs. Rockefeller and maybe Percy on the outside . . . but in fact Nixon's mind-bending failure has effectively castrated the aggressive/activist core of the GOP (all the Bright Young Men, as it were), and barring totally unforeseen circumstances between now and November '76, the GOP looks at a future of carping opposition until at least 1984.

Which would seem to be nice, for Democrats—but I wouldn't know about that, because I share what seems to be a very active and potentially massive sentiment among the erstwhile "youth generation" (between ages twenty-five and forty now) to the effect that *all* career politicians should be put on The Rack—in the name of either poetic or real *justice,* and probably for The Greater Good.

This sentiment, reflected in virtually *all* age, income, and even demographic groups (sic/Caddell . . .) is broad and deep enough now—and entirely justified, to my mind—to have a massive effect not only on the '76 elections, which *might* in turn have a massive effect on the realities of life in America for the next several generations, but also on the life expectancy of the whole concept of Participatory Democracy all over the globe.

As a minor and maybe even debatable forerunner of this, we can look back at what happened in South America (in the time span of five or six years) when it suddenly became obvious in the mid-1960s that the Alliance for Progress was all bullshit. In half a decade, we saw a whole continent revert to various forms of fascism—an almost instinctive reversion that was more inevitable than programmed, and which will take at least five decades to cure.

Ah . . . that word again: "Cure."

Manifest Destiny.

The question raised by the ostensibly complex but essentially simple reality of what happened in South America in the late sixties—and also in Africa and most of Asia, for different reasons—is only now beginning to seriously haunt the so-called civilized or at least industrialized nations in Europe and the northern Americas. President Marcos of the Philippines put it very bluntly about a year ago in a quote I can't find now—but I think it went something like this: "Your idea of 'democracy' was right for *your* development, but it's not what we need for *ours*."

I've been meaning to go to the Philippines to see what kind of working alternative Marcos had in mind, but I haven't had the time. . . .

Maybe later. If we decide even tentatively here in Elko that Marcos was *right,* I want to spend some time over there very soon—because regardless of what happens in the Philippines, the question Marcos raised has a nasty edge on it.

Was Thomas Jefferson a dingbat?

Ten days before he died, on July 4, 1826, Jefferson wrote his own valedictory, which included the following nut:

> All eyes are opened, or opening, to the rights of man. The general spread of the light of science has already laid open to every view the palpable truth, that the mass of mankind has not been born with saddles on their backs, nor a favored few booted and spurred, ready to ride them legitimately, by the grace of God. . . .

President Marcos would probably agree, but he would also probably argue that Jefferson's reality was so different from what was happening

100 years later in Russia or 200 years later in the Philippines that his words, however admirable, are just as dated and even dangerous *now* as Patrick Henry's wild-eyed demand for "liberty or death."

Ah . . . madness, madness . . . where will it end?

I think I know, with regard to the way I live and intend to keep on living *my own* life—but as I grow older and meaner and uglier it becomes more and more clear to me that only a lunatic or an ego-maniacal asshole would try to impose the structure of his own life-style on people who don't entirely understand it, unless he's ready to assume a personal responsibility for the consequences.

When the price of liberty includes the obligation to be drafted and have your legs blown off at the age of twenty-two in a place called "Veet-Naam" for some reason that neither Democratic nor Republican presidents can finally claim to understand, then maybe death is not such an ugly alternative. Thomas Jefferson kept slaves, but there is nothing in history to indicate that he routinely sacrificed any of their lives and limbs for the sake of his fiscal security.

Jesus, here we go again. Is there anyone in this star-crossed group with access to a doctor of psychic-focus drugs? If so, please meet me in the northwest corner of the Commercial Hotel casino at dawn on Saturday.

Meanwhile, I want to wind this thing out and down as quickly as possible . . . and, since I asked most of the other people here to bring some kind of Focus Document for the rest of us to cope with, I think this will have to be mine—if only because it's Wednesday morning now and I've already sunk six pages into what seems like a single idea, and it also strikes me as an idea (or question) that rarely if ever gets mentioned at political conferences.

This is the possibility that maybe we're all kidding ourselves about the intrinsic value of taking politics seriously in 1970's America, and that maybe we (or the rest of you, anyway—since I'm a Doctor of Journalism) are like a gang of hired guns on New Years Eve in 1899. Things changed a bit after that, and the importance of being able to slap leather real fast at High Noon on Main Street seemed to fade very precipitously after 1900. A few amateurs hung on in places like San Diego and Seattle until The War came, but by 1920 the Pros took over for real.

Which is getting off the point, for now. What I want to do is raise the question immediately—so we'll have to deal with it in the same context as all the others—as to whether Frank Mankiewicz was talking in the past, present, or future when he said, in the intro to his book on Nixon, that he learned from Robert Kennedy that "the practice of American politics . . . can be both joyous and honorable."

Whether or not Frank still agrees with that is not important, for now—but in the context of why we're all out here in this god-forsaken place I think it's important *not* to avoid the idea that reality in America might in fact be beyond the point where even the most joyous and honorable kind of politics can have any real effect on it. And I think we should also take a serious look at the health/prognosis for the whole idea of Participatory Democracy, in America or anywhere else.

That, to me, is an absolutely necessary cornerstone for anything else we might or might not put together—because unless we're honestly convinced that the Practice of Politics is worth more than just a short-term high or the kind of short-term money that power pimps pay for hired guns, my own feeling is that we'll be a lot better off avoiding all the traditional liberal bullshit and just saying it straight out: that we're all just a bunch of fine-tuned Politics Junkies and we're ready to turn Main Street into a graveyard for anybody who'll pay the price and even pretend to say the Right Things.

But we don't want to get carried away with this Olde West gig—except to recognize a certain connection between politics/campaign Hit Men in *1974* and hired guns all over the West in *1874*. It's just as hard to know for sure what Matt Dillon thought he was really doing then as it is, today, to know what the fuck Benn Wattenberg might describe as the "far, far better thing" he really has in mind. . . .

One of the primary ideas of this conference, in my own head, is to keep that kind of brutal option open—if that's what we seem to agree on. Maybe tilting with windmills really *is* the best and most honorable way to go these days. I get a definite kick out of it, myself—but I have a feeling that my time is getting short, and I'm becoming unnaturally curious about how much *reality* we're really dealing with.

This is what the rest of you are going to have to come up with. My only role in this trip, as I see it right now, is to eventually write the introduction to some kind of book-form statement that the rest of you (and probably a few others) will eventually crank out. We are dealing with a genuinely ominous power vacuum right now, in terms of political reality. Both major parties seem to be curling back into an ill-disguised fetal crouch—and the stuporous horror of a Jackson-Ford race in '76 is as easily conceivable as the barely avoided reality of another Nixon-Humphrey contest in 1972.

There is no way to get away from names and personalities in any serious talk about the '76 election—but if that's *all* we can talk about, I think we should write this whole project off, as of Sunday, as a strange bummer of sorts that never got untracked. Shit, we'd be better off at the crap tables, or watching the Keno balls.

On the other hand, I don't think we're here to write some kind of an all-purpose Platform for a (presumably) Democratic candidate in '76. Massive evidence suggests that there are plenty of people around who are already into that.

What we *might* do, I think, is at least define some of the critical and unavoidable questions that *any* presidential candidate will have to deal with, in order to be taken seriously in '76. We have a long list of these goddamn things to hassle with, in the very short space of two days—and the best we can do for right now is: (1) Decide if the patient is worth saving . . . (2) What's basically wrong with the patient . . . (3) And if the saving is worth the effort, *how* to define and begin *dealing* with the *basics*.

At the same time, we want to keep in mind that a really fearful (or "fearsome") chunk of the voting population is in a very vengeful and potentially dangerous mood with regard to national or even local politics. If George Metesky decided to run for the Senate in N.Y. against Javits this year, I suspect he would do pretty well. . . .

And, for the same reason(s), I'm absolutely certain I could fatally cripple any Democratic candidate for the U.S. Senate in Colorado by merely entering the race as a serious Independent . . . but that would only guarantee Dominick's reelection, I think, and besides that I have a great fear of having to move back to Washington.*

Which is neither here nor there. My only real concern is to put something together that will force a genuine alteration of consciousness in the realm of national politics, and also in the heads of national politicians. Given the weird temper of all the people I've talked to in the past year, this is the only course that could possibly alter the drift of at least a third of the electorate *away* from politics entirely . . . and without that third, the White House in '76 is going to become the same kind of mine field that Gracie Mansion became about ten years ago, and for many of the same reasons.

*I have formally "withdrawn" from the race.

· · ·

Okay for now. I have to get this bastard Xeroxed and then catch the bush plane for Elko in two hours. The *agenda* will have to wait—not only in terms of time, but also for people who will hopefully have a much better sense of priorities than I do.

If not, you bastards are going to wish you never heard the word "Elko."

Sincerely,
Hunter S. Thompson

ROLLING STONE: ABANDON ALL HOPE YE WHO ENTER HERE

WENNER FOLDED STRAIGHT Arrow Books shortly after the Saigon piece. I had to write that piece because the War had been such a player in my life for ten years. I needed to see the end of it and be a part of it somehow. Wenner folded Straight Arrow at a time when they owed me $75,000. I was enraged to find that out. It had been an advance for Shark Hunt. I wrote a seriously vicious letter—finally saying all I was thinking when I was taking off for Saigon. While in Saigon, I found I'd been fired when Wenner flew into a rage upon receiving the letter. Getting fired didn't mean much to me. I was in Saigon, I was writing— except that I lost health insurance. Here I was in a war zone, and no health insurance. . . .

So, essentially, I refused to write anything once I found out. I found out when I tried to use my Telex card and it was refused. I called Rolling Stone to find out why (perfect phone system right to the end of the war). I talked to Paul Scanlon, who was sitting in for Wenner (off skiing)—he told me I was fired, but fixed my Telex card, etc. The *business department had ignored the memo to fire me because it'd happened too many times before. They didn't want to be bothered with the paperwork, so Wenner's attempt had been derailed.*

Anyone who would fire a correspondent on his way to disaster . . . I vowed not to work for them. It was the end of our working relationship except for special circumstances. About that time, they moved to New York. Rolling Stone began to be run by the advertising and business departments and not by the editorial department. It was a financial leap forward for Wenner and Rolling Stone, but the editorial department lost any real importance.

You shouldn't work for someone who would fire you en route to a War Zone. . . .

I got off the plane greeted by a huge sign that read, "Anyone caught with more than $100 U.S. currency will go immediately to prison." Imagine how I felt with $30,000 taped to my body. I was a pigeon to carry the Newsweek payroll and communication to those in Saigon. I thought we'd all be executed. It was total curfew when we got off the plane so we were herded into this small room with all these men holding machine guns. There I was with 300 times the maximum money allowance. We got out and I leapt on a motor scooter and told the kid to run like hell. I told Loren I wouldn't give him the money until he got me a suite in a hotel. Not an easy task, but he came through.

The Leap of Faith . . . I had already picked up on Carter in '74. It was a special assignment as everything was after Saigon. I was still on the masthead. It was an honor roll of journalists, but the people on it—well, all of them were no longer with Rolling Stone. I didn't like that they put on the cover that I endorsed Carter. I picked him as a gambler. Endorsing isn't something a journalist should do.

Essentially, the fun factor had gone out of Rolling Stone. It was an Outlaw magazine in California. In New York it became an Establishment magazine and I have never worked well with people like that.

Today at Rolling Stone there are rows and rows of white cubicles, each with its own computer. That's how I began to hate computers. They represented all that was wrong with Rolling Stone. It became like an insurance office with people communicating cubicle to cubicle.

But my relationship had ended with the firing. The attempt was enough.

Woody Creek, January 1990

DANCE OF THE DOOMED

Last Notes from Indochina, Lost Memo from the Global Affairs Desk . . . the Fall of Saigon, the Seige of Laos . . . a Way You'll Never Be

"WORLD IDEOLOGIES play little part in Asian thinking and are little understood. What the people strive for is the opportunity for a little more food in their stomachs, a little better clothing on their backs, a little firmer roof over their heads and the realization of the normal, nationalist urge for political freedom. These political, social conditions have but an indirect bearing upon our own national security. But they do form a backdrop to contemporary planning that must be thoughtfully considered if we are to avoid the pitfalls of unrealism."
—General Douglas MacArthur, addressing the U.S. Congress, 1951

COMMUNISTS TAKE OVER SAIGON;
U.S. RESCUE FLEET IS PICKING UP
VIETNAMESE WHO FLED IN BOATS

Communications Cut
Soon After Raising
of Victory Flag

SAIGON, South Vietnam, April 30 (AP). Communist troops of North Vietnam and the Provisional Revolutionary Government of South Vietnam poured into Saigon today as a century of Western influence came to an end.

Scores of North Vietnamese tanks, armored vehicles, and camouflaged Chinese-built trucks rolled to the presidential palace.

The President of the former neo-Communist Government of South Vietnam, Gen. Duong Van Minh, who had gone on radio and television to announce his administration's surrender, was taken to a microphone later by North Vietnamese soldiers for another announcement. He appealed to all Saigon troops to lay down their arms and was taken by the North Vietnamese soldiers to an undisclosed destination. (Soon after, the Saigon radio fell silent, normal telephone and telegraph communications ceased, and the Associated Press said its wire link to the capital was lost at 7 P.M. Wednesday, Saigon time. . . .)

Saigon, April 1975

CHECKING INTO THE LANE XANG

"I'LL TALK WITH Your Daughter Tomorrow . . ."

I have finally arrived in Vientiane after a long and torturous five-day journey from Saigon, via Hong Kong and Bangkok. When I walked into the Lane Xang Hotel, sometime around two-thirty this morning in a drenching monsoon rain, the man at the desk first refused to let me register because he said I had no reservation. Which may or may not have been true, depending on which view of the understandably scrambled Indochinese mind one subscribes to in these menacing times. But, in fact, I had sent a cable from Hong Kong, requesting a large room with a king-size bed, quick access to the pool, and a view of the Mekong River, which flows in front of the hotel.

After a fairly savage argument, the night clerk agreed to a compromise. He would give me the best suite in the hotel for as long as I wanted, provided I gave him twenty green American dollars at once for the company of his daughter for the rest of the night. He described her as a "young and beautiful student, not a bar girl," who spoke excellent English and would certainly have no objection to being awakened at three in the morning and hauled over to the hotel by taxi in a hellish rainstorm, just in order to make me happy.

"Look," I said, "you are dealing with a very tired person. The only thing I want right now is a long sleep in a big bed with nobody bothering me. I have nothing against meeting your daughter; I'm sure she's a wonderful person, but why don't I just give you twenty dollars and never mind about waking her up tonight. If she's free around noon tomorrow, maybe we can have lunch at the White Rose."

The man winced. Nobody's "daughter" goes near the White Rose. It is one of the scurviest and most infamous bangios in all of Indochina, even worse than "Lucy's" in Saigon, and the moment I said that name and saw the man's face, I knew I'd said both the right and wrong thing at the same time. He was deeply insulted, but at least we understood each other. So he carried my bags up to No. 224, a rambling suite of rooms half hidden under the top flight of wide white-tiled stair/ramps that rise out of the middle of the Lane Xang lobby. When I first went into 224, it took me about two minutes to find the bed; it was around the corner and down a fifteen-foot hallway from the refrigerator and the black-leather-topped bar and the ten-foot-long catfish-skin couch and five matching easy chairs and the hardwood writing desk and the sliding glass doors on the pool-facing balcony outside the living room. At the other end of the hallway, half hidden by the foundation of the central stairway, was another big room with a king-size bed, another screened balcony, another telephone, and another air-conditioner, along with a pink-tiled bathroom with two sinks, a toilet and a bidet and a deep pink bathtub about nine feet long. There was no view of the river, but I was in no mood to argue.

I asked the night clerk if he would get me a bucket of ice. Somewhere in the bowels of my luggage I had a film can full of extremely powerful Cambodian red, along with a quart of Jack Daniel's I'd just bought in Hong Kong, and the prospect of a few iced drinks along with a pipeload of paralytic hallucinations seemed just about right for that moment . . . followed by fifteen or sixteen hours of stuporous sleep.

But my new buddy had not yet tied the knot in his half of the bargain. "Very good," he said finally. "I will get your ice when I go downstairs to call my daughter."

"What?"

"Of course," he said. "You will like her. She is very beautiful." Then he smiled and held out his hand. "Twenty dollars, please . . ."

I hesitated for a moment, listening to the rain pounding the palm trees outside my window, then I reluctantly pulled out my wallet and gave him a twenty-dollar bill. I had seen enough of Vientiane on the drive in from the airport to know I'd be in grave trouble if I got thrown out of the Lane Xang at three-thirty in the morning in the middle of a blinding monsoon, hauling an electric typewriter and a soft-leather suitcase, with no currency except U.S. and Hong Kong dollars, and not speaking a word of Laotian or even enough French to beat on somebody's door and ask for directions to another hotel. No, I couldn't stand that; but I wasn't sure I could stand the kind of nasty scene I suspected this humorless, fat little hustler was planning to lay on me, either. As he opened the door to leave, I said, "That money is for ice, okay? Just bring me a bucket of ice and keep the money yourself. I'll talk to your daughter tomorrow."

He paused for a moment, looking back at me, but his eyes were blank and I could tell his brain was busy with other matters. Then he pulled the door shut behind him and left me alone in the room. I slumped back on the couch and opened the bottle of hot bourbon, propping it up on my chest and my chin so I could drink with only a slight movement of my lower lip while I listened to the rain and tried not to think about anything at all.

Laos is as different from Vietnam as Long Island is from Big Sur . . . which is interesting, but not the kind of tangent I want to get off on right now because every time I think of Laos, my mind slips strangely out of focus and I see a chorus line of transvestites dancing crazily in a sort of hypnotic trance at an all-night fertility festival while the government crumbles and grinning little men wearing huge wooden dildoes pass out leaflets saying the first act of the new Communist regime will be to legalize the use and cultivation of opium.

Compared to Laos, the Communist victory in Vietnam seems eminently rational, if only because it was accomplished more or less on American terms, by means of brute force and sheer military skill.

On the day I arrived at Ton San Nhut Airport in Saigon, the afternoon of April 8, the city was almost entirely surrounded by anywhere from fifteen to twenty full-strength Communist divisions, the Saigon branch of the Chase Manhattan Bank announced that it would no longer exchange U.S. dollars for South Vietnamese piastres, the First National City Bank of New York was refusing to cash its own travelers checks, and just a few hours before, a disgruntled South Vietnamese Air Force pilot had flipped out and dropped all the bombs from his American-made F-5 on the presidential palace in the middle of downtown Saigon, causing widespread panic and a twenty-four-hour shoot-to-kill curfew. He made two screaming, low-level runs that almost clipped leaves off the treetops in John F. Kennedy Square and loosened the bowels of a dozen American journalists half relaxing over late-morning breakfast in the garden of the Continental Hotel. But all four of his bombs missed the palace. One killed the presidential gardener, two others destroyed a few trees on the lawn, and the fourth came alarmingly close to landing in the Olympic-size pool of the Cercle Sportif, an almost preternaturally elegant and exclusive French tennis and swimming club just across the street.

This last alleged "eyewitness" report on the trajectory of the fourth bomb was generally dismissed as either unreliable or apocryphal, or both, by almost every correspondent who knew the source—a notorious drunkard, lecher, and foul-mouthed bigot who had just emerged from the Reuters office on Kennedy Square, en route to the Cercle Sportif with his tennis racket in one hand and a thermos of iced gin in the other, when the bombs began falling. His first report on the incident, which he immediately rushed back to the Reuters office and filed on the hot line to London, said the would-be assassin's F-5 came in so low that the pilot was easily recognizable as former South Vietnamese premier and Vice-Air Marshal Nguyn Cao Ky, a one-time favorite of both Lyndon Johnson and former Defense Secretary Robert McNamara. Ky had garnered a certain amount of fame for himself in the days of his ill-fated premiership back in the mid-1960s by making sure that every American correspondent who interviewed him understood that his personal hero was the late Adolf Hitler.

This was as close as the Cercle Sportif ever came to sustaining any damage. The Viet Cong and North Vietnamese generals were very careful to preserve it for their own use, and the swinish French colonels who ran the place became more and more anti-American as the deep rumbling of Communist artillery grew louder and closer to the city. Less than a week before Saigon surrendered, with the advance units of the Red Menace less than five miles away, I was thrown out of the Cercle Sportif by a liver-lipped Frenchman who claimed to be the president of the club and denounced me at poolside for being "improperly dressed." My baggy L. L. Bean shorts were not right for the club's atmosphere, he said. Bikini trunks were the only proper attire, and since I obviously couldn't meet the dress standards of his club, he was giving me exactly two minutes to get off the premises or he would call the police.

What police? Jesus, I thought, we've finally found Martin Bormann. But before I could laugh I had a terrible vision of what it would be like to be locked in a Saigon jail cell while the Communists launched a full-scale assault on the city, totally helpless while the holocaust raged all around me, maybe burned alive in a firestorm or gunned down by crazed jailers, and then waiting in terror when the sounds of battle ceased for whatever fate the victors might decide for me, anything from death by flagellation to being freed as a hero of the people.

No, I thought, not jail. I had brought ten hits of extremely powerful blotter acid with me to Vietnam, taped to the back of my press card for use in a terminal emergency, but if I was going to die in Saigon with my brain on fire from a massive dose of acid, I didn't want to do it in a jail cell. So I left the Cercle Sportif and never returned.

Now, a few weeks later, lounging beside the Lane Xang swimming pool in Laos, I read in the Bangkok *Post* that the Cercle Sportif has been officially seized by the new Communist government in Saigon for use as an officers' club, and no Frenchmen are allowed on the premises. That is the coup de grace for the last remnants of the exotic colonial empire once known as French Indochina. Not even the name remains, except as a quaint and nostalgic designation for what is now just a chunk of Southeast Asia. Saigon, once known as "the Paris of the Orient," had degenerated into an American military ghetto almost a decade before I arrived there in the final weeks of the war. And in the last hours, it became a desperate, overcrowded nightmare full of thieves, losers, pimps, conmen, war junkies, and many, many victims. Including me, although I am just beginning to understand this.

Laos, May 4, 1975

WHOOPING IT UP WITH THE WAR JUNKIES

The Last Great Indochina Reunion . . . Conversations from the Garden of Agony . . . "We Tried Our Best To Save Your Life" . . .

So bye, bye. Miss American Pie . . .
Drove my Chevy to the levee but the levee was dry . . .
And good old boys were drinking whiskey and rye
Singing "This'll be the day that I die . . . this'll be the day that I die."

—DON McLEAN

THAT SONG BOOMING out of the Muzak in the air-conditioned top-floor bar of the Hotel Continental while we sat by the window and watched incoming artillery hitting the rice paddies about five miles south across the Saigon River is one of my clearest memories of those last weird weeks of the thirty-year war in Vietnam.

I was sitting with London Sunday *Times* correspondent Murray Sayle, and we were eating fresh crab salad, pondering a big geophysical map of Indochina and spotting the rumored locations of the fifteen or twenty NVA and VC divisions in the ring around Saigon, drawing arrows and dots on the map while the Muzak kept croaking "Bye, bye, Miss American Pie" and the soft thump of those distant howitzer explosions occasionally made us look up and watch another cloud of muddy white smoke rising out of the rice paddies.

We had just come back in a Harley-Davidson-powered trishaw from the weekly Viet Cong press conference in the heavily guarded VC compound right in the middle of Saigon's Ton San Nhut air base, less than a mile from the city's only commercial air terminal and about halfway between the South Vietnamese Air Force headquarters and the huge American military complex that used to be called "Pentagon East," or "Mac V."

That was one of the last press conferences the Provisional Revolutionary Government (or Viet Cong, as the American press called it) ever held at Ton San Nhut. About ten days later, they emerged from their barbed-wire compound and took over the whole base, along with all the rest of Saigon, just like the carbon-steel voice of PRG spokesman Colonel Vo Dan Giang had told us they would do, whenever they felt like it and a lot sooner than most of us thought. One of the American correspondents had asked Giang how long it would be before he'd feel free to come downtown and have a drink with us at the Hotel Continental, and Giang had replied, with an oddly gentle smile, that he wasn't much of a drinker but that we might run into him in one of the downtown markets "sometime next week" if we were still in town.

At that point and all the way up to the morning less than two weeks later when the American evacuation dissolved in a panic, about half the round-eyed press corps in Saigon had seriously considered staying on, after South Vietnam finally fell and the PRG took over, and at least a half dozen of the questions Col. Giang had dealt with that morning were phrased, in one way or another, to find out how the PRG planned to treat any foreign journalists who stayed on after the fall.

Giang had not gone out of his way to reassure the questioners. The fate of the foreign press, he said, was low on the list of the PRG's priorities, but the only ones who had anything to worry about were "the many American military personnel posing as journalists." He had used this phrase three or four times, and each time I noticed that he was looking directly at me, which was not especially surprising, to me or anyone else, because if there was anybody among the hundred or so journalists crowded into the sweaty, screened-in barracks press room that morning who looked like every career VC colonel's perfect image of an ex-Green Beret major trying to pass for a journalist, it was me.

Here was a tall, bow-legged thug of some kind, wearing white Converse sneakers, tan L. L. Bean hiking shorts, black-rimmed Ray-Ban shades and an Arnold Palmer sport shirt straight out of the Baron's men's store on Lincoln Road in Miami Beach . . . constantly taking pictures with a black, nonreflecting 35mm camera, taping the whole press conference with a mini-cassette recorder, and pouring an inordinate volume of sweat off an almost completely hairless head while consuming one warm beer after another and never even trying to ask a question.

The only thing Giang missed was the silver "McGovern 72" belt buckle I was wearing, and since I was one of the journalists giving serious thought, at that time, to staying on in Saigon and taking my chances with the new owners, rather than suffer the humiliation of having to be rescued by the U.S. Marines, I went back to the Global Affairs Suite in the Continental that night and wrote Col. Giang a letter, explaining that if he was even half as smart as he seemed to be, he might at least go to the trouble of having me and my writings checked out with his Intelligence people in Hanoi before deciding to have me beheaded on the diving board of the U.S. Embassy swimming pool or shot out of the barrel of a 90mm cannon on one of his captured U.S. tanks in the middle of Tu Do Street.

It had taken me about forty-four minutes of watching and listening to Giang's act that morning to know that we were dealing with a genuine razor-edged heavy. There was nothing particularly impressive in what he said. It was mainly gibberish, in fact; a stale mix of canned VC propaganda and Kissinger-style non sequiturs, but there was no mistaking the fact that this mean-looking, flinty-eyed bastard understood exactly what he was doing and that he was getting a definite kick out of making us listen to it.

There was also an unmistakable hint of humor in some of his off-camera talk with the handful of American correspondents who had been around Saigon long enough to get to know him personally. In this small circle, Giang was universally admired and regarded as more of a friendly adversary than some kind of natural, robot enemy. AP photographer Neil Vukovitch, for instance, invited Col. Giang to his wedding in Saigon, and got a friendly sort of black-humored note in return, saying that due to circumstances beyond his control (de facto imprisonment in the PRG compound at Ton San Nhut), the Colonel had to regretfully decline the invitation, which he nonetheless valued and appreciated.

Another correspondent, Loren Jenkins of *Newsweek,* discovered almost by accident that Col. Giang spoke excellent Spanish—the result of a two-year apprenticeship in Cuba with Che Guevara. Jenkins was born in South America, so whenever he wanted to talk personally with Giang, he would find him outside the press barracks after one of the Saturday press conferences and ask all his questions in Spanish.

I noticed this, and since Giang speaks no English—or none that he admits to—and I speak no Vietnamese, I figured the next best thing would be to seize on the Colonel and begin rambling at him in my bastard, street-level Spanish and maybe learn something more than he'd been telling us for the record through his young English-speaking interpreters.

"Don't bother," Jenkins told me. "I've been talking to him for almost a year in Spanish, and we've become pretty good friends, on one level, but when it comes to the kind of stuff you want to ask him, it wouldn't even help if you spoke perfect Vietnamese. He hasn't spent twenty years fighting the round-eyes for nothing."

I met Nick Profit, a *Newsweek* correspondent, in the garden of the Hotel Continental about the time *Newsweek* and the *Washington Post* were trying to get their people out of Saigon. It was about ten days too early and everybody knew it, but Ben Bradley or Katherine Graham supposedly had some inside information, and it was a question of which two of the four correspondents had to go.

PROFIT: I called the foreign editor, Kline, and said, "Look, I've got my airplane ticket, I've got my exit visa, but I really don't want to go and I really don't think I should go, and I want to make a pitch to stay." And he said, "Well. I'll switch you over to Kosner, but you're going to have to really be persuasive because he really wants you out of there." So I get on with Kosner and Auchincloss and Kline, and Kosner's got this sort of high, whiny . . .

HST: Yeah, I know.

PROFIT: Madison Avenue (imitates high, whiny, Madison Avenue voice), "Hi, Nick, baby. What's happening?" And I said, "I, uh . . ." He said, "Speak, speak." So I said, "Well, I want to stay." He said, "Reasons, reasons." So I told him the reasons. Number one. I don't think it's dangerous. Number two, the *Washington Post* has been taking a lot of shit because they were hysterical for a while and I don't want to see *Newsweek* join the joke. And I resent . . . I don't relish the professional and personal embarrassment of bugging out of here at this time. And I don't want to spend the next three fucking years of my life explaining just how I was ordered out and trying to make colleagues believe it. And if you want an evacuation story, the way to do it is not from the ship but from here. So he says, "All right, all right. You're a grown man. If your assessment is it's okay to stay, stay. We tried our best to save your life. We tried to get you out of there. If you want to get yourself killed, go ahead. Go ahead."

HST: That's something I wouldn't have thought about, this fear of being ostracized behind your back.

PROFIT: Oh well, look, the press corps is the most suspicious little group around. And especially for the people who cover wars, the guys that become war correspondents. I mean, they're always looking for cracks in the armor. A guy decides that he's feeling sick or he's just tired, and he wants to leave the front, well, he really has to consider it, because the minute he's gone . . . "Oooh, bugging out early. Well, he used to be a damn good war correspondent, but they all get the shakes at one time or another."
And you can't just go off and say, "Well, I was ordered out," because that's not good enough. People say. "Well, fuck you. Why didn't you tell them to fuck off?" It's always easy for them to say. It's not a matter of being afraid to have your nuts questioned. I mean, this is my third or fourth war, if I really wanted to count them. And you know, all you need is one. One, and you've proven yourself. You don't have to prove any more shit, except you just don't like those kind of stories going around. They start, who knows, sometimes justifiably, sometimes not justifiably. And it really undermines you. I mean, all you got in this fucking profession is your reputation.

HST: Yeah, I was a little surprised at the heaviness of it. You people are all nuts, aren't you? It's almost unanimous among war correspondents.

PROFIT: Well, it's stupid, because everybody is always watching everybody else and judging all the time. And so you find yourself doing stupid things. You find yourself standing around out in the open when you should be groveling on your fucking face someplace, simply because if you hit the ground too early and try to burrow too deep, the story goes about how you freaked out and then tried to crawl to China.

HST: You tried to lay that one on me.

PROFIT: No, I was just joking. You did the exact right thing. You heard a bang and you jumped for the ditch. I knew the artillery was outgoing, so I didn't move. I mean, I just knew it. I saw them loading up and that tank was getting ready to fire a round. I knew it was coming.

HST: I don't worry about the macho number. I'd rather be down in some ditch like a fool and be alive than to be walking around with my head knocked off by some shrapnel.

It was not long thereafter that Loren Jenkins, the *Newsweek* bureau chief, recounted to those of us in the garden the embassy's official evacuation plans. Jenkins had just been summoned to a high-powered briefing for the bureau chiefs, people who were going to be in charge of getting the press out of Saigon. The embassy really didn't have much obligation to do anything, and nobody was really planning on their doing anything. Whatever they did, it was free-fall. There was no real belief, I don't think, that the North Vietnamese were going to sweep into town and butcher the populace. The evacuation was always seen as a matter of inconvenience. You worried only about being locked up or wounded by some drunken American running around with a .45 in a panic. Or having your arm jerked out of its socket by a frantic Vietnamese collaborator, desperate to get on a plane.

JENKINS: They're so fucked up. The embassy wants us to organize our own evacuation because they obviously don't seem to be able to organize anything. Apparently this plan was designed in 1969. They said it was revised, updated, in January of this year, which means it was updated before they had any idea of what could happen in Danang. It was based on the assumption that they would have friendly South Vietnamese to protect their retreat, that there would be a secure city, that you would be evacuating among friendly people and friendly soldiers. And there'd be no interference by their allies, by the South Vietnamese. They admit they did not anticipate a breakdown of order.

They're now revising like mad. They've got all sorts of different grades of contingency plans, but the basic plan is to evacuate five to ten thousand people. This includes Americans, Vietnamese dependents of Americans, and other foreigners—the British embassy, the Japanese, you know, various others.

HST: Where do they draw the line?

JENKINS: The U.S. apparently has a lot of arrangements with other nations, third-country nationals, as they call them. I mean, they're pushing people out, but almost as fast as they do, new people come out of the woodwork. Some ex-GI who retired here, who wasn't registered here, you know, got a Vietnamese wife, six, seven kids— they've all been appearing.

They were talking about there being five thousand Americans still here. It's clear there's a hell of a lot more that they had no fucking knowledge of. So if you talk about five thousand Americans, what they're talking about evacuating is something like six times that— thirty thousand, not five thousand. I talked to a guy this morning who's trying to get his wife's sister on. The guy said, "We can't have sisters-in-law. Why don't you say she's your adopted daughter?" I don't think they're being overly strict on it.

HST: Well, it doesn't matter now.

JENKINS: Yeah, I mean, that's good. What they gotta do is get as many of these people out as possible before they have to try a helicopter evacuation. Obviously, the whole state of events in Danang has just shell-shocked them. It put the kibosh on their whole fucking plan, and there's no fucking way it's gonna work. They thought they'd have a secure air base, a secure port—we're not gonna have any of those. We're not gonna have secure streets. The fucking ARVN may be running around shooting, chaos. They originally had twenty-five assembly points; they've now reduced that to thirteen. They realize that more assembly points are going to be harder to defend from anything. They were going to move on foot to these assembly points, where they would be bused out to Ton San Nhut where American planes would take everyone on. Now they've had to modify that.

These thirteen assembly points are too small to handle big Marine helicopters. So now they'll have to take these people out of here on Hueys, which carry only eight to ten people, to another staging area. They're setting up really big, secure defense areas, three in particular: the U.S. embassy, the military advisory committee headquarters (now called the DAO headquarters) out at Ton San Nhut, and another place in town, at the DAO annex, I'm not sure where. They're apparently fortifying these places so they can defend them against charging, rampaging mobs—which means they're putting in Marines and barbed wire and bunkers and everything else.

Now these three centers, the next range of centers, are gonna be big enough to take these big Marine helicopters, the CH53 and CH46s, which is what the Marines use, these Jolly Green Giant fucking birds that they used in Phnom Penh. So the next contingency plan is to get people into these centers, where they'll be housed, and flown out of there. If conditions permit, people would only be flown to the air base and flown out of there, but if the air base is under fire, and they can't get the planes in, they'll just try to fly people straight out to carriers. They've talked about plans to just put some Navy ships up the Saigon River—which would be absurd, since the river can be mined, has been mined in the past. It's also open to attack. But that's another contingency that they're toying with. They figure if they have a large evacuation, they'll try to make it at night. Get people to these assembly points just before the curfew. They figure they can move about fifteen hundred people an hour out to Ton San Nhut.

HST: By Huey? Are they assuming there's gonna be a panic?

JENKINS: Yeah, I have a feeling they're assuming the worst. They are obviously trying to buy off key people, like the police chief, the colonels who are in command of Ton San Nhut air base, and people like that, by saying "Look, when it comes to the crunch, we need you and you need us. We will get you and your family out. But you have to help us maintain security." So they're hoping that they will have a certain segment of the South Vietnamese under control, maybe certain police forces. At Ton San Nhut they may have the base people themselves. Now, whether or not the officers can control their men, obviously, is another matter. They certainly couldn't control them in Da Nang.

They're scared shitless about being followed by local Vietnamese who are watching the Americans like hawks. Afraid that when an American takes off, five cars of Vietnamese are gonna follow him to find out where they're planning to leave from. They're sort of issuing warnings: "Don't tell your Vietnamese about this. Don't leave your fucking evacuation plans lying around so your servants can read them." Really frightening, which again leads me to believe that this whole fucking thing about taking the Vietnamese out is a hoax. A real cruel fucking hoax. They keep talking about two hundred thousand. The only plan they have is this plan to take out Americans, their dependents, foreigners, and obviously a few select people like the president and his family and any other goddamned collaborators that they've held on a string for so long.

Now, they figure it will take two hours to get the Marines to defend this place.

HST: When they first call. When the whistle blows.

JENKINS: The Marines have to come in from the ship, but they don't have enough Marines to defend all these places. Until they get helicopters in from the Marine ships, from the aircraft carriers, they can only operate with twenty-five or twenty-eight small Hueys. That's all Air America has, apparently, which isn't much at all. It sort of shows you how ridiculous this whole plan is. It really comes down to trying to ship people out on choppers. But big choppers can't land at these collection points, and all they've got are twenty-eight small choppers that can carry eight to ten people.

HST: On the theory that only the first one will get out of any assembly point, that means that only two hundred people are likely to escape. Good God.

JENKINS: They were asked, "What were the conditions which would trigger this?" This guy delivering the briefing says that once artillery got into range and started popping into Saigon, when that happened, that would be time to really haul ass out of here.

HST: Since I've never heard artillery popping around me, what does that constitute? The first rocket? The first three rockets? The first one hundred thirty?

JENKINS: It would probably depend. I think what they're really worried about is one hundred thirties. If artillery shells start popping in here, and with regularity—I think a couple of rockets probably wouldn't do it—if they go screaming in here wild, one or two would probably hit. One would explode, another one wouldn't. I've seen this happen. It doesn't come immediately. There's not gonna be a fucking Stalingrad rumble all of a sudden one night. There will probably be days when the first early elements will put a few rockets in, and maybe the next night there'll be a few more, and then three or four nights later maybe they'll have artillery in range. And then it might start getting hotter.

And when this thing goes, the press is not going to be any different than any other Americans. People are gonna come in waving Japanese passports, American passports, and it's gonna be: Get on the choppers. Get 'em out.

It was nearly a fortnight after Pyle's death before I saw Vigot again. I was going up the Boulevard Charner when his voice called me from Le Club. It was the restaurant most favored in those days by members of the Sûreté, who, as a defiant gesture to those who hated them, would lunch and drink on the ground floor while the general public fed upstairs out of reach of a partisan with a hand grenade.

I joined him and he ordered me a vermouth cassis. "Play for it?"

"If you like," and I took out my dice for the ritual game of Quatre Cent Vingt-et-Un. How those figures and the sight of dice bring back to mind the war years in Indochina. Anywhere in the world when I see two men dicing I am back in the streets of Hanoi or Saigon or among the blasted buildings of Phat Diem. I see the parachutists, protected like caterpillars by their strange markings, patrolling by the canals, I hear the sound of mortars closing in, and perhaps I see a dead child.

　　　　—From *The Quiet American* by Graham Greene, 1955

My own sharpest memories of Indochina are not the same as Greene's, but he was there twenty years earlier, in the ruins of a different empire, when the losers still had plenty of time to spend their afternoons "dicing for drinks" on the shaded patios of French colonial hotels while they pondered the terrible cancer that was growing on The White Man's Burden; and to occasionally glance up from their dice and gin tonics to look for the faithful dwarf newsboy who delivered two copies of the Paris *Herald Tribune* to their table every afternoon about this time . . . a friendly little bugger, with big brown eyes and legs like wet spaghetti from some kind of congenital syphilis that his mother picked up from the Japs back in World War II, which was tragic, but no fault of theirs, and they always tipped him well. But whenever he was late with the newspapers, they would start to feel slightly nervous, because when he was late they would have to *think* about him, and whenever that happened they'd start wondering if maybe this was the day they had known would come sooner or later—when the evil little monster would show up with the same friendly smile on his face and toss a hand grenade onto their table, instead of the newspaper.

That kind of subliminal tension was always a part of the charm of living the soft colonial life in an outpost of progress like Saigon. It lent just enough hint of menace to "the mystery of the Orient" to keep life interesting for the "round-eyes" who were sent out from France and England to protect the natural resources of this weird subcontinent from the opium-crazed natives.

Saigon, Hotel Continental Plaza, in the Garden, May 1975

CONFIDENTIAL MEMO TO COLONEL GIANG VO DON GIANG

May 1975
Col. Vo Dan Giang, PRG
c/o Tan Son Nhut Air Base
Saigon

Dear Colonel Giang,

I am the National Affairs editor of *Rolling Stone,* a San Francisco–based magazine, with offices in New York, Washington, and London, that is one of the most influential journalistic voices in America right now—particularly among the young and admittedly left-oriented survivors of the antiwar Peace Movement in the 1960s. I'm not an especially good typist, but I am one of the best writers currently using the English language as both a musical instrument and a political weapon . . . and if there is any way you can possibly arrange it in the near future, I'd be very honored to have a private meeting with you and talk for an hour or so about your own personal thoughts right now.

We would need the help of one of your interpreters, because my French is a joke, my Spanish is embarrassing, and my command of Vietnamese is nonexistent. I came to Saigon two weeks ago, just after the panic at Da Nang, because I wanted to see the end of this stinking war with my own eyes after fighting it in the streets of Berkeley and Washington for the past ten years.

And the reason I'm writing you this note is that I was very much impressed by the way you handled your Saturday press conference the first time I attended, on the Saturday before last. That was the one in which you made three or four specific references to the dark fate awaiting "American military advisers posing as journalists"—and each time you mentioned that phrase, you seemed to be looking directly at me.

Which is understandable, on one level, because I've been told by my friend Jean-Claude Labbe that I definitely look like that type. But we both know that "looks" are very often deceiving, and almost anybody among the American press in Saigon today will tell you that— despite my grim appearance—I am the most obvious and most well known politically radical journalist in your country today.

In any case: shortly after leaving your press conference I called my associate, Tom Hayden, at his home in Los Angeles and asked him what he knew about you. Tom, as you know, is married to the American actress Jane Fonda, and they have both been among the strongest voices in the Peace Movement for the past ten years. Tom Hayden is also an editor of *Rolling Stone,* as you can see by the enclosed masthead . . . and when I asked him about you on the phone, he said I should make every effort to meet you because he considered you one of the most intelligent and humane leaders of the PRG. He also said you have a sense of humor and that I'd probably like you personally.

I had already picked up that feeling, after watching your press conference, and I am writing you now with the hope that we can arrange a brief and informal private meeting very soon. I think I understand the political reality of the PRG, but I'm not sure I understand the Human reality—and I have a sense that you could help me on that latter point. You might be surprised to know how many of the American journalists in Saigon today admire you and call you their friend.

I understand that a letter like this one puts you in a difficult position at this time, so I won't be personally offended if you decide against having a talk with me . . . but I trust you to understand that, as a professional para-journalist, I am in the same situation today that you were as a para-military professional about three years ago . . . and if you have any serious doubts about my personal and political views, please ask one of your friends to stop by the Hotel Continental, #37, and pick up a copy of my book on the 1972 presidential campaign in

America. I will give the book to anybody who asks me for "the book for Che." Or I'll bring it to you myself, if there is any way you can invite me into your compound out there. . . . And, as a matter of fact, if there is going to be any real "battle for Saigon," I think I'd feel safer out there with you and your people than I would in the midst of some doomed and stupid "American Evacuation Plan" dreamed up by that senile death-monger, Graham Martin.

If you think it might be of any help to you to have a well-known American writer with you out there in the compound when the "battle" starts, I'll be happy to join you for a few days in your bunker. . . . But that is not the kind of arrangement I can make on my own; it would require some help from you, to let me pass quietly through the check-points outside your compound . . . and I give you my word that I'll do that, if you can make the arrangements and let me know.

Okay for now. I hope to see you soon . . . but even if I don't, allow me to offer my personal congratulations for the work you've done and the very pure and dramatic victory you've accomplished. I can only feel saddened by all the pain and death and suffering this ugly war has caused on all sides . . . but your victory, I think, is a victory for all of us who believe that man is still capable of making this world a better, more peaceful and generous place for all our sons and daughters to live in.

This is the kind of thing I'd like to talk to you about—not such things as "battle strategy" or your current political plans. That is not my style—as a journalist or a human being—and besides, you'll soon be getting all the questions you can handle on those subjects. No pack of jackals has ever been more single-mindedly obtuse in their hunger for news/meat than the army of standard-brand American journalists who will soon be hounding you for wisdom and explanations. I can only wish you luck with that problem, and I hope we can have a quick and friendly private visit before you get caught up on that tiresome merry-go-round.

As for me, I won't stay in Vietnam much longer, unless I hear from you in the next few days. I may return in a few months, but I am homesick for the peace and quiet of my log house in Colorado and I want to get back there as soon as possible. My home address in America is Owl Farm, Woody Creek, Colorado 81656—or you can reach me in care of any one of the *Rolling Stone* offices listed on the enclosed masthead. I am also a friend of Senator George McGovern, Senators Gary Hart and Ted Kennedy, and former Senators Eugene McCarthy and Fred Harris . . . so if I can be of any help to you as a friendly contact in Washington, feel free to communicate with me at any time and I'll do whatever I can . . . but in the meantime, I hope you'll let me know, by whatever means you think best, if there is any chance for us to get together: perhaps even here in the Continental for a quiet bit of drink and talk with a few of your friends in the American press. I have a feeling you'll be a welcome guest in this place fairly soon and I think you'll enjoy it.

And that's all I have to say at this time. It is five minutes before six in the morning and I need to get some sleep, so I'll end this letter now and take it around to my friend who plans to deliver it to you.

Very sincerely,

Hunter S. Thompson
Suite 37
Hotel Continental Plaza
Saigon, Vietnam

MEMO TO JIM SILBERMAN ON THE DEATH OF THE AMERICAN DREAM

THE CORD IS cut now: I have quit that outpost of progress called the National Affairs Desk that I founded at *Rolling Stone,* and in the slow process of quitting I drifted so far from the backstairs complexities of national politics that I couldn't go back to it now, even if I wanted to . . . and that, I think, is a point I had to reach and recognize on my own, and for my own reasons. As long as the constant speedy lure of political journalism seemed more essential and important to me than the ugly, slow-burning reality of writing a novel, any effort to write fiction would have been a part-time, left-handed gig (like my recent journalism). . . . And in any other line of work except writing, people who try to deal with the world and life and reality off a split-focus base are called "schizoid" and taken off the streets, as it were, for their own and the greater good.

Now, after more than a week of extremely disorienting conversations regarding the ultimate fate of this story—a novel? a screenplay? or both?—I feel in the grip of a serious confusion, to wit: the story as I originally conceived it, more than two years ago, was a first-person "journalistic novel," set in Texas and rooted in a genuine conflict between Innocence and Violence, that seemed to be the source of a unique and classically "American" style of energy that I hadn't felt since my first visit to Brazil in 1962, or to California in 1959. It was the same level of energy that I sensed on my first contact with the Hell's Angels, my first visit to Las Vegas, and my first few days in the frenzied vortex of a U.S. presidential campaign. . . . But I knew that, in order to deal properly with any story set in Texas, I would have to move for a year to Houston or Dallas or Austin and actually live there; and this was the harsh reality that I wasn't quite ready to face two years ago. There were other stories to get involved in, other places to go, and the sudden millstone of personal notoriety that caused so many unexpected changes in my life stance that I still haven't regained my balance. . . . It was one thing to slip into Texas as an anonymous young journalist with a subsistence-level book contract, and quite another to boom into a state full of boomers with a national reputation as some kind of lunatic felon, a journalistic Billy the Kid and a cartoon character that appeared every day in newspapers all over Texas. That kind of act is known, among boomers, as a "hard dollar"—and anybody who thinks otherwise should try it for a while.

In any case, that and a few other good reasons is why I kept postponing the book on Texas. . . . But I continued to brood on it, and one of the people I brooded with from time to time was Bob Rafelson, a film director and personal friend who listened to my gibberish about Texas and violence and energy for so long that he eventually began brooding on the story himself, and finally suggested that it might work better as a film than as a book.

At that point I was still thinking vaguely about writing a book on the '76 presidential campaign and taking all the 50–1 bets I could get on my own lonely dark horse—some yahoo from Georgia named Carter—and so for all the obvious reasons that seemed at the time to mandate another HST/Campaign book, my "Texas Project" remained in an oddly intense state of "talking limbo" for most of 1975. Rafelson was totally involved in the making of *Stay Hungry*, and since there was nobody else to prod me along in "Texas," I ignored my own fast-rising conviction that another HST/Campaign book would be a fatal mistake that would lock me for life into Teddy White's footsteps, and fell prey to the natural gambler's affection for his own long shot—and it was not until I went up to New Hampshire to cover the first primary that I understood the finality of the choice I was drifting into. The New Hampshire results were all I needed to prove my point as a gambler and a seer, but the personal notoriety I'd accrued since 1972 had changed my role as a journalist so drastically that even the Secret Service treated me with embarrassing deference, and I couldn't walk into a bar without total strangers wanting to argue with me or ask for my autograph. . . . And for two days after the New Hampshire primary I sat around Charles Gaines' house on a hill near a hamlet called Contoocook, trying to decide whether I should keep on covering the '76 campaign and adjust to my new persona, or to quit political journalism altogether and get seriously to work on a novel—which is something I've been planning to do ever since I finished my ill-fated "Rum Diary" almost fifteen years ago. I have never had much respect or affection for journalism, but for the past ten years it has been both a dependable meal ticket and a valid passport to the cockpit(s) of whatever action, crisis, movement, or instant history I wanted to be a part of.

And it worked, folks. Between 1962, when I was working for the *National Observer* and got the first private interview with the new president of Peru in the wake of a military takeover, until 1975 when I failed to get the first interview with the VC/NVA colonel who orchestrated the fifth-column seizure of Saigon as the last Americans fled, I managed—by using almost any kind of valid or invalid journalistic credentials I could get my hands on—to get myself personally involved in just about everything that interested me: from Berkeley to Chicago, Las Vegas to the White House, shark-fishing, street-fighting, dope-smuggling, Hell's Angels, Super Bowls, local politics, and a few things I'd prefer not to mention until various statutes of limitations expire.

Indeed. Those were good years for almost any kind of journalism; it was the main language of a very public and political decade. . . . But I suspect it will not be the main language of the 1970s, or at least not for me and most of the people I know. Very few of them subscribe to the same papers or magazines now that they subscribed to five or even two years ago, and even fewer plan to vote in the '76 general election. Not even the best and most perceptive journalists covering the pres-

idential campaign seem to care who will win it, or why. . . . And
neither do I, for that matter: after ten years of the most intense kind
of personal and professional involvement in national politics, it occurs
to me now that I could have left it all alone, and—except for my role
as a journalist and all the constant action it plunged me into—my life
would not have been much different, regardless of who won or lost
any one of the myriad clashes, causes, confrontations, elections,
brawls, chases, and other high-adrenaline situations that I found myself
drawn to.

Ah . . . but this is a hasty judgment, and probably not true: I can
think of at least a half-dozen public realities that I managed, for good
or ill, to affect by my presence, participation, or journalistic advo-
cacy—and in retrospect I'm about 98 percent happy with whatever
ripples I caused in the great swamp of history—and there were also
those handful of moments when my life might have been drastically
changed by what did *not* happen: like dying a violent death, a fate I
seem to narrowly avoid about once every year, or going to prison, or
becoming a junkie, or becoming an indentured servant to Jann Wenner, or running off to Bermuda with Eleanor McGovern, or becoming
sheriff of Pitkin County, the governor of American Samoa, or a speech
writer for Jimmy Carter. . . .

Indeed . . . and on balance, my behavior as a person, writer, ad-
vocate, midnight strategist, hatchet man, and serious gambler for at
least the past ten years has been generally beneficial to myself, my
friends, my wife and son, and most of the people I tend to side with,
whenever the deal goes down. . . . Which is not a bad thing to look
back on: and if I seem a bit cynical, at this point, or a trifle uncertain
about The Meaning of It All, it is probably because of my secret
conviction that a whole generation of journalists and journalism went
over the hump with the Nixon/Watergate story, and that the odds
against any of us ever hitting that kind of peak again are impossibly
long. It was not just the Watergate story itself, but the fact that nobody
who worked on the leading edge of journalism in the years between
1960 and 1975 could have asked for or even hoped for a better or more
dramatically perfect climax to what now seems like one long violent
and incredibly active story. When I proposed that book on "The Death
of the American Dream" back in 1967 and then rushed off to cover
the first act of Nixon's political "comeback" in the '68 New Hampshire
primary, my instinct was better than any of us knew at the time—
because the saga of Richard Nixon *is* The Death of the American
Dream. He was our Gatsby, but the light at the end of his pier was

black instead of green. . . . Whoever writes the true biography of Richard Nixon will write the definitive book on "The Death of the American Dream."

We should keep that in mind, because that is the book I was just beginning to scent ten years ago. I was hearing the music, but I am not a musician and I couldn't "put it to words," and even when I found the right lyrics, in bits and pieces of almost everything I wrote in those years, it was not until I stood in the wet grass of the White House rose garden and watched Nixon stumble onto the helicopter that would carry him into exile that I heard the music again. . . .

And I am still hearing it; but I am not quite ready to write the lyrics yet—and in the meantime I want to write a story that will leap and roll and crackle, a quick and brutal tale of life in a world without Nixon. What I need right now, I think, is a bit of a workout, something more along the lines of *Fear and Loathing in Las Vegas* than *The Saga of Horatio Nixon and the Death of the American Dream.*

(NO . . . don't say it, Jim. Don't even *think* it right now. We both know what kind of pain and suffering and preternatural concentration the Nixon book will require, and I simply can't stand it right now. It's too goddamn heavy, and it would take at least two and probably three years of extremely focused research, thinking, and writing; because it is obviously the one book I've been instinctively gearing down to write for these many years. . . . But that one will have to wait at least until we get Nixon's own version of his ugly rise and fall, and in the meantime I think I've paid enough dues to justify another sort of busman's vacation, on the order of *Fear and Loathing in Las Vegas,* which is far and away my personal favorite of the three books I've written: it was also the most fun to write, the best and most economical piece of sustained "pure writing" I've ever done, and sooner or later it will prove to be the most financially successful of the three. . . . Which is fitting, because *Vegas* is a book that no other living writer could have written. . . .

Indeed, and to hell with all that. What I'm saying now is that I think it's about time for me to indulge, once again, that whole high-powered stratum of my writer's energy that keeps bubbling up to the surface of all my journalism and confusing my standard-brand colleagues so badly that even the ones who consistently feel free to plagiarize my best concepts and perceptions seem almost personally offended by the style and stance of my "gonzo journalism."

Which rarely bothers me—but Rarely is different from Never, and every once in a while I think it's healthy to clear the deck and lay a serious fireball on some of these bastards who lack either the grace or the integrity or both to understand that they can't have it both ways. There are numerous lame and sterile ways to counter *surface* plagiarism, but the only sure and final cure is to write something so clearly and brutally original that only a fool would risk plagiarizing it . . . and that's what I'd like to do now: if "gonzo journalism" is essentially the "art" (or compulsion) of imposing a novelistic form on journalistic content then the next logical step in the "gonzo process" would seem to be a 180-degree reversal of that process, by writing a "journalistic novel."

Which is bullshit, of course, because on the high end there is only one real difference between the two forms—and that is the rigidly vested interest in the maintenance of a polar (or strictly polarized) separation of "fiction" and "journalism" by at least two generations of New York–anchored writers who spent most of their working lives learning, practicing, and finally insisting on the esthetic validity of that separation.

And what the hell? I suspect it's genuinely important to them, so why not concede it? Ten years from now I might feel in a mood to force that kind of merger, but for now the formal separation works in my favor, because it gives me a straw man to beat on, and stir the buggers up. (Just for the record, however—and one of these days I hope to find enough time to explain this notion properly—the only real difference between "journalism" and "fiction" in my own mind is *legalistic:* with our contemporary, standard-brand journalism as nothing more than a sloppy lay extension of the Rules of Evidence, rooted in the Adversary Relationship that governs our twentieth-century American trial procedure; and the best and highest kind of contemporary fiction or even High Novelistic Journalism with its roots in the thinking of those essentially Jeffersonian pragmatists often referred to by historians as "the great Stoic lawyers of ancient Rome. . . ."

And, mother of babbling Jesus, how did I get into this? The only point I wanted to make was that—by conceding what I consider a false distinction between journalism and fiction—I can jangle the rules even further by claiming to have made a 180-degree turn, quitting journalism and going back to The Novel, while in fact making no turn at all, and holding exactly the same course I began with *Hell's Angels*. . . . Selah.)

Woody Creek, 1977

LETTER TO RUSSELL
CHATHAM

Woody Creek, Colorado
February 17, 1979

Dear Russell,

Thanks for the elegant print. It arrived yesterday by UPS and I took it down to the Woody Creek Tavern to show to the cowboys. It is a bleak landscape, for sure, and some of them recognized it. One of them called it ugly and we had a brief scuffle, but in the end they agreed it was Art.

Which is true, and it was a moment of pure pleasure to reach into that finely packed box and lift the bugger out and hold it up in the sunlight, a fine little unexpected surprise on my way to the tavern for lunch. It was one of those moments that can change a man's whole attitude for a while. . . .

You should stay away from inscriptions, however; history is rife with tragic examples of what happens when primitive artists try to express themselves in words. I have had this argument with Steadman for many years. Stay away from words, I tell him, but he persists, he fouls his art with the kind of jabbering you'd normally expect to hear from an old woman weeding a garden.

Take it as a lesson, Russell. Nobody needs that kind of confusion. It is no accident that Ralph's hair turned white when he was sixteen years old. His nuts shriveled up and fell off his body like raisins off a bush, and he has been like a chow ever since. He has sired five children, all with obvious brain damage, and he says he wants to sire more . . . horrible, horrible.

In any case, I'm enclosing a copy of our LONO Experiment. It is a noble effort, although flawed in certain ways, to push back the barriers of art. Somewhere in this three-legged crank is the seed of a good idea—the same thing we briefly discussed at the bar that night in Aspen and which you and Tom [McGuane] seem to be coming at, from a slightly different direction, with *In the Crazies*. I'll be curious to see what kind of a mix you'll come up with. I suspect we're on the brink of a whole new format that will make us all dangerously rich. We can travel in the style of young Buddhas all over the globe for the rest of our lives. It is definitely a thing worth pondering, the next time we get together.

I am planning to be down in the Keys for most of the spring. I issued a bad check to the landlord yesterday and told him I would be taking the house through June. The idea is to hunker down and finish my Cuban novel, then sell my passport and become a citizen of Hong Kong, living on coupons and taking my lunch alone each day at a table near the window in the Press Club, drinking gin in the morning and playing cards at night with strangers. . . .

Jesus. I think it's time to quit. I just smoked a bowl of hash and then had to change the ribbon, which took about twenty-five minutes. And now I seem to have lost my will to write . . . let me know if you think you'll be in Florida; we can go out on my boat and run the Flats like real men.

Okay. That's it, for me. Some animal killed one of my peacocks last night and I am sitting here with the 12-gauge, hoping the thing will come back for another one. Probably I will end up killing the neighbor's dog, and the neighbor. . . . Anyway, thanks again for the Art.

Hunter

The EIGHTIES

HOW MUCH MONEY DO YOU HAVE?

WELCOME TO THE '80s

THERE'S NO SANE reason for all these runners. Only a fool would try to explain why four thousand Japanese ran at top speed past the U.S.S. *Arizona*, sunken memorial in the middle of Pearl Harbor, along with another four or five thousand certified American *liberals* cranked up on beer and spaghetti and all taking the whole thing so seriously that only one in two thousand could even smile at the idea of a twenty-six-mile race featuring four thousand Japanese that begins and ends within a stone's throw of Pearl Harbor on the morning of December 7, 1980. . . .

Thirty-nine years later. What are these people celebrating? And why on this bloodstained anniversary? . . .

At least one person has suggested that we may be looking at the Last Refuge of the Liberal Mind, or at least the Last Thing That Works.

Run for your life, sport, because that's all you have left. The same people who burned their draft cards in the sixties and got lost in the seventies are now into *running*. When politics failed and personal relationships became unmanageable; after McGovern went down and Nixon exploded right in front of our eyes . . . after Ted Kennedy got Stassenized and Jimmy Carter put the fork to everybody who ever believed anything he said about anything at all, and after the nation turned *en masse* to the atavistic wisdom of Ronald Reagan.

Well, these are, after all, the eighties and the time has finally come to see who has teeth, and who doesn't. . . . Which may or may not account for the odd spectacle of two generations of political activists and social anarchists finally turning—twenty years later—into *runners*.

Why is this?

This is what we came out here to examine. Ralph came all the way from London—with his wife and eight-year-old daughter—to grapple with this odd question that I told him was vital but which in fact might not mean anything at all.

Why not come to Aspen and have some fun with the New Dumb?

Or why not skewer Hollywood? If only to get even with that scum . . . or even back to Washington, for the last act of *Bedtime for Bonzo*?

Why did we come all the way out here to what used to be called "the Sandwich Islands" to confront some half-wit spectacle like eight thousand rich people torturing themselves in the streets of Honolulu and calling it sport?

Well . . . there is a reason; or at least there was, when we agreed to do this thing.

The Fata Morgana.

Yes, that was the reason—some wild and elegant hallucination in the sky. We had both retired from journalism; but then years of working harder and harder for less and less money can make a man kinky. Once you understand that you can make more money simply by answering your telephone once a week than by churning out gibberish for the public prints at a pace keyed to something like three hours of sleep a night for thirty, sixty, or even eighty-odd hours in a stretch, it is hard to get up for the idea of going back into hock to American Express and MasterCharge for just another low-rent look at what's happening.

Journalism is a Ticket to Ride, to get personally involved in the same news other people watch on TV—which is nice, but it won't pay the rent, and people who can't pay their rent in the '80s are going to be in trouble. We are into a very nasty decade, a brutal Darwinian crunch that will not be a happy time for free-lancers.

Indeed. The time has come to write *books*—or even movies, for those who can keep a straight face. Because there is money in these things; and there is no money in journalism.

But there is *action,* and action is an easy thing to get hooked on. It is a nice thing to know that you can pick up a phone and be off to anywhere in the world that interests you—on twenty-four hours' notice, and especially on somebody else's tab.

That is what you miss: not the money, but the action—and that is why I finally drilled Ralph out of his castle in Kent for a trip to Hawaii and a look at this strange new phenomenon called "running." There was no good reason for it; I just felt it was time to get out in the world . . . get angry and tune the instruments . . . go to Hawaii for Christmas.

Honolulu, December 7, 1980

BAD CRAZINESS IN PALM BEACH: I TOLD HER IT WAS WRONG . . .

Notes from the Behavioral Sink and Other Queer Tales from Palm Beach . . . and Wild Lies and Relentless Perjury . . . a Fishhead Judge Meets a Naked Cinderella . . . Dark, Dark Days on the Gold Coast, Long Nights for Animals

THERE IS A lot of wreckage in the fast lane these days. Not even the rich feel safe from it, and people are looking for reasons. The smart say they can't understand it, and the dumb snort cocaine in rich discos and stomp to a feverish beat. Which is heard all over the country, or at least felt. The stomping of the rich is not a noise to be ignored in troubled times. It usually means they are feeling anxious or confused about something, and when the rich feel anxious and confused, they act like wild animals.

That is the situation in Palm Beach these days, and the natives are not happy with it. The rich have certain rules, and these are two of the big ones: maintain the privacy and the pipeline at all costs—although not necessarily in that order—it depends on the situation, they say; and everything has its price, even women.

There are no jails or hospitals in Palm Beach. It is the ultimate residential community, a lush sandbar lined with palm trees and mansions on the Gold Coast of Florida—millionaires and old people, an elaborately protected colony for the seriously rich, a very small island and a very small world. The rules are different here, or at least they seem to be, and the people like it that way.

There are hideous scandals occasionally—savage lawsuits over money, bizarre orgies at the Bath and Tennis Club or some genuine outrage like a half-mad eighty-eight-year-old heiress trying to marry her teenage Cuban butler—but scandals pass like winter storms in Palm Beach, and it has been a long time since anybody got locked up for degeneracy in this town. The community is very tight, connected to the real world by only four bridges, and is as deeply mistrustful of strangers as any lost tribe in the Amazon.

The rich like their privacy, and they have a powerful sense of turf. God has given them the wisdom, they feel, to handle their own problems in their own way. In Palm Beach there is nothing so warped and horrible that it can't be fixed, or at least tolerated, just as long as it stays in the family.

The family lives on the island, but not everybody on the island is family. The difference is very important, a main fact of life for the people who live here, and few of them misunderstand it. At least not for long. The penalty for forgetting your place can be swift and terrible. I have friends in Palm Beach who are normally very gracious, but when word got out that I was in town asking questions about the Pulitzer divorce trial, I was shunned like a leper.

The *Miami Herald* called it the nastiest divorce trial in Palm Beach history, a scandal so foul and far-reaching that half the town fled to France or Majorca for fear of being dragged into it. People who normally stay home in the fall to have all their bedrooms redecorated or to put a new roof on the boathouse found reasons to visit Brazil. The hammer of Palm Beach justice was coming down on young Roxanne Pulitzer, a girl from the wrong side of the tracks who had married the town's most eligible bachelor a few years back and was now in the throes of divorce. Divorce is routine in Palm Beach, but this one had a very different and dangerous look to it. The whole life-style of the town was suddenly on trial, and prominent people were being accused of things that were not fashionable.

A headline in the *Denver Post* said PULITZER TRIAL SEETHING WITH TALES OF SEX, DRUGS, OCCULT. The *New York Post* upped the ante with TYCOON'S WIFE NAMED IN PULITZER DIVORCE SHOCKER and I SLEPT WITH A TRUMPET. The Boston *Herald American* made a whole generation of journalists uneasy with a front-page banner saying PULITZER WAS A DIRTY OLD MAN.

Some of the first families of Palm Beach society will bear permanent scars from the *Pulitzer v. Pulitzer* proceedings. The Filthy Rich in America were depicted as genuinely *filthy,* a tribe of wild sots and sodomites run amok on their own private island and crazed all day and all night on cocaine. The very name *Palm Beach,* long synonymous with old wealth and aristocratic style, was coming to be associated with berserk sleaziness, a place where price tags mean nothing and the rich are always in heat, where pampered animals are openly wor-

shiped in church and naked millionaires gnaw brassieres off the chests
of their own daughters in public.

I arrived in Palm Beach on a rainy night in November, for no particular
reason. I was on my way south, to Miami, and then on to Nassau for
a wedding. But it would not be happening for two weeks, so I had
some time to kill, and Miami, I felt, was not the place to do it. Two
weeks on the loose in Miami can change a man's life forever. It is the
Hong Kong of the Western world. Not even the guilty feel safe in
Miami these days.

Money is cheap on the Gold Coast, and there is a lot of it floating
around. A thirteen-year-old boy recently found a million dollars' worth
of big, finely cut diamonds in a brown bag on the railroad tracks near
Hollywood. His aunt made him turn in the loot, but nobody claimed
it, and his neighbors called him a fool. Which was true. There is no
place for Horatio Algers down here on the Gold Coast; hard work
and clean living will get you a bag of potato chips and a weekend job
scraping scum off the hull of your neighbor's new Cigarette boat.

There is a whole new ethic taking shape in South Florida these days,
and despite the rich Latin overlay, it is not so far from the taproot of
the old American Dream. It is free enterprise in the raw, a wide-open
Spanish-speaking kind of Darwinism, like the Sicilians brought to New
York a hundred years ago and like the Japanese brought to Hawaii
after World War II, and not really much different from what the Israelis
are bringing to Lebanon today. The language is different, the music
is faster, the food is not meat and potatoes, but the message is still
the same. Rich is strong, poor is weak, and the government works for
whoever pays its salaries.

The Palm Beach County Courthouse is not much different from others
all over the country. It is just another clearinghouse on the street of
broken dreams, a grim maze of long corridors full of people who would
rather not be there. Young girls wearing neck braces sit patiently on
wooden benches, waiting to testify against young men wearing handcuffs and jail denim. Old women weep hysterically in crowded elevators. Wild blacks with gold teeth are dragged out of courtrooms by
huge bailiffs. Elderly jurors are herded around like criminals, not
knowing what to expect.

Only lawyers can smile in this atmosphere. They rush from one trial to another with bulging briefcases, followed by dull-eyed clerks carrying cardboard boxes filled with every kind of evidence, from rusty syringes to human fingers and sworn depositions from the criminally insane with serious grudges to settle.

The Pulitzer divorce trial was held in a small hearing room at the end of a hall on the third floor. There was no room for spectators, and the only way to get one of the nine press seats was to be there in person at seven o'clock in the morning—or even earlier, on some days—and put your name on the list. Under Florida law, however, Judge Carl Harper was compelled to allow one stationary TV camera in the courtroom so that the trial could be filmed for the public and watched on closed circuit in a room across the hall, where anybody could watch the proceedings in relative comfort, with cigarettes and doughnuts from the courthouse coffee shop.

These were the bleacher seats at the Pulitzer trial, a strange and sometimes rowdy mixture of everything from CBS-TV producers to lanky six-foot women with no bras and foreign accents who claimed to be from *Der Spiegel* and *Paris Match*. It was a lusty crowd, following the action intently, sometimes cheering, sometimes booing. It was like a crowd of strangers who came together each day in some musty public room to watch a TV soap opera like "General Hospital." On one afternoon, when Roxanne Pulitzer lost her temper at some particularly degenerate drift in the testimony, the bleachers erupted with shouting: "Go get 'em, Roxy! Kick ass! That's it, Rox baby! Don't let 'em talk that way about you!"

Some people made notes, and others played constantly with tape-recording equipment. A man from the *National Enquirer* came in one day but left quickly and never returned. "We don't need it," he said later. "It's too serious."

On the surface, the story was not complex. Basically, it was just another tale of Cinderella gone wrong, a wiggy little saga of crime, hubris, and punishment: Herbert "Pete" Pulitzer, Jr., fifty-two-year-old millionaire grandson of the famous newspaper publisher and heir to the family name as well as the fortune, had finally come to his senses and cast out the evil golddigger who'd caused him so much grief. She was an incorrigible coke slut, he said, and a totally unfit mother. She stayed up all night at discos and slept openly with her dope pusher, among others. There was a house painter, a real-estate agent, a race-car driver, and a French baker—and on top of all that, she was a lesbian, or at least some kind of pansexual troilist. In six-and-a-half years of marriage, she had humped almost everything she could get her hands on.

Finally, his attorneys explained, Mr. Pulitzer had no choice but to rid himself of his woman. She was more like Marilyn Chambers than Cinderella. When she wasn't squawking wantonly in front of the children with Grand Prix driver Jacky Ickx or accused Palm Beach cocaine dealer Brian Richards, she was in bed with her beautiful friend Jacquie Kimberly, thirty-two, wife of seventy-six-year-old socialite James Kimberly, heir to the Kleenex fortune. There was no end to it, they said. Not even when Pulitzer held a loaded .45-caliber automatic pistol to her head—and then to his own—in a desperate last-ditch attempt to make her seek help for her drug habits, which she finally agreed to do.

And *did,* for that matter, but five days in Highland Park General Hospital was not enough. The cure didn't take, Pete's attorneys charged, and she soon went back on the whiff and also back to the pusher, who described himself in the courtroom as a "self-employed handyman" and gave his age as twenty-nine.

Roxanne Pulitzer is not a beautiful woman. There is nothing especially striking about her body or facial bone structure, and at age thirty-one, she looks more like a jaded senior stewardess from Pan Am than an international sex symbol. Ten years on the Palm Beach Express have taken their toll, and she would have to do more than just sweat off ten pounds to compete for naked space in the men's magazines. Her legs are too thin, her hips are too wide, and her skin is a bit too loose for modeling work. But she has a definite physical presence. There is no mistaking the aura of good-humored, out-front sexuality. This is clearly a woman who likes to sleep late in the morning.

Roxanne blew into town more than ten years ago, driving a Lincoln Continental with a sixty-foot house trailer in tow, a ripe little cheerleader just a year or so out of high school in Cassadaga, New York, a small town of 900 near Buffalo. After graduation from Cassadaga High, she got a job in nearby Jamestown as a personal secretary to the general counsel for the American Voting Machine Corporation— a serious young man named Lloyd Dixon III, who eventually committed suicide. His father, who was later sent to prison, was president of AVM at the time and took such a shine to the new secretary that he hastened to marry her off to his other son, a callow youth named Peter, just back from the Air Force Reserve.

The newlyweds hauled their trailer down to West Palm Beach, where young Peter had often spent winter vacations with the family, and set up housekeeping in a local trailer park. They both enrolled in local colleges and lived more or less like their neighbors. But the marriage turned sour and the couple soon separated. The trailer was sold to gypsies, and Roxanne got half, which she used to finance the rest of her education at Palm Beach Junior College in West Palm Beach. After she graduated, she went immediately to work for a local insurance agency, selling policies.

That is where she met Randy Hopkins, who at the time was also selling policies to supplement his income as an heir to the Listerine mouthwash fortune. Everybody in Palm Beach is an heir to something, and there is no point in checking them out unless you want to get married. Hopkins was the real thing, for Roxanne, and soon they were living together.

These were the weird years in Palm Beach, with a sort of late-blooming rock and roll crowd, champagne hippies who drove Porsches and smoked marijuana and bought Rolling Stones records and even snorted cocaine from time to time. Some ate LSD and ran naked on the beach until they were caught and dragged home by the police, who were almost always polite. Their parties got out of hand occasionally, and the servants wept openly at some of the things they witnessed, but it was mainly a crowd of harmless rich kids with too many drugs.

It was in the heat of the mid-seventies that Roxanne Dixon moved in with Randy Hopkins and took herself a seat on the Palm Beach Express.

One of Hopkins' good friends at the time was Pete Pulitzer, a forty-five-year-old recently divorced millionaire playboy who bore a certain resemblance to Alexander Haig on an ether binge and was known in some circles as the most eligible bachelor in town. Pulitzer was also the owner of Doherty's, a fashionable downtown pub and late-night headquarters for the rock and roll set. Doherty's was a fast and randy place in the years when Pete owned it. John and Yoko would drop in for lunch, the bartenders were from Harvard, and Pete's patrons were anything but discreet about their predilection for dirty cocaine and a good orgy now and then.

It was the place to be seen, and Pulitzer was the man to be seen with. He had his pick of the ladies, and he particularly enjoyed the young ones. When his friend Randy Hopkins introduced him to Roxanne one night, he liked her immediately.

• • •

All the evidence in the case was trundled around the courthouse in a grocery cart that some bailiff had apparently borrowed from a local supermarket. It contained everything from family tax returns to the tin trumpet Roxanne allegedly slept with while trying to communicate with the dead. The cart was parked next to a Xerox machine in the county clerk's office on all days when the court was not in session, and under the curious provisions of Florida's much-admired public-records statute, it was open to public inspection at all times. The contents of the cart were shuffled and reshuffled by so many people that not even the judge could have made any sense of it by the time the trial was over, but journalists found it a source of endless amusement. You could go in there with a satchel of cold beers on a rainy afternoon and whoop it up for hours by just treating the cart like a grab bag and copying anything you wanted.

I spent a lot of time poring over copies of the Pulitzers' personal tax returns and financial ledgers submitted as evidence by the Pulitzer family accountants, and I have made a certain amount of wild sense of it all, but not enough. I understood, for instance, that these people were seriously rich. Family expenditures for 1981 totaled $972,980 for a family of four: one man, one woman, two four-year-old children, and a nanny who was paid $150 a week.

That is a lot of money, but so what? We are not talking about poor people here, and a million dollars a year for family expenditures is not out of line in Palm Beach. The rich have special problems. The Pulitzers spent $49,000 on basic "household expenditures" in 1981 and another $272,000 for "household improvements." That is about $320,000 a year just to have a place to sleep and play house. There was another $79,600 listed for "personal expenses" and $79,000 for boat maintenance. "Business" expenditures came in at $11,000 and there was no listing at all for taxes. As for "charity," the Pulitzers apparently followed the example of Ronald Reagan that year and gave in private, so as not to embarrass the poor.

There was, however, one item that begged for attention. The figure was $441,000 and the column was "miscellaneous and unknown." Right. Miscellaneous and unknown: $441,000. And nobody in the courtroom even blinked. Here were two coke fiends who came into court because their marriage didn't seem to be working and the children were getting nervous.

And the servants were turning weird and on some nights there were naked people running around on the lawn and throwing rocks at the upstairs bedroom windows and people with white foam in their

*mouths were jacking off like apes in the hallways . . . people screeching
frantically on the telephone at four in the morning about volcanic erup-
tions in the Pacific that were changing the temperature of the ocean
forever and causing the jet stream to move south, which would bring
on a new Ice Age—and that's why neither of us could get any sleep,
Your Honor, and the sky was full of vultures so we called a plastic
surgeon because her tits were starting to sag and my eyes didn't look
right anymore and then we drove halfway to Miami at 100 miles an
hour before we realized it was Sunday and the hospital wouldn't be
open so we checked into the Holiday Inn with Jim's wife and ye gods,
Your Honor, this woman is a whore and I can't really tell you what it
means because the children are in danger and we're afraid they might
freeze in their sleep and I can't trust you anyway but what else can I
do, I'm desperate—and, by the way, we spent $441,000 last year on
things I can't remember.*

Welcome to cocaine country. White line fever. Bad craziness. What
is a judge to make of two coke fiends who spent $441,000 last year on
"miscellaneous and unknown"? The figure for the previous year was
only $99,000, at a time when the Pulitzers' cocaine use was admittedly
getting out of hand. They said they were holding it down to just a few
grams a week, at that point, a relatively moderate figure among the
Brotherhood of the Bindle, but the evidence suggests a genuinely
awesome rate of consumption—something like thirteen grams a day—
by the time they finally staggered into divorce court and went public
with the whole wretched saga.

The numbers are staggering, even in the context of Palm Beach.
Thirteen grams a day would kill a whole family of polar bears.

With Mrs. Pulitzer sitting at a table only an arm's length away, Cheatham
went on to say, "Your Honor, Jamie told me Roxanne was the wildest,
strongest piece of ass that he ever had in his whole life."
—*New York Post*, October 4, 1982

That is not bad publicity in some towns, but it is definitely wrong
for Palm Beach. And it is not the kind of thing most men want to read
about their wives in the morning paper. A pimp might call it a windfall,
but it is bad press with bells on for a fifty-two-year-old socialite known
to big-time society page writers as a dashing millionaire sportsman
from Palm Beach. Or maybe not. History has judged F. Scott Fitzgerald harshly for allegedly saying to Hemingway that "the very rich

are different from you and me," but perhaps he was on to something Ernest couldn't grasp.

What is the *real* price, for instance, of a seat on the Palm Beach Express? The island is more like a private club than a city. It is ten miles long and one mile wide, more or less, with a permanent population of 9,700. But these figures are too generous, the real ones are lower by half. The real Palm Beach—the colony itself, the gilded nexus—is only about five miles long and three blocks wide, bordered on the east by a fine stretch of white beach and Atlantic Ocean, and on the west by palm trees, private piers, and million-dollar boathouses on the Intracoastal Waterway. There is North Palm Beach and South Palm Beach and the vast honky-tonk wasteland of West Palm Beach on the mainland, but these are not the people we're talking about. These are servants and suckfish, and they don't really matter in the real Palm Beach, except when they have to testify.

That is the weak reed, a cruel and incurable problem the rich have never solved—how to live in peace with the servants. Sooner or later, the maid has to come in the bedroom, and if you're only paying her $150 a week, she is going to come in hungry, or at least curious, and the time is long past when it was legal to cut their tongues out to keep them from talking.

The servant problem is the Achilles' heel of the rich. The only solution is robots, but we are still a generation or so away from that, and in the meantime it is just about impossible to hire a maid who is smart enough to make a bed but too dumb to wonder why it is full of naked people every morning. The gardener will not be comfortable with the sight of rope ladders hanging from the master-bedroom windows when he mows the lawn at noon, and any chauffeur with the brains to work a stick shift on a Rolls will also understand what's happening when you send him across the bridge to a goat farm in Loxahatchee for a pair of mature billies and a pound of animal stimulant.

Nakedness is a way of life in Palm Beach, and the difference between a picnic and an orgy is not always easy to grasp. If a woman worth $40 million wants to swim naked in the pool with her billy goat at four in the morning, it's nobody's business but hers. There are laws in Florida against sexual congress with beasts, but not everybody feels it is wrong.

"My roommate fucks dogs at parties," said a sleek blonde in her late twenties who sells cashmere and gold gimcracks in a stylish boutique on Worth Avenue. "So what? Who gets hurt by it?"

I shrugged and went back to fondling the goods on the shirt rack. The concept of victimless crime is well understood in Palm Beach, and the logic is hard to argue. No harm, no crime. If a pretty girl from Atlanta can sleep late in the morning, have lunch at the Everglades Clubs and make $50,000 tax-free a year fucking dogs in rich people's bedrooms on weekends, why should she fear the police? What's the difference between bestiality and common sodomy? Is it better to fuck swine at the Holiday Inn or donkeys in a penthouse on Tarpon Island? And what's wrong with incest, anyway? It takes 200 years of careful inbreeding to produce a line of beautiful daughters, and only a madman would turn them out to strangers. Feed them cocaine and teach them to love their stepsisters—or even their fathers and brothers, if that's what it takes to keep ugliness out of the family.

Look at the servants. They have warts and fat ankles. Their children are too dumb to learn and too mean to live, and there is no sense of family continuity. There is a lot more to breeding than teaching children good table manners, and a lot more to being rich than just spending money and wearing alligator shirts. The real difference between the Rich and the Others is not just that "they have more money," as Hemingway noted, but that money is not a governing factor in their lives, as it is with people who work for a living. The truly rich are born free, like dolphins; they will never feel hungry, and their credit will never be questioned. Their daughters will be debutantes and their sons will go to prep schools, and if their cousins are junkies and lesbians, so what? The breeding of humans is still an imperfect art, even with all the advantages.

Where are the Aryan thoroughbreds that Hitler bred so carefully in the early days of the Third Reich? Where are the best and the brightest children of Bel Air and Palm Beach?

These are awkward questions in some circles, and the answers can be disturbing. Why do the finest flowers of the American Dream so often turn up in asylums, divorce courts, and other gray hallways of the living doomed? What is it about being born free and rich beyond worry that makes people crazy?

Nobody on the Palm Beach Express seemed very interested in that question. Instead, the community rallied around poor Pete Pulitzer when the deal started going down—even through eighteen days of weird courtroom testimony that mortified his friends and shocked half the civilized world. The most intimate aspects of his wild six-year marriage to an ambitious young cheerleader from Buffalo were splayed out in big headlines on the front pages of newspapers in New York,

Paris, and London. Total strangers from places like Pittsburgh and Houston called Pulitzer's wife at home on the telephone, raving obscene proposals. Vicious lawyers subpoenaed his most private belongings and leaked whatever they pleased to giggling reporters. Any tourist with a handful of dimes could buy Xerox copies of his personal tax returns or even his medical records for ten cents a page in the Palm Beach County Courthouse. His privacy was violated so totally that it ceased to exist. At the age of fifty-two, with no real warning at all, Herbert Pulitzer became a very public figure. Every morning he would wake up and go downtown with his lawyers and hear himself accused of everything from smuggling drugs to degrading the morals of minors and even committing incest with his daughter.

The only charge Judge Harper took seriously, though, was Roxanne's "adultery," which was defined so many times by so many people that it came to be taken for granted. No adultery was ever proved, as I recall, but in the context of all the other wild charges it didn't seem to matter.

> "He told me that if I didn't sign those documents, he would take my children. He said he had the power, the money and the name. He said he would bury me."
> —Roxanne Pulitzer in court, November 15, 1982

The husband was never pressed to confirm that quote. The judge performed the burial for his own reasons, which he explained in a brutal nineteen-page final opinion that destroyed Roxanne's case like a hurricane. In the end she got even less than her lawyer, Joe Farish, whose fee was reduced by two-thirds. He got $102,500 for his efforts, and the wife came away with $2,000 a month for two years, no house, no children, a warning to get a job quick, and the right to keep her own personal jewelry and her own car. The whole package came to not much more than Pulitzer had spent on the day-to-day maintenance of his boats in 1981, which his accountants listed at $79,000.

The $441,000 the couple spent that year on "miscellaneous and unknown" was four times what the wife was awarded as a final settlement after six-and-a-half years of marriage and two children. It was nothing at all. A little more than $100,000 on paper and in fact less than $50,000. There are dentists all over Los Angeles who pay more alimony than that. But we are not talking about dentists here. We are talking about a dashing millionaire sportsman from Palm Beach, a wealthy jade of sorts who married an ex-cheerleader from the outskirts of Buffalo and took her to live sex shows and gave her jars of cocaine for Christmas.

In a nut, Herbert "Pete" Pulitzer rented the Best Piece of Ass in Palm Beach for six-and-a-half years at a net cost of $1,000 a month in alimony, and when it was over, he got the house and the children, along with everything else. That is not a bad deal, on the face of it. The *worst* piece of ass in San Francisco goes for at least a hundred dollars a night at the Siamese Massage Parlor, and that can add up to a lot more than $1,000 a month. Dumb brutes. Women so mean and ugly that you don't want to be seen with them, even by a late-night room-service waiter. There is a bull market for whoremongers all over the country these days, and the price of women is still not going up.

Judge Harper had run the whole show with an evil glint in his eye enduring a shit train of perjury from both sides and day after day of relentless haggling and posturing by teams of Palm Beach lawyers and a circus parade of rich fools, dumb hustlers, and dope fiends who were all getting famous just for being in his courtroom—where smoking was not allowed, except for the judge, who smoked constantly.

That should have been the tip-off, but we missed it. The judge had made up his mind early on, and the rest was all show business, a blizzard of strange publicity that amused half the English-speaking world for a few months and in the end meant nothing at all.

Toward the end of the trial, it rained almost constantly. Logistics got difficult, and my suite overlooking the beach at the Ocean Hotel was lashed by wild squalls every night. It was like sleeping in a boathouse at the end of some pier in Nova Scotia. Big waves on the beach, strange winds banging the doors around like hurricane shutters, plastic garbage cans blowing across the parking lot at thirty miles an hour, darkness in chaos, sharks in the water, no room service tonight.

It was a fine place to sleep, wild storms on the edge of the sea—warm blankets, good whiskey, color TV, roast beef hash and poached eggs in the morning. . . . Fat City, a hard place to wake up at six o'clock in the morning and drive across the long, wet bridge to the courthouse in West Palm.

One morning, when I got there too late to make the list for a courtroom seat and too early to think straight, I found myself drifting aimlessly in a dimly lit bar on the fringes of the courthouse district, the kind of place where lawyers and bailiffs eat lunch and the bartender has a machine pistol and the waitresses are all on probation, and where nobody reads anything in the newspapers except local gossip and legal notices. . . .

The bartender was trying to find limes for a Bloody Mary when I asked him what he thought about the Pulitzer divorce case. He stiffened, then leaned quickly across the bar to seize my bicep, and he said to me: "You know what I think? You know what it makes me feel like?"

"Well . . . ," I said, "not really. I only came in here to have a drink and read the newspaper until my trial breaks for lunch and—"

"Never mind your goddamn trial," he shouted, still squeezing my arm and staring intently into my eyes—not blinking—no humor.

I jerked out of his grasp, unsettled by the frenzy.

"It's *not* the goddamn Pulitzers," he shouted. "It's nothing personal—but I know how those people behave, and I know how it makes me feel!"

"Fuck off!" I snapped. "Who cares how you feel?"

"Like a goddamn animal!" he screamed. "Like a *beast.* I look at this scum and I look at the way they live and I see those shit-eating grins on their faces *and I feel like a dog took my place.*"

"What?" I said.

"It's a term of art," he replied, shooting his cuffs as he turned to deal with the cash register.

"Congratulations," I said. "You are now a Doctor of Torts."

He stiffened again and backed off.

"Torts?" he said. "What do you mean, *torts?*"

I leaned over the bar and smacked him hard on the side of the head.

"*That's* a tort," I said. Then I tossed him a handful of bills and asked for a cold beer to go. The man was slumped back on his rack of cheap bottles, breathing heavily: "You whoreface bastard," he said. "I'll kill you."

I laughed. "Shiteyes! People like you are a dime a dozen!" I reached over and grabbed him by the flesh on his cheek. "Where is your dog, swinesucker? I want to *see* the dog that did this to you. I want to *kill* that dog." I snapped him away from me and he fell back on the duckboards.

"Get out!" he screamed. "*You're* the one who should be on trial in this town! These Pulitzers are *nothing* compared to monsters like you."

I slapped him again, then I gathered my change and my mail and my newspapers and my notebooks and my drugs and my whiskey and my various leather satchels full of weapons and evidence and photographs. . . . I packed it all up and walked slowly out to my red Chrysler convertible, which was still holding two feet of water from the previous night's rain.

"You skunk!" he was yelling. "I'll see you in court."

"You must be a lawyer," I said. "What's your name? I work for the IRS."

"Get out!" he screamed.

"I'll be back," I said, lifting a small can of Mace out of my pocket and squirting it at him. "You'd better find a *dog* to take your place before you see me again—because once I croak these scumbags I'm working on now, I'm going to come back here and rip the nuts right off your ugly goddamn body."

The man was still screaming about dogs and lawyers as I got in my car and drove off. People in the street stopped to stare—but when he begged them for help, they laughed at him.

He was a Doctor of Torts, but in the end it didn't matter. A dog had taken his place anyway.

Long after the Pulitzer divorce case was finally over—after the verdict was in and there were no more headlines, and the honor of Palm Beach had been salvaged by running Roxanne out of town; after all the lawyers had been paid off and the disloyal servants had been punished and reporters who covered the trial were finally coming down from that long-running high that the story had been for so long that some of them suffered withdrawal symptoms when it ended . . . long after this, I was still brooding darkly on the case, still trying to make a higher kind of sense from it.

I have a fatal compulsion to find a higher kind of sense in things that make no sense at all. We were talking about hubris, delusions of wisdom and prowess that can only lead to trouble.

Or maybe we are talking about cocaine. That thought occurred to me more than once in the course of the Pulitzer divorce trial. Cocaine is the closest thing to instant hubris on the market these days, and there is plenty of it around. Any fool with an extra hundred-dollar bill in his pocket can whip a gram of cocaine into his head and make sense of just about anything.

Ah, yes. Wonderful. Thank you very much. I see it all very clearly now. These bastards have been lying to me all along. I should never have trusted them in the first place. Stand aside. Let the big dog eat. Take my word for it, folks. I know how these things work.

In the end it was basically a cocaine trial, which it had to be from the start. There was no real money at stake: Peter Pulitzer ended up paying more money to lawyers, accountants, "expert witnesses," and other trial-related bozos than Roxanne would have happily settled for if the case had never gone to court in the first place.

I am living the Palm Beach life now, trying to get the feel of it: royal palms and raw silks, cruising the beach at dawn in a red Chrysler convertible with George Shearing on the radio and a head full of bogus cocaine and two beautiful lesbians in the front seat beside me, telling jokes to each other in French. . . .

We are on our way to an orgy, in a mansion not far from the sea, and the girls are drinking champagne from a magnum we brought from Dunhills, the chic and famous restaurant. There is a wet parking ticket flapping under the windshield wiper in front of me, and it bores me. I am giddy from drink, and the lesbians are waving their champagne glasses at oncoming police cars, laughing gaily and smoking strong marijuana in a black pipe as we cruise along Ocean Boulevard at sunrise, living our lives like dolphins. . . .

The girls are naked now, long hair in the wind and perfumed nipples bouncing in the dull blue light of the dashboard, white legs on red leather seats. One of them is tipping a glass of champagne to my mouth as we slow down for a curve near the ocean and very slowly and stylishly lose the rear end at seventy miles an hour and start sliding sideways with a terrible screeching of rubber past Roxanne Pulitzer's house, barely missing the rear end of a black Porsche that protrudes from her driveway. . . .

The girls shriek crazily and spill champagne on themselves, and the radio is playing "The Ballad of Claus von Bulow," a song I wrote last year with Jimmy Buffett and James Brown and which makes me nine cents richer every time it gets played on the radio, in Palm Beach or anywhere else. That is a lot of money when my people start adding it up. I am making ninety-nine cents a day out of Palm Beach alone, and ten times that much from Miami. The take from New York and L.A. is so massive that my accountant won't even discuss the numbers with me, and my agent is embarrassed by my wealth.

But not me, Jack. Not at all. I like being rich and crazy in Palm Beach on a pink Sunday morning in a new red Chrysler convertible on my way to an orgy with a magnum of French champagne and two gold-plated lesbian bimbos exposing themselves to traffic while my own song croaks from the radio and palm trees flap in the early morning wind and the local police call me "Doc" and ask after my general health when we speak to each other at stoplights on the boulevard. . . .

The police are no problem in Palm Beach. We own them and they know it. They work for us, like any other servant, and most of them seem to like it. When we run out of gas in this town, we call the police and they bring it, because it is boring to run out of gas. The rich have special problems, and running out of gas on Ocean Boulevard on the way to an orgy at six o'clock on Sunday morning is one of them. Nobody needs that. Not with naked women and huge bags of cocaine in the car. The rich love music, and we don't want it interrupted.

A state trooper was recently arrested in Miami for trying to fuck a drunk woman on the highway, in exchange for dropping all charges. But that would not happen in Palm Beach. Drunk women roam free in this town, and they cause a lot of trouble—but one thing they don't have to worry about, thank God, is the menace of getting pulled over and fondled by armed white trash wearing uniforms. We don't pay these people much, but we pay them every week, and if they occasionally forget who really pays their salaries, we have ways of reminding them. The whole West Coast of Florida is full of people who got fired from responsible jobs in Palm Beach, if only because they failed to understand the nature of the Social Contract.

Which brings us back to the story, for good or ill: not everybody who failed to understand the nature of the Social Contract has been terminally banished to the West Coast. Some of them still live here, and every once in a while they cause problems that make headlines all over the world. The strange and terrible case of young Roxanne Pulitzer is one of these, and that is the reason I came to Palm Beach, because I feel a bond with these people that runs deeper and stronger than mere money and orgies and drugs and witchcraft and lesbians and whiskey and red Chrysler convertibles.

Bestiality is the key to it, I think. I have always loved animals. They are different from us and their brains are not complex, but their hearts are pure and there is usually no fat on their bodies and they will never call the police on you or take you in front of a judge or run off and hide with your money. . . .

Animals don't hire lawyers.

Rolling Stone, July 21/August 4, 1983

SUGARLOAF KEY: TALES OF THE SWINE FAMILY

Adventures in the Conch Republic . . . Raw and Primitive People, Living Their Lives Like Sharks . . . Today's Pig Is Tomorrow's Victim

FUCK THESE PEOPLE

THERE IS NOT much time to tell this story. The sun will come up in two hours and I want to be gone by then. But it will not be easy. I have a whole room full of weight to move out of this motel room by dawn— and, as always, there is nobody around to help. One friend could make a big difference now, but it is four o'clock in the morning and all decent people are in bed. So much for friends.

I am sitting in a motel room on the edge of a private marina in the Florida Keys. It is room number 202 at Sugarloaf Lodge, to be exact, and I am looking across the canal at a tall red, white, and blue Pepsi-Cola machine in front of the main marina building on the other side. The Pepsi-Cola machine is the brightest thing in my universe right now. It lights up the gasoline dock and the big white ice lockers where the fishing guides will be leaving from in two or three hours.

There are a dozen or so boats tied up around the canal, mostly white Makos—22- and 25-footers, pure fishing boats, center consoles, most with big white outboard engines, Johnsons and Evinrudes, 175 and 200 horsepower, white shrouds on the consoles to keep saltwater fog off the dashboard equipment, bait boxes floating off the stern, resting easy in the water on this wet black night.

My own boat—a 17-foot Mako with a big black Mercury engine on the back—is tied up about twenty feet in front of my typewriter, and I know the gas tank is full. I filled it up last night around seven o'clock in the evening, and when they asked me why I was gassing my boat up at the start of a bad moonless night, I said I might want to go to Cuba. The fishhead woman laughed but I didn't. I went back to mixing the oil: one quart to twelve gallons, be careful; give the engine what it needs—or whatever it wants, for that matter—because when you are out on the ocean at night the engine is going to be your best friend. Cuba is only ninety miles away, and I think I could get to Havana on a night like this a lot easier than I am going to get even ten miles away from the nightmare situation I have got myself into in this place.

Sugarloaf Lodge is a "fishing resort," they say; just another place to stay in the Keys if you want to bring your boat down and get serious about the water. Which is true, as far as it goes. This is a nice place. It is a sprawling 200-acre complex with its own airstrip, a twenty-four-hour liquor license, sixty-five waterfront rooms at sixty-five dollars a night, its own grocery store and gas station, a massive generator for electrical power, and even its own water tank. It is a completely self-contained community, secure in every way from the storms of the outside world. And it is worth about twenty $20,000,000.

The owner is Lloyd Good, a one-time district attorney from Philadelphia who bought the whole place on a whim about ten years ago and moved into a position of considerable power in the low end of the Florida Keys, where there is basically no law at all that can't be broken or bought or at least casually ignored by the right people.

I am a paying guest in Lloyd Good's motel, and from my desk I can see his apartment behind the General Store about 100 yards away from me across the canal . . . and I know he is sleeping heavily on a king-size bed over there with his wife, Miriam, a fine and friendly woman about fifty years old who has always been my friend. She has been asleep since midnight, and she will wake up early to supervise the breakfast shift at the restaurant.

Lloyd will wake up later. Or at least he would on most days, but on this one I suspect he will be an early riser. It could happen at any moment, in fact, and that is why I want to get this story down quick and get out of this place before dawn. Because ugly things are about to happen.

There is a huge pig's head in Lloyd Good's toilet tonight. I put it there about three hours ago, just before he walked home from the bar. The snout is poking straight up out of the family toilet and the pig's lips are glistening with Ruby Red lipstick and the eyes are propped open and the toilet bowl is filled with red commercial catsup.

The first time anybody in that house goes into the bathroom and turns the light on, I am going to have to be very alert. We will have serious action. Hysteria, wild rage. I have seen a lot of hideous things in my time, but the sight of that eerie-white pig's head in the white toilet bowl with its mouth covered with lipstick and its dead gray eyes looking straight up at me—or at anyone else who comes near that toilet—will live in my memory forever as one of the most genuinely hideous things I've ever seen. The idea of waking up half drunk in the middle of the night and wandering into your own bathroom and pissing distractedly into your own toilet and realizing after not many seconds that there is something basically wrong with the noise that normally happens when you piss into a bowl full of water in the middle of the night, and feeling the splash of warm urine on your knees because it is bouncing off the lipstick-smeared snout of a dead pig's head that is clogging up your toilet . . . that is a bad thing to see when you're drunk.

And Lloyd will see it soon. He should have seen it a long time ago, in fact, but tonight he broke his normal routine of relieving himself before falling into bed. And at that point the joke went out of control. I thought, What have I done?

What if his wife wakes up first? Which she almost certainly will. . . . Or maybe John, the thirteen-year-old son, will be the first to visit the bathroom. I was not counting on this. My plan has turned weird on me, and now I have to flee. The thing is so ugly that I almost got sick while I was putting the lipstick on it. We all enjoy humor, but this is very far over the line. We are not talking about jokes here; we are talking about Crazy Ugly, real malice, terrible shock and weeping for a fifty-year-old lady or a thirteen-year-old child, people screaming out of control at a sight too vile to see. Innocent people crawling out of the bathroom on their knees and calling wildly for help from the father. . . .

And that evil drunken bastard is going to be jerked out of his sleep very soon, by the terrified screams of his loved ones—and when that happens he is going to turn crazy and want to kill somebody; or maybe send others to do it, and they will come to number 202.

My room is the only one with lights on tonight. I am still up, and I will be on the road very soon. I have a friend up the road on Ramrod Key who will take me in and hide me for a while, and my partner in the Gonzo Salvage Co. will get my boat out of the marina, if we do it early enough, and we will hide it up there in the trailer court on Summerland.

Jesus! I just looked to my left and saw the curtains moving. My sliding glass door is wide open, and he could jump me at any moment. That is why I have this big gray flashlight sitting next to me on the desk. It is a fully charged Taser, a savage little tool capable of delivering a 50,000-volt whack on anybody who comes within eighteen feet, and I have the bugger primed. . . . WHAPPO! Fifty thousand volts, flapping around like a fish, eyes rolled back in the head, screeching helplessly and then taking another shock. The Taser will deliver five separate and distinctly massive jolts, once the barbs are fired into the victim. You can keep the buggers jumping around on the end of the little wire lines for almost an hour, if the machine is fully charged. I don't want to have to do it; the Taser is a felony crime in some states and I am not sure right now about Florida—but I know that anybody who comes through my door at this hour of the night will not have good news for me, and they will have to be shot with something. I am not a violent person, but I know there is a time and place for everything, and this is unfortunately one of them.

I sawed the head off the pig around midnight. Lloyd had it stored in the meat locker at the Lodge, planning to marinate it for a big barbeque for his friends on Sunday, with the head as a main piece of art. I chopped it off with a meat saw in forty-five seconds, and it took about forty-five more to put the lipstick on. The tube broke, so I had to do it by hand, rubbing a lump of red lipstick around that dead thing's gums like I was waxing up some kind of dummy. . . . And meanwhile his wife was asleep in the next room, ten feet away, and then the head wouldn't sit right in the bowl so I had to jerk it up by the ears and jam it back in a proper position. And I also had to prop the eyes open, so they would be looking straight up at him. . . . All this took about ninety more seconds, sneaking into his home and putting a pig's head in his toilet.

Okay. The joke's over now. I have to flee. It is 6:25 on a wet Thursday morning and I know that somebody over there will be using the bathroom very soon. The time has come. I don't want to be around here when it happens, despite a pressing deadline that will cost me a lot of money to miss. That bastard will not take this thing gently— and besides that I owe him about $3,000, my food and beverage bill for the past three months, and he is worried about getting the money.

Indeed. I am preparing to flee, even now. I told him that pig was going to be very expensive. He and his boys put it in my bed the other night, tied up and drugged and half hidden under the covers so that I sat down on the bed right next to the beast and began talking seriously on the telephone to my accountant, who was not amused when the thing suddenly began moving and I said, "I'm sorry, I'll have to call you back, there's a pig in my bed."

Which was true. I calmed the beast down with a billyclub and then hauled it up to the restaurant, where I cut it loose in the dining room at the peak of the dinner hour. People screamed and cursed me and ran around like rats while I was chopping the pig loose. Two of the fishing guides cornered it and dragged it out to a van . . . and then they slit its throat the next day, and hung it up to bleed; and then they put it in the meat locker, to cool off.

The moral of this story is Never Let Strangers Get Their Hands on the Key to Your Meat Locker. And also, Get Out While You Can. Which I will have to do now. Immediately. The fat is in the fire. Selah.

EPILOGUE

The boy found it, when he woke up to go to school. His mother heard him screaming on his way out of the house. And then she saw it. Ye gods, she thought. What has he thrown up *now*?

I couldn't make that up. You have to live here a long time before you start thinking that way.

"I ate three or four Valiums," she said, "then I called Ernie to take the thing away. It was three and a half hours before we could use the toilet. Lloyd didn't wake up until noon and by the time he went into the bathroom, the head was lying in the bathtub."

And I was gone.

But I am back now, standing around the bar at night, and people are a lot nicer to me. I buy drinks for women and put liters of Chivas Regal on my tab, and I may be here for a while.

Florida Keys, March 18, 1983

THE SILK ROAD

FISHHEAD BOYS

We WERE CALLING a cab in the Key West airport when I saw these two Fishhead boys grab my bags off the carousel. The skinny one was halfway to the parking lot with the big red, white, and blue seabag full of diving gear before I realized what was happening. . . .

No, I thought. No, this can't be true. Not right here in front of my eyes, in the blue-lit glare of the breezeway in this friendly little airport, with palm trees all around and Mother Ocean rolling up on the beach just a few hundred yards to the south.

It *must* be a setup, I thought; some nark in the pay of the White House; that evil bastard Hamilton has been trying to bust me ever since I set him on fire in Orlando . . . and this was, after all, another election year.

In the good old days I might have thought it was Gordon Liddy, just running one of his capers. But Gordon doesn't work for the White House anymore, and Hamilton has other problems—like trying to reelect what Dick Goodwin calls "the only truly Republican president since Herbert Hoover" on the Democratic ticket.

So I was puzzled. Election years tend to create their own priorities, for the White House and even the DEA . . . and on a "need to be busted" basis, I figured my name was not even on the list for 1980. I was not even covering the campaign.

I still had the phone in my hand when I saw the fat one. He came shuffling out of the darkness, where he'd obviously been standing lookout for his buddy; he glanced around to see that nobody was watching, then reached down and picked up my triple-locked leather satchel.

Whoops, I thought, let's have a word with these boys. They were locals—punks, maybe nineteen or twenty years old, and they did it so casually that I knew they had been here before. Semi-pro luggage thieves, the lowest and cruelest kind of scum. I felt the phone pulling out of the wall as I suddenly moved toward the action.

Cut the thumbs off these vultures, I thought. *Carve* on them.

Then I remembered that my bone knife was in the red, white, and blue diving bag. All I had for leverage was this baby blue telephone receiver that I'd just ripped off the wall by the Travelers' Aid counter. It was trailing about six feet of coiled blue rubber wire as I ran.

"Goddamn you rotten bastards I'll kill you goddamn brainless—"

This savage screaming confused me for a moment. Then I realized it was *me*. Was I moving faster than my own sounds?

Maybe not. But pure rage is a serious fuel, and now I was moving at least like Dick Butkus on speed toward this poor doomed screwhead who had already staggered and fallen to one knee under the weight of my leather satchel. I was still about 100 feet away when he heard my screams and saw me coming. I knew I had the angle on him, even before he staggered . . . he was out in the open now and his face was stupid with terror.

"Eat shit and die!"

It was a thundering brutal scream, and for a moment I thought it was me again, still moving faster than sound. . . .

But this time the scream was *really* behind me. It was Skinner: He'd been raving, drooling drunk all the way from Aruba, but the sudden screech of battle had jerked him awake from his stupor and now he was right behind me, screaming as he ran. I pointed left toward the parking lot, at the skinny geek with my diving bag. I smelled the whiskey pumping up from Skinner's lungs as he passed me and angled left to where I'd pointed.

It was not quite an hour after sunset. We had come in on the last flight and then lingered for a while in the pilots' lounge, so now there was nobody else in that end of the airport. A magic moment in the tropics: just the four of us, like beasts gone into a frenzy, back to the fang and the claw . . . and for just a few seconds the only other sound in that empty white corridor where we were closing with terrible speed and craziness on these two Fishhead boys was the high-speed rubbery slap of Skinner's new Topsiders on the tile as we bore down on them . . . wild shouts and the squeal of new rubber. . . .

A punk's nightmare: like getting sucked into the blades of a jet engine, for no good reason at all. . . .

Right. Just another late gig at the airport. . . . Just you and Bubba, like always; maybe two or three times a week: just hang around the baggage area until something worth stealing shows up late on the carousel . . . and then, with perfect dumb style and timing, you seize the bags you've been watching and . . .

YE FUCKING GODS! Two drunken screaming brutes, coming wild out of nowhere and moving with awesome speed . . .

"Hey Bubba! Who's all that screaming? I thought there was nobody—

"O God, *no!* Run, Bubba, *run!*"

Killer Drunks! They jumped us like mad dogs. At first I saw only one of them. He had big brown eyes and no hair . . . I was *scared*, man. I mean the way he was running and screaming just scared the shit out of me. . . . It was CRAZY.

Bubba never had a chance. These were serious Killer Drunks, man.

I mean they were out of their fucking *minds*. The last thing I remember is when Bubba started to scream and then all of a sudden I didn't hear *anything* . . . and that's when the other one hit me. It almost broke my back, and all I remember after that is pain all over my head and somebody yelling, "Eat Shit and Die!" They were *serious*, man. They were trying to *kill* us. They were *crazy!*

Well . . . maybe so. But we were there to cover the Boat Races, not to act crazy.

And certainly not to kill Fishhead boys . . . although Skinner was so crazed on whiskey that for a while I thought he really *was* going to kill that skinny bleeder he ran down out there in the parking lot.

"You screwhead bastard!" he was yelling. Then I heard the awful smack of bone against bone. . . . The sound drove me wild; somewhere in that madness I recall a flash of remorse, but it had to be very brief. My last coherent thought before we made physical contact with these people was, Why are we doing this?

There was not much time to think. All of a sudden the whole airport came alive with the sounds of violence. A pitiful cry drifted in from the palm-shrouded darkness of the parking lot as Skinner made his hit . . . and then I crashed into the fat boy at top speed, leg-whipping him in the groin as we collided and then tumbled wildly across the tile floor and into the wall of the Avis booth.

I grabbed him by the hair and bit deeply into the flesh on the side of his neck. The sudden taste of hot blood caused me to bite him twice again before he went stiff and started making sounds like a chicken. I got a grip on his hair and dragged him out to the parking lot, where I heard Skinner still whipping on the other one.

"Let's tie these bastards to a tree and play hurricane," I said. He was still kicking the body of the unconscious thief—but he heard what I said, and smiled.

So we lashed these two Fishhead boys to a palm tree with some yellow nylon cord from my diving bag; then we beat them with tree limbs for twenty or thirty minutes. Finally, when we were too exhausted to whip on them anymore, I wanted to cut off their thumbs with the bone knife, but Skinner said it would be wrong.

Later, in my penthouse suite at the Pier House, I felt vaguely unsatisfied.

"We don't need it," Skinner insisted. "The joke's over when you start mutilating people—hacking off thumbs and weird shit like that. We're not in Damascus, Doc. Get a grip on yourself."

I shrugged. Why not? Why push it?

Skinner was drinking heavily now, but his mind seemed clear. "There could be a few questions when they find those boys tied up to that tree in the morning," he said.

"Never mind that," I told him. "We have *work* to do in the morning; we have our own questions to ask."

He stared into his drink for a long moment. "Ah yes," he said finally, "The Race."

Indeed. We were there to cover the boat race—big off-shore boomers like Cigarettes and Scarabs and Panteras, ninety miles an hour on the open sea. When I asked if I could ride in one of the race boats, the driver replied, "Sure you can—but if you have any fillings in your teeth, you'll probably lose them."

"What?"

"That's right," he said. "We kick ass. We *never* slow down."

"Okay," I said. "I guess I'll ride with *you*."

The driver looked up at me from his seat in the cockpit of the boat. It was forty feet long and the whole rear end was two 300-horsepower Chrysler engines. "No you won't," he said after waiting a moment while Skinner took some pictures of his boat. "It's against the rules."

Skinner spit down into the cockpit. "Fuck you, man," he said. "We're riding on this boat. We're taking it to Cuba."

The driver seized a wrench handle and quickly stood up in the cockpit. "You conch bastard!" he snarled. "You *spit* on my boat!"

Skinner was wearing three Nikons around his neck, and I grabbed him by one of the straps. "Are you *sick?*" I said quietly. "Is *this* how you act when I finally get you a decent assignment?"

OVERVIEW

"The Silk Road" is a story about people who got caught in the fast and violent undercurrents and, finally, the core of the action of the great Cuba-to-Key West Freedom Flotilla in the spring of 1980—a bizarre and massively illegal "sea lift" which involved literally thousands of small private boats that brought more than 100,000 very volatile Cuban refugees to this country in less than three months and drastically altered the social, political, and economic realities of South Florida for the rest of this century.

By 1980, the billion-dollar drug-smuggling industry and influx of Latin-American millionaire refugees had turned Miami into the Hong Kong of the Western World and the cash capital of the United States. It was also the nation's murder capital, with a boom-town economy based on the smuggling of everything from drugs and gold bullion to guns and human beings. What Havana was to the 1950s, Marseilles to the '60s, and Bangkok to the '70s, Miami is to the '80s.

The Freedom Flotilla began on April Fool's Day. In less than two weeks the Coast Guard had abandoned all hope of stopping the boat traffic; the port of Key West was overwhelmed, and any boat longer than fifteen feet was for sale or rent. Cubans from Miami roamed the bars and local docks with fistfuls of hundred-dollar bills, and drug smugglers had already begun to take advantage of the general confusion and the helplessness of the Coast Guard. Not even the White House or the U.S. Marines could stop the tidal wave of Cubans pouring into South Florida.

To accelerate the exodus of refugees already granted asylum at the Peruvian embassy in Havana, Castro put out the word: Miami's Cubans could take out one relative for every four refugees taken from Cuba to America. The reaction of the Miami Cuban community was near hysteria. The 150-mile length of Highway A1A—from Key West to Miami—became strangled by a huge caravan of destitute refugees in busloads with blacked-out windows, headed north, and the south-bound lane was jammed with Cuban-Americans towing a strange armada of fiberglass speedboats, cabin cruisers, and ungainly fishing boats. . . . All this in a constant frenzy of traffic through police and military roadblocks all along the way.

As the traffic jam got worse, pockets of stranded people began to build up in places along the way. There was simply no way to move on the highway without risk or delay.

People who lived in the Keys were afraid to go anywhere at all: you could go out for a drink on Wednesday night and not get back home until Friday. What was "easy money" in April became a shit train by May . . . but by that time the thing was out of control; and the going price for refugees was *still* $1,000 a head.

The locals began turning on each other, and growing resentment over the Cuban refugee invasion was compounded by constant TV news bulletins about the national humiliation of the Iran Hostage Crisis. People began carrying guns and hunkering down wherever they could be sure of getting a drink.

One of these pockets of doom along Highway A1A was an isolated fishing resort called Spanish Key Lodge, about twenty miles up the island chain from Key West—a sprawling, run-down motel and marina with its own airstrip and a twenty-four-hour liquor license, owned by an ex-commodities broker from Chicago named Frank Mont, who came to the Keys to get rich.

The chaos of the Cuban refugee invasion and the resulting nightmare at Spanish Key is the baseline of the narrative: a once-lazy backwater fishing resort is transmogrified, overnight, into a seething fortress of thieves, smugglers, and criminally insane Cuban refugees, who soon take it over completely, by force of sheer numbers.

The raw elements of the story are (in no special order): sex, violence, greed, treachery, big money, fast boats, blue water, Cuba, CIA politics, Fidel Castro's sense of humor, one murder, several rapes, heavy gambling, massive drug smuggling, naked women, mean dogs, total breakdown of law and order, huge public cash transactions, the Iran Hostage Crisis, overloaded boats catching fire and sinking at night in the Gulf Stream, the nervous breakdown of a U.S. Coast Guard commander, fast cars running roadblocks on Highway A1A, savage brawls in Key West bars, Boog Powell, sunken treasure, wild runs on the ocean at night, personality disintegration, desperate wagering on NBA playoff (TV) games and 1980 presidential primaries, a grim and violent look at American politics in the eighties, dangerously tangled love affairs, warm nights and full moons, one hurricane, stolen credit cards, false passports, deep-cover CIA agents, the U.S. Marines, a jailbreak in Key West at the peak of the refugee invasion, political corruption in South Florida, the emergence of Miami as the Hong Kong of the Western World, Colombian coke dealers, crooked shrimp-fishermen, scuba diving with shotguns (powerheads, mounted on spears) . . . and all the other aspects of high crime, bad craziness, and human degradation that emerged from that strange and shameful episode in our history.

I could list a few more, on request . . . but this seems like enough, for now. The true story of the Freedom Flotilla is weird enough, on its own, to be a good book if it were written as pure and factual journalism. And the fact that I happened to be there at the time, with my own boat, almost convinced me to write it that way.

But there was not enough room in a journalistic format for the characters I wanted. So I finally decided to write the story as a novel, told in the first person by a narrator who is also a main character and who speaks from a POV not unlike that of Nick Carraway in *The Great Gatsby*—and Gene Skinner, the main character and high-rolling protagonist of *The Silk Road*, may in fact be a lineal descendant of Jay Gatsby, in a different time and a very different place.

Gene Skinner is a professional adventurer who worked in Vietnam as a helicopter pilot for a CIA-owned property called Air America and who now lives (at the time of the Freedom Flotilla) with his beautiful half-Cuban fiancée in a double-wide Airstream mobile home in a trailer park on Marathon Key . . . which is nine worlds away from Long Island in every way except that it sits on the edge of the sea and fits Skinner's idea of The American Dream in the same way that West Egg fit Gatsby's.

And Skinner's hired fiancée, Anita, is an ex-debutante from Miami whose life has been changed more than once by her own strange lust . . . which need not be described, at this time, but will figure strongly in the story.

There was no way I could fit an exotic creature like Anita into a purely journalistic story about the Freedom Flotilla—and no way I can describe her in a 1,000-word outline, either. The odd and eventually unspeakable "love triangle" involving Anita, Gene Skinner, and The Narrator is one aspect of the story that I think we can save for later. . . . Except to say that Bill Buckley and all the rest of those lame masturbators who've been whipping on me for "not writing about sex" are about to get what they wanted. Or at least what they need.

In any case, these are the main characters in a story of free enterprise gone amok in the tropics. The narrator goes to Key West (Chap. 1) to cover a boat race and to do some scuba diving with his old friend Gene Skinner, but the boat race is disrupted when the whole city of Key West is plunged into a feeding frenzy by what amounts to a hurricane of suddenly available cash. Anybody who can get his hands on a boat seaworthy enough to make the ninety-mile run over to Cuba can make $1,000 a head for every refugee he brings back.

Which was true, for a while, and a lot of local boat captains got instantly rich on the refugee traffic. I was on the Coast Guard pier in Key West one night when a huge cruise boat called *The Viking Starship* came in with 500 passengers. It looked like a scene from the last days of the war in Vietnam. The crew was armed, the refugees were being herded into pens by U.S. Marines with bullhorns and spotlights, and huge fines were being levied on boat captains who came in with *illegal* refugees.

But not all of them were technically illegal, and in the chaos on the docks it was impossible to sort out the legal ones from all the others. Castro, in a flash of high humor, had turned what began as a political embarrassment for Cuba into a nightmare for the U.S. by emptying his jails and insane asylums and loading the boats in Mariel Bay with all the "undesirables" he could round up.

These were the ones the Coast Guard were doing their best to arrest and detain on the pier of Key West—and these were also the ones that boat captains were being fined $1,000 a head for bringing in.

Skinner's idea, then, was to use the narrator's boat to off-load the most obvious of these undesirables from bigger boats, out at sea, and bring them in *somewhere else*—for $500 a head, instead of $1,000. The math, laws, and logistics of the scheme are too complex to explain here. . . .

The place where we decided to bring them in was the marina at Spanish Key Lodge, where they would be immediately crammed into rental cars and sent up the road to Miami. The idea was to skim off the scum, as it were, and smuggle them through the undermanned roadblocks like so many bales of marijuana.

Which worked well enough, for a while, but the scheme began coming apart when Key West ran out of rental cars and a nasty backlog of refugees started building up at the headquarters of the operation at Spanish Key.

The situation becomes more and more intolerable as the rooms and cabins fill up with a nasty crowd of stranded refugees and paranoid drug smugglers. The whole place turns into a madhouse, a wild microcosm of the larger madness in Key West. Gangs of Cuban thugs roam the grounds and naked prostitutes lounge by the swimming pool. Fights break out between the Cubans and the smugglers. The Lodge runs short of food and refugees begin stealing chickens from local backyards and roasting them over driftwood bonfires on the beach.

The local police are too busy controlling street crime in Key West to respond to the increasingly desperate phone calls from Frank Mont, the owner of Spanish Key Lodge, who is slowly going to pieces under the strain of trying to control the lawless mob that has taken over his resort. He is afraid to sleep and begins living on a diet of cocaine and Chivas Regal. His family flees to Miami, leaving him to run the Lodge with a flaky skeleton staff of dope addicts and rummies.

The only nonlethal forms of amusement for the criminal mob at the

Lodge are orgies, wild boat races in the bay, and frantic gambling on TV basketball games and the presidential primaries. Thousands of dollars change hands in the bar every night. Mont is going broke and fears for his life.

The first half of the story is basically a building process and a tale of wild humor, fast boats, and big profits—along with a relentlessly cranked-up tale of day-to-day events in the eye of the human hurricane at the Lodge—but the humor suddenly gets thin when a mid-level character (a local politico named Colonel Evans—USAF Ret.) gets killed in a sudden gunfight in the bar at Spanish Key, while raging at a TV special on the Iranian Hostage Crisis.

Gene Skinner, whose CIA background is one of the continuing mysteries of the story, is accused of the murder by Frank Mont, who finally goes over the edge.

Skinner flees to Cuba, leaving his girlfriend and the narrator to run the Scum-Lift operation, which eventually gets busted and cleaned out by the U.S. Marines. Frank Mont is arrested for Trading With The Enemy* and is sentenced to nineteen years in prison and the Lodge is destroyed by fire in the midst of a hurricane.

Meanwhile—before the holocaust—the narrator and Anita receive a desperate radio call from Skinner and set off in the narrator's boat to rescue him off a rocky beach in Cuba, where he's hiding from Russian soldiers. . . . This is the climax of the story, but not quite the end. There is one more brutal twist to come.

But we'll save that. This is all ye know (for now) and all ye need to know. Selah.

THE MURDER OF COLONEL EVANS

Our room-service bills are massive—Frank is now in a state of frantic, drunken fear. He is a lawyer from New York who bought the Lodge five years ago on a whim and got himself on a very strange train; he became—with his magic marina and his private airstrip—a man of leverage in a business he knew nothing about except that if he ever got arrested for what he was doing there was no doubt at all that his picture would be on the front page of the next day's *Miami Herald,* over a headline saying: FEDS BUST CUD JOE CONNECTION; RINGLEADER

---

*An obscure 1917 federal statute, unused for fifty years.

SEIZED WITH 2 TONS—DISBARRED NEW YORK ATTORNEY NAMED AS MAIN
LINK IN KEY WEST MIAMI DRUG PIPELINE.

Frank had come to grips with this reality.

But five years in the Keys had made him a serious bigot on the question of Cubans (not "Castro"—but *Cubans*). The mayor of Cud Joe was alleged to be Cuban and Frank brooded constantly on what he called the Cuban Cancer. . . .

So now he was half mad with rage and greed at the sight of his lodge filling up with illegal Cuban refugees.

And also with drugs—the Sunday hurricane that knocked out the TV cable for the basketball games had also ripped the huge U.S. Navy observation blimp out of its moorings on Cud Joe Key and sent it off at 80 mph in the general direction of Cuba. The blimp was the Navy's eye in the sky, scanning the whole southern horizon of the Caribbean twenty-four hours a day with NASA-style cameras that could take stunningly detailed photos of Havana Harbor—and fatally detailed photos of any boat on the ocean within 100 miles of Florida. Smugglers feared the blimp—and they rejoiced when the hurricane blew it away.

The Freedom Flotilla was now joined by literally hundreds of boats full of weed, coke, and Quaaludes from Colombia.

The Coast Guard was totally tied up with the Cubans (50,000 by now) and the seas were open for smugglers.

We now had nine rooms rented—and out-front smugglers were operating out of at least ten more.

Frank was sinking deeper into fear and still no Avis cars or anything else—except one or two strays every day from no-shows, so we kept going out to meet Steve's boats full of *dangerous Cubans.*

They got weirder and weirder. These people were nobody's relatives—they were the first wave of the *criminally insane* that Castro had decided to set free.

They were not easy people to board at Frank's place while we scavenged for cars to ship these savage buggers off to Miami.

They began to drink heavily in their rooms, screaming all night and lying around the pool during the day (hookers, cockfights, brawls). Finally they got into the *bar;* they drank on our bill and Frank was too far in the hole to object.

Our bill for less than three weeks was already $9,000—and now with nine rooms and two suites rented and anywhere from fifteen to fifty-five hysterical Cubans eating and drinking on our bill at any given time, we were running a tab with Frank of about $1,000 a day.

The place became a sleepless nightmare of gambling and fighting and nervous breakdowns . . . along with the constant loading and unloading of ton-level week shipments by a crew of at least twenty top professionals working twenty-four hours a day.

The place hummed constantly with movement—either scammers moving their loads or us moving our Cubans.

The whole compound—the Lodge and the marina and all the rooms and grounds—was also alive with cocaine, which compounded and lent frenzy to the prevailing madness.

I never slept. Despite the violent ravings of Colonel Evans and other conch regulars at the bar, we still managed to bring in two loads a day, but we were building up a dangerous backlog in the Lodge because we still couldn't move them out fast enough to Miami.

Frank appeared to be losing his grip—we now had sixteen rooms on our tab and the dopers had all the others. Millions of dollars' worth of illegal contraband was moving out of his parking lot every day, along with dozens of what he now *knew* to be criminally insane Cuban convicts, lepers, and spies.

He was $8,000 down to me on the NBA playoffs at this point; the local sheriff was warning him that things were getting out of control: too many Cubans, too much dope, too much traffic for *anybody's* off-season . . . and the governor was appointing a special prosecutor to investigate "drugs and corruption" in the Keys (see *Miami Herald* series: April '80).

It was too much. On paper the Lodge was functioning at supermaximum capacity. The dopers were paying $500 a night for every room that was empty the next morning—a long-standing arrangement that had made Frank rich almost by accident in the five years since he'd come down from New York—but the dopers refused to pay until the weed was out of the room and on the road . . . they had a dozen boats waiting full of marijuana out there in the mangrove creeks; waiting for an empty room at the marina.

But it was too dangerous to move the weed now—roadblocks everywhere, 600 border patrol agents imported from Texas to "screen Cubans"—Marines in Jeeps on the streets, TV cameras everywhere . . . and no Avis cars for our Cubans.

Convoys of freshly painted black buses moved by on the highway at all hours. There was so much traffic in and out of the Boca Chica Naval Air Station that the air for ten miles in both directions was so heavy with jet fuel that you had to close the windows and punch Max AC just to breathe air.

They were moving the refugees up to north Florida and Arkansas now—there was no more room in Miami and Alabama was closed to refugees.

This ugly limbo was in full force at the Lodge when the TV brought us news of Carter's failed *Rescue Attempt* in Iran—total rage and despair.

Colonel Evans cried after hearing the first bulletins and he threatened to *blow Skinner's head off* for calling it all a bad joke. The colonel was seriously shaken. "This is the worst tragedy for the human race since the killing of Christ," he told us one afternoon in the bar.

"Bullshit," said Skinner. "It's two thousand years of white trash dumbness."

"You evil bastard!" Evans screamed. "You can mock everything else in this world—but you can't mock *this!*" (he raged back from the bar). *"Those men gave their lives!"*

"So what?" said Skinner. Evans went visibly stiff at the bar and nobody laughed. "So what?" Skinner said again. "Who *asked* for their lives, Colonel? Who *needs* their fucking lives!"

There was a high wild edge in his voice that I hadn't heard in a while. He kept his eyes on the blank TV set while he talked.

"They didn't give their lives, Colonel—they *wasted* their lives!" He was suddenly on his feet and pointing a finger at Evans. "Those men *failed,* Colonel! *They blew the mission!* They killed each other for no good reason at all. . . ." He smacked both palms on the bar. . . ."And you don't know the *difference,* do you?" He stared at Evans. "You don't know the *fucking difference!*" He was screaming now and so was Colonel Evans.

"God *damn* you!" the old man blurted . . . and then he raised a big chrome-plated automatic and fired point blank at Skinner.

One shot, like a bomb going off in the room—a blank white shock of a noise that paralyzed everybody. Skinner disappeared without a sound and the rest of us scrambled around on the floor for what seemed like eighty or ninety terrible seconds . . . until we heard the second shot and I looked up just in time to see the colonel die on his feet as another deafening blast of gunfire lit up the room. Colonel Evans walked backward away from the bar for two steps and then fell face down on the tile floor with both hands dangling at his sides. His body fell almost on top of me, hitting with a nasty, dead-sounding thump that shook the whole room.

For a moment nobody moved—and then everybody moved, including Skinner. "Jesus Christ," he muttered. "Who *did* that?"

The bar was suddenly empty. No Cubans, no dopers—just me and Skinner and Frank and the high smell of cordite—and Colonel Evans, bleeding quietly from three or four holes. "Mother of God," said Frank. "I don't *need* this shit." He was leaning with both arms on the bar, looking down at the colonel's body.

Skinner was already gone. . . . Evans had somehow missed him at point-blank range; but at least one other person in the room had *not* missed.

"Those Cuban bastards!" Frank said quietly. "They shot him *fifteen times*." He looked up at me, tears rolling down from his eyes. "That's it for you, Jocko," he said. "Take your scum and get out of this place!" He banged on the bar with his fist. "Right *now!*" he screamed. "Get out! You bastards can't *murder* people in my place!"

I picked up a long-handled broom from the end of the bar and hit him, a two-handed shot on the back of his head. He fell forward and I hit him again, swinging the broom like an axe. He fell on the duck-boards, screaming. "No! Please! No!"

"*You* shot him," I said. "You warned him first, then you killed him."

"What?"

I rattled the handful of 9mm auto casings I'd picked off the floor. "You shot him," I said. "These are *your* bullets."

"What?" He was wall-eyed with shock and confusion.

I walked around the bar and got a cold Heineken out of the cooler. "Where's your weapon?" I asked him. I knew he had a SM #59 behind the bar; he'd showed it to me several times since we'd been there.

"Fuck you," he snapped. "It's *right here*—and it's *clean!*" He lifted the 9mm auto out of the cash-register drawer and held it up to show me.

I took it from him and fired two shots into Colonel Evans' body. The noise almost blinded me, and Frank went down to his knees with a groan.

I wiped off the gun with a wet bar towel and handed it back to him . . . but he backed away.

"Here," I said. "It's loaded. Take it."

He backed farther away from me, so I put the gun down on the bar. "You better do it now," I said. "I'm going back to the room." I smiled as I walked away. "You're a lawyer," I said. "You know how to handle a witness. . . ."

His eyes were wild and bright. "No!" he said finally—still crouching away from the gun. "No! I didn't!"

I shrugged and walked out to the parking lot. The sun was hot and nobody else was around the office as I passed and went into the trees to keep out of sight on my way to the room. The door was locked, but it opened before I could use my key . . . the girl was standing there in the dark hallway, wearing a blue string bikini and looking about thirteen years old.

"Gene's gone to Cuba," she said calmly. "He said he'd call on the radio." I nodded and put the chain on the door, then I hung out the DO NOT DISTURB flag and turned on the TV.

"Call room service," I said. "We need food and whiskey."

She shook her head and sat down on the bed beside me. "What happened?" she said. "Gene wouldn't tell me."

"Frank will," I said; and just as I said it the phone rang.

"How's your boat running?" he asked.

"Fine," I said. "We'll need club sandwiches and a quart of gin . . . and some tonic; I have limes and ice on the boat."

There was no response for a moment, then he said, "Okay . . . nobody knows; we just dump him . . . right?"

"Why not?" I said.

"I'll bring him down to the dock in my van," he said. "He's all wrapped up."

"That's good," I said. "Maybe he went swimming—we'll go look for him."

"Sure," he said. "We'll check the Gulf Stream first—see you in twenty minutes."

I hung up and watched the girl grind on the Deering. She took a long hit and then passed it over to me.

"Where's Steve?" I said finally after the fire had cooled in my head.

"Cuba," she said. "They both went. . . ." She lay down beside me on the bed and I put my arm around her. "We're going for a ride out to the blue water," I told her. "You and me and Frank—somebody died and we have to bury it."

I felt her shudder against me. We lay there in silence for a while and then she whispered, *"Who* died?"

"Never mind," I said. "We're into the chute on this one."

"We?" she said.

I smiled. "That's right." I said—*"We."*

She stood up and walked over to look at the boat. "Jesus!" she muttered. "I knew that son of a bitch would *kill somebody.*"

"He didn't," I said. "The dopers did it."

She wandered around the room for a while and I could hear her mind working.

The phone rang again and I quickly picked it up.

"You ready?" Frank asked.

"Never mind," I said. "Just put the stuff in my boat, then go back to the bar and get real drunk."

"What? Are you *crazy?* You'll never find that channel alone!"

"Don't worry," I said. "I won't be alone."

"What?" he shouted. "I told you—*nobody else knows!*"

"Right," I said. "That's why we'll do it ourselves."

"Who?" he screamed.

"Calm down, Jocko," I said. "We're all friends here—you do your business and I'll do mine."

"You bastard," he hissed. "You're worse than Skinner."

"Maybe," I said. "What time is the game tonight?"

There was a long silence and then I heard him say, very faintly— "It's delayed—eleven o'clock."

"Okay," I said. "We'll be there."

"We?"

"Yeah," I said, "and if you see that welshing bastard Evans, tell him to *bring money!*"

"What?"

"He *owes* me," I said.

"God *damn!*" he said after a long pause. "You bastards are *all* Cubans, aren't you?"

Key West, 1980

LETTER TO RALPH
STEADMAN

June 30, 1981

Dear Ralph,

Enclosed please find some pages I did in Kona, and a photograph suitable for framing.

Your letter of 24/6 arrived today, along with the book on shark care, which I suspect we can use. . . . And I also like your notion of the Cro-Magnon man reemerging on the point of a new Ice Age, both ahead *and* behind his time. Which is a serious trick to pull off, as you know, and it has given me no end of trouble, in both the personal and the professional arenas. Few people are comfortable with this concept, and even fewer can live with it. Thank God I have at least one smart friend like you.

But there is one thing I feel you should know, Ralph, before you take your theory any further: *I am Lono*.

Yeah. That's me, Ralph. I am the one they've been waiting for all these years. Captain Cook was just another drunken sailor who got lucky in the South Seas.

Or maybe not—and this gets into religion and the realm of the mystic, so I want you to listen carefully; because you alone might understand the full and terrible meaning of it.

A quick look back to the origins of this saga will raise, I'm sure, the same inescapable questions in *your* mind that it did in mine, for a while. . . .

Think back on it, Ralph—how did this thing happen? What mix of queer and (until now) hopelessly confused reasons brought me to Kona in the first place? What kind of awful power was it that caused me— after years of refusing all (and even the most lucrative) magazine assignments as cheap and unworthy—to suddenly agree to cover the Honolulu marathon for one of the most obscure magazines in the history of publishing? I could have gone off with a plane-load of reporters to roam the world with Alexander Haig, or down to Plains for a talk with Jimmy Carter. There were many things to write, for many people and many dollars—but I spurned them all, until the strange call came from Hawaii.

And then I persuaded *you*, Ralph—my smartest friend—not only to come with me, but to bring your whole family halfway around the world from London, for no good or rational reason, to spend what might turn out to be the weirdest month of our lives on a treacherous pile of black lava rocks called The Kona Coast . . . and then to come back *again* six months later, at your own expense, for something as dumb and silly as the Jackpot Fishing Tournament.

Strange, eh?

But not really. Not when I look back on it all and finally see the pattern . . . which was not so clearly apparent to me then as it is now, and that's why I never mentioned these things to you in Kona. We had enough problems, as I recall, without having to come face to face with the Genuinely Weird. Merely getting on and off the island required thousands of dollars and hundreds of man hours; and the simple act of sending a packet from Kona to Portland, Oregon, was a full-time job for both of us, for three or four days.

And then, when you came back, the massive shame and humiliation we suffered at the hands of those fools made us both too crazy to talk about what I was only then beginning to understand was the *real reason* for it all . . . and in fact I failed to see it clearly, myself, until last night.

I had known, of course, from the start. But the idea was not acceptable. . . .

I *am* Lono. And you're not. . . . Indeed, and that explains a lot of things, eh?

Right. It tells us all we need to know about this goddamn maddening story that has driven at least thirteen people to madness and despair, since it started. Think of all the editors, agents, and realtors who tried to get a grip on it, along with all the bartenders, fishermen, and even the innocent, who went down on this gig, for reasons they will never understand . . . and, yes, think also of our good friends and loved ones.

It was not an easy thing for me to accept the fact that I was born 1,700 years ago in an ocean-going canoe somewhere off the Kona coast of Hawaii, a prince of royal Polynesian blood, and lived my first life as King Lono, ruler of all the islands.

According to our missionary journalist, James Ellis, I "governed Hawaii during what may in its chronology be called the Fabulous

Age. . . . Until I became offended with my wife, and murdered her; but afterward lamented the act so much as to induce a state of mental derangement. In this state I traveled through all the islands, boxing and wrestling with everyone I met. . . . I subsequently set sail in a singularly shaped canoe for Tahiti, or a foreign country. After my departure I was deified by my countrymen, and annual games of boxing and wrestling were instituted in my honor."

How's that for roots?

What?

Don't argue with me, Ralph. You come from a race of eccentric degenerates; I was promoting my own fights all over Hawaii 1,500 years before you people even learned to take a bath.

And, besides, this *is* the story. I don't know music, but I have a good ear for the high white sound . . . and when this Lono gig flashed in front of my eyes about thirty-three hours ago, I knew it for what it was. My body trembled, my eyes rolled back in my head, and I said, "Yes! Tell me more!"

And then I thought, You bitch! It's about time!

Suddenly, the whole thing made sense. It was like seeing the Green Light for the first time. I immediately shed all religious and rational constraints, and embraced the New Truth with all my heart.

Many things happened after you left, Ralph, and that is why I am writing you, now, from what appears to be my new home in The City; so make note of the address:

c/o Haleokeawe

City of Refuge

Kona Coast, Hawaii

You remember the Haleokeawe, Ralph—it's the hut where you told me they were keeping King Kam's bones; the place where you dared to climb over the wall and pose in the yard for some Polaroid shots, like the buggering fool you are and always will be. . . .

What?

Did I say that?

Well . . . yeah, I did . . . but never mind these idle jabs, Ralph; you weren't there when the deal went down.

The trouble began on the day I caught the fish—or, more specifically, it began when I came into the harbor on the flying bridge of the *Humdinger* and started bellowing at the crowd on the dock about "filthy drunken sons of missionaries" and "lying scum" and "doomed pigfuckers" and all those other things I mentioned in my last update letter.

What I *didn't* tell you, old sport, is that I was also screaming *"I am Lono!"* in a thundering voice that could be heard by every Kanaka on the whole waterfront, from the Hilton to the King Kam—and that many of these people were deeply disturbed by the spectacle.

I don't know what got into me, Ralph; I didn't mean to say it—at least not that loud, with all those natives listening. Because they are *superstitious* people, as you know, and they take their legends seriously. Which is understandable, I think, in the minds of people who still shudder (and quake) at the memory of what happened when they bungled *Lono's* last visit.

That was in 1778 when some unwashed English bastard traveling under the name of "Captain Cook" arrived in the islands and caused such *Angst und Wagling* among the natives that they finally killed him, for reasons they still can't properly explain. All they know for sure is that his death touched off a terminal shit train of grief, death, and perversion that has endured for 200 years.

They are still not sure about Cook's credentials, but they know what happened after they killed him and they don't want to make that kind of mistake again. If history has taught us anything at all about what happens to primitive tribes who fail to recognize the second coming of a long-lost God, it is the absolute necessity of taking a very long look at all strangers, no matter how strange and brutal they might seem at first glance.

Nobody makes quick judgments out here, Ralph—which accounts, I think, for the native tradition of greeting all strangers with flower leis and nervous cries of "Aloha." That is why these Kanakas are so friendly and polite on the surface, and so savage underneath. Ever since they killed the Captain and ate his heart for the power that was in it, things have not gone well for them. First came the missionaries, then syphilis, and finally a dose of raw capitalism that changed the face of the islands forever. The grandchildren of King Kamehameha The Great, wherever they are, no longer control their own fates. They live on the outskirts of town, catching fish or growing marijuana for a living, and the one thing they know is that Lono *will* return someday—and when he does, they don't want to hurt him. One more mistake like the last one could finish off the whole race.

So it was not surprising, in retrospect, that my King Kong–style arrival in Kailua Bay on a hot afternoon in the spring of 1981 had a bad effect on the natives. The word traveled swiftly, up and down the coast, and by nightfall the downtown streets were crowded with people who had come from as far away as South Point and the Waipio Valley to see for themselves if the rumor was really true—that Lono had, in fact, returned in the form of a huge drunken maniac who dragged fish out of the sea with his bare hands and then beat them to death on the dock with a short-handled Samoan war club.

By noon the next day these rumors of native unrest had reached our friends in the real estate bund, who saw it as the "last straw," they said later, and reached a consensus decision to get me out of town on the next plane. This news was conveyed to me by Bob Mardian at the bar of the Kona Inn, which he owns. "These guys are not kidding," he warned me. "They want to put you in Hilo Prison." He glanced nervously around the bar to see who was listening, then grasped my arm firmly and leaned his head close to mine. "This is *serious*," he whispered. "I've got three waiters who won't come to work until you're gone."

"Gone?" I said. "What do you mean?"

He stared at me, drumming his fingers on the bar. "Look," he said finally. "You've gone too far this time. It's not funny anymore. You're fucking with their *religion*. The whole town is stirred up. The realtors had a big meeting today, and they tried to blame it on me."

I called for another brace of margaritas—which Mardian declined, so I drank both of them while I listened. (It was the first time I'd ever seen Mardian take anything seriously.)

"This Lono thing is dangerous," he was saying. "It's the *one* thing they really believe in."

I nodded.

"I wasn't here when it happened," he went on, "but it was the first thing I heard about when I got off the plane—Lono is back, Lono is back." He laughed nervously. "Jesus, we can get away with almost anything out here—but not *that*."

The bar was quiet. People were staring at us. Mardian had obviously been chosen.

> *Get out of this town by noon*
> *You're coming on way too soon*
> *And we never really liked you,*
> *Anyway."*
>
> —JOHN PRINE

Indeed. They never liked us, Ralph, despite all the money we gave them. And when the natives started calling me Lono, they decided to make their move. That article we did on the Marathon was not received warmly in Kona, and the real reason they invited us back for the tournament was to turn our minds around and convince us to write something nice about the place. So they could unload their property on the millions of rich dopers who would naturally flock to Kona, after reading our book.

They thought they could *use* us, Ralph. I feel sick just thinking about it. Ex-Captain Steve doesn't realize he admitted this to me, but he did. The realtors took up a collection to pay off any charter captain on the island who could catch me a fish, and thus put a cork in my mouth. Steve lied all the way to the end—and if it hadn't been for Lono, we'd have been in serious trouble. I was not eager to publish a lightweight collection of half-connected vignettes that would have left me wide open for a savage beating from the critics.

But I think I can go with this one. By the time I finish whipping on those lying bastards, they will have to close the airport for lack of traffic.

Thank God I brought the big white rock back with me—on your advice, of course—to change my luck and pull the story together, which it did. There is still a lot of work to do, but now it seems worth doing. Selah.

Okay, I want to finish this and get it mailed off. The story ends with me living in that hut at the City of Refuge to which I was forced to flee after the realtors hired thugs to finish me off. (But they killed a local haole fisherman instead, by mistake.) This is true—on the day before I left, thugs beat a local fisherman to death and left him either floating face down in the harbor, or strangled to death with a brake cable and left in a Jeep on the street in front of the Hotel Manago. (News accounts of the murder varied widely.)

That's when I got scared and took off for The City. I came down the hill at ninety miles an hour and drove the car as far as I could out on the rocks, then I ran like a bastard for the Haleokeawe—over the fence like a big kangaroo, kick down the door, then crawl inside and start screaming *"I am LONO"* at my pursuers, a gang of hired thugs and realtors who were turned back by native Park Rangers.

They can't touch me now, Ralph. I am in here with a battery-powered typewriter, two blankets from the Bali Kai, my miner's head-lamp, a kitbag full of speed and other vitals, and my fine Samoan war club. Laila brings me food and whiskey twice a day, and the natives send me women. But they won't come into the hut—for the same reason nobody else will—so I have to sneak out at night and fuck them out there on the black rocks. We scream a lot, but . . .

So what? It's not a bad life. I like it in here. But I can't leave, because they're waiting for me out there by the parking lot. The natives won't let them come any closer. They killed me once, and they're not about to do it again.

Because I *am* Lono, and as long as I stay in The City those lying swine can't touch me. I want a telephone installed, but Steve won't pay the deposit until Laila gives him 600 more dollars for bad drugs.

Which is No Problem, Ralph; no problem at all. I've already had several seven-figure offers for my life story, and every night around sundown I crawl out and collect all the joints, coins, and other strange offerings thrown over the stake fence by natives and others of my own kind.

So don't worry about me, Ralph. I've got mine. But I would naturally appreciate a visit, and perhaps a bit of money for the odd expense here and there. The place comes rent-free, but I have to pay for the whiskey.

It's a queer life, for sure, but right now it's all I have. Last night, around midnight, I heard somebody scratching on the thatch and then a female voice whispered, "When the going gets weird, the Weird turn pro."

"That's right!" I shouted. "I love you!"

There was no reply. Only the sound of this vast and bottomless sea, which talks to me every night, and makes me smile in my sleep.

Hunter

LETTER TO KEN KESEY

December 12, '81
Mobile

Dear Ken,

If you thought the air was bad in China, you should smell Mobile in the rain at four-thirty on a cold Saturday morning. I just got back from the Waffle House across the bay, where I spent about two hours eating steakburgers and reading your Beijing piece in *Running* . . . and drinking a hell of a lot of coffee, because a man with no hair and short pants can't just *hang around* a Waffle House on the edge of Mobile Bay at four o'clock in the morning without running up a tab, especially when he's laughing a lot and ducking outside in the rain every once in a while to hunker down in a big red Cadillac car for a drink of good whiskey and a few whacks of rotten cocaine. . . .

Risky business, all in all. You want to get down under the dashboard for that kind of action, and lock the electric doors. The parking lot of a Waffle House on Interstate 10 is a bad place to get weird, and it's even worse if you keep coming back inside and reading the same goddamn magazine and make the waitress jumpy by laughing out loud every few minutes and smacking the orange countertop and smoking Dunhill cigarettes in a holder. . . .

Jesus Christ, that was a hell of a *long* article. I kept thinking I could finish it off with maybe just one more whack of Wild Turkey and two more quick snorts—but the fucker kept on going, like a thing I might have written myself, and when I finally finished the bastard I tipped that fishhead bitch five dollars and drove like a bastard across the bridge, eight miles in five minutes.

It was the most fun I've had in a while, and a really fine piece of writing. I'm going to have a word with Perry about the unfortunate slip into damaging personal libel, with regard to my own persona and future earning power, but I figure that's something we can settle out of court. An ounce should cover it, I think. . . .

Anyway, it's good to see that you're finally beginning to learn something from the fine example I've been trying to provide, for lo these

many years. And never mind those jack-offs who keep saying you'll
never make it as a sportswriter. Fuck those people. You just keep *at*
it, Ken, and someday you'll be like me.

Okay, see you next time I get up there into Rape Country . . . and
meanwhile, write just a *little* more often. I could use a few more good
nights in the Waffle House. That was *fun,* man. If the piece had gone
on for a few more pages, I'd have ripped the apron off that fishhead
woman and fucked her right there on the stove.

Hello to Babbs and the family. And tell Perry that I'm into serious
training for London. By the time I get through with those dilettante
limey bastards, they'll wish they were back in Dunkirk. . . .

But, until then, you've set a new standard, and it gives me real
pleasure to salute it.

Your friend,
Hunter

LAST MEMO FROM THE
NATIONAL AFFAIRS DESK

THERE ARE A LOT of ways to get finally and completely out of political
journalism—and a lot of good reasons, for that matter—but it is not
quite as easy as it seems. The journalism part is easy to dump, and
until about three hours ago I thought I had more or less done that.
There is no money in it, for one thing, unless you want to spend the
rest of your life on television and never knowing from one day to the
next when some freakish shift in the Nielsen ratings or a sudden change
in network management might end your career forever. A bald spot,
a double chin, even a giddy decision to wear a pink shirt on camera
can finish you off just as quick as getting drunk—or even being totally
sober and innocent and getting punched by some drunk in a public

place. Nobody needs an anchorman who gets named in a paternity suit or . . .

Right. And we can get back to these hazards, etc., later if necessary. But they are not really pertinent in my case. I made a conscious decision about five years ago to get out of both politics and journalism, if only because I'd been personally and intensely involved in both of them for twenty years—everything from the Alliance for Progress in Peru and Brazil to the Free Speech Movement in Berkeley and getting gassed in the Pump Room in Chicago to the Black Panthers and the Drug Revolution and Fishing Rights for Indians to four presidential campaigns and ten years on the road with Richard Nixon. And then two wild years of Watergate and even having my life and medical insurance cut off while I was flying at 37,000 feet across the Pacific to cover the last days of the Vietnam War.

So I have done politics, folks. And I have been right most of the time. Or maybe just crazy, but it didn't really matter at the time, and I didn't really care. There was no time to worry about whether I was right or wrong about Ed Muskie or Richard Nixon or even Sonny Barger. There were too many deadlines, and barely enough time to write, much less think. It was like a twenty-year war, and at one point I got so involved—after a quick little beating at the corner of Michigan and Balboa by a Chicago cop with a three-foot billyclub—that I came back home and ran for sheriff of Aspen on the Freak Power ticket, one of the most savage and unnatural political campaigns in the history of American politics, a genuinely radical experiment that came within four percentage points of winning over the Democratic incumbent and beat the Republican challenger by something like thirty-three points.

After that I decided that almost anything was possible, once you understood the machinery—even running for president, or at least senator—and one of the key points I want to make in this screed is that my involvement with political journalism was always more political than journalistic. Somewhere between Chicago in 1968 and Watergate in '74, I became dangerously comfortable with the notion that journalism was an honorable means to a valid end, or maybe vice versa.

And then hubris set in—which is a long story, and there is no point in rehashing it now, except to say that I got myself so deeply involved in presidential politics by the summer of 1976 *Time* magazine devoted two whole pages to a full-bore assault on everything I stood for (except Jimmy Carter, the dark-horse peanut farmer candidate for the Democratic nomination that I had picked, more as a gambler and a politician than a journalist, about a year before *Time* saw him coming).

Okay, and so much for that, too. History will absolve me on the Carter question, I think, and not even the most confidential files or internal advisory memos in the Time Inc. morgue will ever come close to the weird and occasionally heinous truth of my personal involvement with the Carter campaign. Those silly hacks devoted more space to a vicious personal assault on me than they ever used on Mussolini—two facing pages in the issue that appeared during the week of the Democratic National Convention in New York.

It made my life difficult and I had to lay a bit low for most of the convention, but if they had done their work as well as I did mine that year, I would still be locked up, etc . . . .

Indeed, and so much for that. We can get into the criminal, and carnal, aspects of the thing later, if necessary—but it is 5:55 on a snowy, cold morning in the Rockies right now and I want to get this thing done before the morning network news comes on—because I have been watching the news on a TV satellite dish all night in a log cabin in an abandoned logging camp 10,000 feet up in a snowstorm at the end of a treacherous jeep road and on my way back down the mountain about an hour ago, creeping through a blizzard at ten or fifteen miles an hour in my ancient and honorable Volvo, I had time to reflect on the nature of the news we'd been watching, and I think I finally came on a way to get out of both journalism and politics forever.

I have a whole legal pad full of my notes on the news of yesterday's astonishing and unprecedented assault on the U.S. Embassy in Lebanon—total destruction, fifty dead and one hundred wounded, with many more buried in the rubble and nobody to blame for it except some mysterious gang of presumably Arab fanatics called the "Moslem Holy War."

There were endless films of mangled bodies being carried out of the burning rubble on stretchers—a sight that not many people in my generation or anybody else alive today has ever seen, on TV or even in newsreels. I could call New York and get some people scanning files for examples of previous attacks on U.S. Embassies, if I thought it was really necessary—but I don't, and that is not the point of this screed anyway. What I want to do here is record my own perceptions and conclusions before the morning TV news comes on. In an hour "The CBS Morning News," "The Today Show" and "Good Morning, America" will be all over my screen with the capsule commentaries and distilled judgments of hundreds of TV wizards and political experts who have been working all night long, just as I have, to make some kind of sense of the thing. And I want to get my own thoughts on paper before I get overrun by theirs, for good or ill.

If I can get the wisdom of the desk on the mojo wire or even read into the ear of some shockproof Western Union operator before dawn, I will do it—just to make sure my own views of the incident will be on record before I get any input from the networks. Maybe they will agree with me, but probably not. And one of the first rules of survival in political journalism is to make sure—absolutely sure—that at least one other reputable newspaper or network or even some vaguely maverick but half-credible political columnist or wizard or correspondent agrees with you—especially when you are about to call the president of the United States a treacherous liar and a cynical monster beyond the wildest dreams of Richard Nixon.

And I have usually followed this rule in the past, or at least been nervously aware of it when I didn't, but this time I mean to violate and ignore it with a vengeance, if only as a scientific experiment. I am, after all, a Doctor, and I have a legitimate interest in the question of whether or not twenty-five years without sleep might alter or perhaps even warp in some way the ability of a good ole boy from Kentucky to fully comprehend the meaning of a major, fast-breaking news story as on the brink of 1984 it unfolds between midnight and dawn on a system that brings in sixty-six TV channels all at once with at least nine of them tracking the Embassy bombing story on a live minute-to-minute basis reminiscent of a presidential assassination story with anchormen clearly confused and no explanation at all for a genuinely monumental political move on the U.S.—*nobody* blows up a U.S. Embassy. It is one of those things that is simply not done. I remember watching TV film of the '68 Tet assault on the American Embassy in Saigon with Richard Nixon in a room at the Holiday Inn in Manchester, New Hampshire. It appeared on the evening news, with no warning, while we were having a drink and talking about something else—and Nixon went half mad with rage at the very idea of such a thing, much less the televised reality of a few dozen gooks in black pajamas actually *firing weapons* into the U.S. Embassy compound. There were no immediate reports of American casualties, but the mere sight of foreigners crazy enough to assault Our Embassy drove Nixon into a frenzy, as if we were witnessing the end of the civilized world as we knew it. A thing like that had not happened since the time of the first Roosevelt, and even then they were punished with the same kind of terrible ferocity that Harry Truman visited on the Japs for bombing Pearl Harbor. It was unthinkable, to Nixon, no matter what he said later in his memoirs, that *anybody* would physically attack a U.S. Embassy. I remember that moment very clearly, and in truth I was almost as shocked as he was. The incident, a mere firecracker compared to what happened yesterday in Lebanon, blew George Romney out of the race for the GOP nomination almost overnight and confused Nelson Rockefeller's long-awaited challenge so totally that Nixon was able to walk away with New Hampshire and ultimately the White House. It sent his staff into a convulsion of all-night rewrites and rescheduling of speeches and focus, all of it based on the fearful notion that America could not, should not, and in fact *would* not tolerate an insult of that magnitude. It raised serious questions about our status as Number One, and what followed was two years of the most savage and relentless bombing of any nation in the history of warfare. Laos and Cambodia were bombed back to the Stone Age—as recently defeated presidential candidate Barry Goldwater had been mocked and brutally beaten for even suggesting four years earlier—just for being in the same neighborhood with people who would dare to attack the Embassy of the number-one nation in the world, and at least half of those 55,000 white crosses from Maine to California were a direct consequence of that insult, etc.

So it was not without a keen and profoundly morbid sense of curiosity that kept me and Cromwell locked into the TV news all night—mainly waiting to see who was going to get blamed for an outrage so awful and massive (a whole Embassy destroyed, hundreds killed or wounded) as to snap the mind of Richard Nixon just as surely as if Pittsburgh had been suddenly blown up like Hiroshima by a nuclear warhead fired from some unknown base for unknown reasons by some queer Muslim sect that nobody had ever heard of.

My first thought, after scanning enough channels to be sure that the thing had actually happened, was Ye fucking gods, the bastards have done it now. Whoever put that bomb in the Embassy made sure that the U.S. can't get out of the Middle East, peacefully or any other way . . . and sure enough, here came Sen. John Tower (R-Tex) saying that every American Embassy in the world would be in danger and "the U.S. will lose its power in the world if this act is ignored."

"Well," I said to Cromwell, who was frantically switching channels and satellites. "A lot of people are going to die for this one. Here we are in the middle of extremely delicate 'peace talks' designed to get both us and the Israelis out of Lebanon and somehow calm the place down, and somebody blows up the whole goddamn embassy."

"Who?" he asked.

"I don't know," I said. "But if there's one man in the world who had better have a good alibi for every minute of where he was last night, I'd say it would be Muammar el-Qaddafi. If somebody is going to pay for this—and somebody will—Qaddafi is the only Arab in the world that we can hit without starting World War III, and he's been on thin ice for years anyway. As a gambler, I'd give Muammar about three weeks. He's the only one both crazy enough to do it and safe enough to punish."

Cromwell nodded and hit the scanner again. Somewhere outside in the blizzard I could hear the low grinding noise of the big white dish changing positions as he went from Comsat One to Comsat Two and back. Constant news, mounting casualties, still no hint of an explanation for one of the most flagrant and warlike attacks on not just the reality but the whole myth and image of any world power since the rape of Nanking.

Whoever rolled that pickup full of what CNN said was 160 pounds of explosives was into some very serious business, extreme escalation. The only thing close to it in recent memory was the seizure of the American Embassy and eighty-nine hostages by Iranian fanatics in 1979, a breach of traditional diplomatic assumptions that made the whole world nervous.

You can spend twenty-five hours a day in political journalism for twenty years or even forty without ever expecting to witness the crazed seizure of an American Embassy, much less the total destruction of one in a hypersensitive de facto war zone. Not even Muammar el-Qaddafi would be dumb enough to do a thing like that. It is off the board, a whole new set of rules.

I was trying to explain this to Cromwell—the sheer magnitude and craziness of the thing—when something like three minutes later I heard another profoundly original notion erupt from the tube. The president of the United States, according to *The Wall Street Journal,* had publicly written off the "Jewish vote" in his campaign for reelection in 1984.

"Wait a minute," I said. "That's impossible. Nobody running for president—not even some weird mix of Washington and Lincoln and Eisenhower and Franklin D. Roosevelt—would even think about saying a thing like that, and certainly not to *The Wall Street Journal.* We must have heard wrong. Let's hit another channel. In the past three minutes I've been forced to confront two of the strangest things I've ever even thought about in twenty years of even listening to crazy people in bars, much less *The Wall Street Journal* and the press secretary for the Israeli government back to back."

But it was true. It took awhile to run it down, and even to run it all down—and as it turned out, the *Journal* was giving Reagan every possible benefit of the doubt, by attributing his alleged dismissal of the Jewish vote in '84 by attributing it to King Hussein of Jordan and/or other unnamed Washington sources and generally writing the whole thing off to madness and politics and gossip. . . . But one thing the *Journal* didn't mention was a secret White House memo. Reagan's pollster Richard Wirthlin showed him a poll losing 94 percent of the Jewish vote (up from 6 percent)—due to economics and Mideast priorities—so they have decided to try to make him be perceived as a peacemaker instead of pandering to special interest groups. On Thursday Reagan told Hussein he could win without the Jewish vote.

Woody Creek, 1985

MEMO FROM THE SPORTS DESK

Dear David,

I am watching the fat people dance on television, right now: Channel 23 out of Aspen, "The Morning Stretch," blonde women in zebra-skin bodysuits dancing and stretching, aerobics, physical fitness—which The Desk has always strongly endorsed. Nobody is against physical fitness, or even this goddamn relentless barrage of fat people dancing on television; you can get these programs twenty-four hours a day if you have a satellite earth station, and about twenty hours a day with the cable.

And I don't mean to hurry along, here . . . I could tell you about the Ron Harris Aerobicise films that I used to watch on TV in Mobile and which affected me very profoundly, at the time. But I think we can save that for later. The TV has suddenly come alive with news of U.S. Marines being killed in "a firefight" at the Beirut airport.

I am not sure what this means, precisely, but it interests me. The Beatles are on television now, and a CNN story out of Hollywood says Debbie Reynolds has doomed her career by doing a benefit for AIDS victims. Nobody came, apparently; or at least not the smart people. AIDS is not chic. It is one of those extremely contemporary gigs, like herpes and poison rain, that not everybody wants to discuss. The news is fast these days, and a lot of it makes people nervous. U.S. Marines are fighting to the death in some corner of a Lebanese airport with some enemy army that the State Department can't even name.

What?

Who killed these U.S. Marines? Whom were they fighting when they died?

These questions make me uneasy, David. There is something ugly afoot. It is not normal to get news bulletins about American casualties in some foreign war that not even the president can explain, or wants to. That is a strange thing, and however they finally explain it, it will not be satisfactory. They will blame it on the Druze, or "the rebels" or maybe Qaddafi. WILD ARAB RENEGADES SLAY MARINES WHILE JEWS WATCH.

Okay. Never mind that. We are business people and we have serious things to discuss. . . . There is *money*, of course, but so what? I have many receipts—maybe $200/220K on file *now*—and let me *assure* you, bro, that it is *all* well spent, like an ever-ripening investment in the condom market. . . . We are on a roll: The Shit Train that I predicted in my memo of last week is now upon us. The Democrats have gone into the tank for good. The party has sold its soul to robot whores from the PACs and local PBA networks who will guarantee the deal to destabilize Hart and nominate Mondale, then sabotage his candidacy by saddling him with a floozy for VP and a personal staff of Judas Goats and Greedheads. . . . Call me quick.

—Doc

Woody Creek, 1985

"I've been evicted from every place I've ever lived except the one where I live now. I finally had to buy that so I wouldn't get evicted."

May 17, 1985

VIA CERTIFIED MAIL

Dear ———:

As you know, I have spoken with you on the telephone on two occasions recently about the constant disturbances from your tenant who lives below us. We listened to the loud music, loud playing of the television, arguing in loud voices, apparent beatings, and a person screaming for approximately one month before I called you to complain about the noise.

During our first discussion you reacted in what I consider to be a very condescending manner when I informed you of the disturbances. I find his disturbances frightening to listen to and the only reason I have not called the Police Department to report the screaming is that once the Police left the house after responding to the call, we would have been left with your tenant as a neighbor.

There is no insulation between where we live and where he lives and when we are sleeping in the upstairs bedroom it sounds as though the arguments and beatings are happening in our living room.

When we had our second discussion about the same subject you told me that he had been told about the noise. However, the situation has not improved. The loud arguments have always occurred at between approximately 3:30 A.M. and 4:30 A.M., with the exception of one evening this week when a loud argument started at 8:15 P.M.

The very worst thing about having this man for a neighbor is the noise and the violence that surround him, but we are also experiencing much difficulty with the parking situation. Whenever he is here we have problems with the huge Jeep he drives being parked in the area in front of the gate. We cannot see clearly enough to safely enter the avenue, assuming that he leaves enough space for us to back the car out.

To sum it all up we are finding life at the house, since this person moved in, to be intolerable. We spend as little time as possible at the house. We only sleep here (when he keeps quiet enough to allow such sleep). We spend no time at all at the house on weekends, if we can possibly help it. The parking difficulties are a problem. We can only assume, from the fact that nothing has been done by you as the landlord about the unpleasant situation we find ourselves in, that you have very little concern for our comfort at the house. It also appears that nothing you say to your other tenant will change matters in any way.

We have consulted an attorney who has advised us to notify you, by way of this letter, of our last day at the above premises. This letter is also to demand the return of the $4,000.00 security deposit which we paid to your agent.

     Very truly yours,

                                       May 23, 1985

VIA CERTIFIED MAIL

Dear ———:

Enclosed is a copy of a book by your tenant the "author." I am sure you have not read it, otherwise you would never have let this person move into your house. The very best thing about this book is that it can be read from cover to cover in a very short period of time and therefore one does not have to invest much of one's time in reading it.

You will particularly enjoy his descriptions of all the drugs he takes, the weapons he enjoys, and how he likes to damage hotel rooms and leave without paying the bills.

I had told you in our telephone conversations that I had never heard of him and you assured me that he was a very well-known writer. With some difficulty I finally did find a copy of this book. I am amazed at how accurately I described him when I told you that he sounds like a crazy person who is on drugs and more than likely armed. This turns out to be an interesting observation as this is very close to the way he describes himself.

Incidentally, the banging and screaming occurred again last night.

     Very truly yours,

Enclosure—*Fear and Loathing in Las Vegas* by Hunter S. Thompson

Intercepted letters to the landlord complaining about Dr. Thompson's alleged behavior the last time he moved down the mountain— temporarily

THE DUKAKIS PROBLEM: ANOTHER VICIOUS BEATING FOR THE NEW WHIGS

Another Dunce, Another Dollar, Another Foul Halloween
. . . and, Ye Gods! Another Dead Election Day . . . What
Does It All Mean, Dr. Oliver? They Laughed at Thomas
Edison and They Killed Old Black Joe . . . Quoth the
Raven, "Nevermore."

SOMETHING IS WRONG here. George Bush has done everything
wrong—from lying on the record about the Iran-Contra Arms Deal
and selecting a giddy little right-wing yo-yo as his running mate to ever
being vice-president of the U.S. in the first place.

The worst bet in American politics is an incumbent vice-president
with a fool-proof first-class ticket to the Oval Office. . . . It is one of
those "guaranteed" gigs like "the check is in the mail" that seems to
make perfect sense at the time but somehow never works.

The last time anybody beat that jinx was Martin Van Buren in 1836.
Ever since then the vice-presidency has been a sinkhole of failure,
shame, and humiliation—except when the president died unexpect-
edly. . . . Which has happened often enough (nine times out of forty)
to make the odds on a sitting vice-president taking over the presidency
a comfortable five to one bet, but if he has to *run* for the office and
campaign in a general election, the odds go up forty-four to one.

There are damn few people in the politics business who feel more
personally menaced by the specter of a George Bush victory in November than I do. . . . Or at least than I *should*, on the evidence of
everything I've said about the man and the bedrock worship of the
Revenge Ethic in politics. . . .

But I am in the gambling business, for good or ill; it is the business
I have chosen, and the only governing rule that we all recognize is:
always sit close to an exit and never trust a man who doesn't sweat.

Be ready to run at all times, like Ed Meese, and do a lot of knee
bends. . . . Quick eyes, fast hands, and legs like bands of steel. It is

like living in the heart of Saturday night with no music and cheap friends and the knowledge that everything you believe in might turn out to be wrong and crazy by the time the polls close on the first Tuesday in November.

Shit happens, like they say in California, and you don't always need music to play musical chairs. In a business where money always talks and sharks never sleep, and the difference between victory and defeat is winning or losing the most powerful office in the world, never leave home without a fistful of speed and a gold credit card.

Indeed. And so much for wisdom. The business is full of smart fools who won't learn, and on some days I am one of them. I have gone down with more ships than Captain Ahab—and usually for honorable reasons—but I am getting tired of it, and I am getting especially tired of getting out on these seas with dumb bastards who punch holes in the bottom of the boat and call it smart.

The names change and the details vary from one year to another, but the bottom line is consistent. It is like taking the Denver Broncos to the Super Bowl every January and watching them get beaten stupid by slower teams with amateur quarterbacks and coaches with one-year contracts.

Nobody can explain it, except as the annual manifestation of an indomitable Will to Lose.

This election is not turning out like it was supposed to. It has been going on for so long that it is hard to remember when it wasn't, but nothing has really happened. The main questions have not even been asked, much less answered, and now as we come creeping down to the wire it is beginning to look like *this is really it,* that what you see is absolutely what you're going to get. Either way, for good or ill, take it or leave it.

It is a grim thing to face—that one of the nation's highest arts has fallen so low, and there seems to be no cure for it. We are looking at the first presidential election in American history to be decided by less than 50 percent of the eligible voters.

This is taken for granted and nobody seems to be worried about it. The hog is back in the tunnel. There is no more talk about "getting out the vote," and the last Voter Registration Drive was a long time ago—way back in the spring, before either one of the party conventions.

There is no pulse.

That is the nut of it, and on some nights it is a very spooky thing to contemplate. . . .

There is a strange new factor at work in this election, and Mr. Jones is not the only who doesn't know what it is.

On the whole spectrum of politics there is none of that angst or anger or urgency that normally comes with a presidential election. Nobody is going crazy in public from traditional motivators like fear and greed and vengeance. There is a blizzard of news, lies, and other thick information coming back from these poor yuppie bastards out there on the campaign trail with their Perrier water and their lap transmitters—but none of it seems to have any meaning to more than one person at a time. . . .

THE UGLY MAN COMETH

The air is uncommonly slow. It is hard to find anybody from coast to coast who feels any real sense of Winning or Losing in this thing. Nobody is *afraid*. There are no marching songs, none of that high white noise and wild music that comes with the feeling of big risk in the air—"Big Doings," like they say in the hills—when the fat is in the fire and the deal is going down and the only thing for sure is that a lot of people are going to wish that wolves had stolen them from their cradles when the votes get finally counted on election day.

The fun has gone out of it. There is no hum of madness or adventure, no festering backwaters of hate and alienation. . . .

You can't feel properly alienated from a process you never knew, or from a choice you never had. We are raising a whole generation in this country that will never know what it feels like to rise up together and flog a crooked president out of the White House, or to wake up in the morning and know that the name of the U.S. Attorney General is Robert Kennedy, instead of Ed Meese.

There is not much justice in big-time American politics—but it happens now and then, and in those moments it is a very elegant thing to see, and no drug can match the high that comes from being a part of it.

All of that is missing in this goddamn dreary mess. The only original voice in this leveraged buyout of an election was Jesse Jackson's, and the last person who had any real fun on the '88 campaign trail was Gary Hart.

DUKAKIS ÜBER ALLES

What happened to the Big Debate—the Bush–Dukakis showdown that the political wizards said was going to decide the whole election in one stroke?

Well . . . shucks. The answer is "not much."

The Great Debate turned out to be a false alarm, more or less. It meant nothing, it solved nothing, it decided nothing, it addressed nothing, and it *was* nothing. . . . A clean sweep, except for a frantic ripple effect that petered out before noon the next day, when the Ronald Reagan Show hit the United Nations and the tabloids hit the supermarkets with a front-page headline that said:

FOUND ON MARS—A STATUE OF ELVIS

When I saw it I went limp with a shock of recognition. It was one of those sudden fiery instants that Herman Melville had in mind when he said, "Genius all over the world stands hand in hand, and one shock of recognition runs the whole circle round."

True headline junkies are a rare breed, almost extinct, and our art is a very fragile thing. Dying, in fact—a dying art, arcane to the point of perversion, with only a few practitioners.

But I like to think I am one of them, and when I saw that ELVIS/MARS head, I felt a high flash in my spine.

The headline was so good that it made the story redundant. . . . It was a masterpiece of the headline-writing art: it told the whole story in six words so sharp and loaded that the article itself became redundant, except to mystics and libel lawyers.

Nobody else cared. Only those of us in the headline trade, but we rarely talk to each other and we know that our art means nothing.

Things are not quite the same in the politics business. The stakes are higher and the talk tends to be a lot looser—but it is the same kind of high-end frequency, like a dog whistle, that normal ears can't hear.

It was a good week for high notes: first came the bizarre ELVIS ON MARS headline, and after that it was Reagan's sudden decision to fly up to New York on Monday morning and deliver his "final, farewell speech" to the entire United Nations assembly.

It came on short notice, they said—but not so short that it couldn't dump most of the Debate stories off the top of the front page and out of the number-one rung on the evening TV news. . . . The debate story was *hazy,* and it made people nervous to have to read about it; but a breaking story about Dutch doing his swan song at the U.N. had a definite zang to it.

JOHN WAYNE SAYS TEARFUL GOODBYE TO PYGMY PEOPLE

Emotional Farewell at World Forum;
Many Weep Shamelessly as President
Gives $144 Million for World Peace

There was nothing hazy about *that* one, and for sheer impact it ripped the tits off of that creepy, neurotic Debate story.

In the gray world of professional politics it was recognized for what it was—a move so high and suave that in the end it was not even necessary. . . . But it was *there,* just in case. If George had faltered badly and turned the Sunday night debate into a nightmare for himself and his people, the Big Man would have been there on Monday morning to cover for him.

It was blue-chip advance work. George could afford the handful of stupid gaffes he blurted out sporadically during the debate. It wouldn't matter, they said. Dutch could always take off for the U.N. a few hours early. It was a lock.

Which was true. George "lost" the debate by a few points, but not by enough to change anything. . . . Dukakis "won," but three days later he was still running five points behind in the polls.

Dukakis is in trouble now. He fired his best shots but George never noticed. He was too busy strutting around the stage like Mussolini. His eyes turned to slits and he even winked brazenly at the audience, to let them in on the joke. Nobody knew why he did it, but by that time it didn't matter. He was, after all, the vice-president, and his opponent was running scared. All George has to do now is to hang tough and deny everything. He will be hard to beat now. He is in the catbird seat, with time on his hands and plenty of money and handsome Danny Quayle to take his place, if anything goes wrong.

Veni, Vidi, Vici.

Woody Creek, October 1988

SECRET CABLES TO WILLIE HEARST

RE: QADDAFI

September 2, 1986

Dear Will,

We *must* get rid of MaCumber. (What? Sp? . . . MacCumber? M'Cumbr? Jesus, this is embarrassing. We shouldn't be hiring people if we can't spell their names. No wonder they can't be trusted.) McCumber has altered the spelling of Muammar el-Qaddafi in my column for something like nineteen straight weeks, and it drives me crazy with rage every time. I have tried to talk to him about it, but he won't listen. Maria says she never trusted him anyway, and now I find out that he has a drinking problem.

Jesus. Where will it end? How many of these goddamn treacherous sots can we afford to keep on the payroll? Get rid of that bastard. He should be humiliated, as a lesson to the others. Have him dragged out of his new office by four huge thugs wearing stockings over their heads and black jumpsuits with the Hearst eagle emblazoned on their backs. Never heard of again. That will settle things down.

Fire him quick and let me know. Thanx,

Hunter

RE: THE COLUMN

September 11, 1987

Dear Will,

I have called you repeatedly, at the office and also at home, but I never seem to get through. Why *is* that?

Anyway, I have some things to discuss with you. I have A LIST, in fact. Here it is:

1. I have written Denny Allen at King Features with a strongly worded proposal in re: *Traveling Expenses* for THE COLUMN—which I will obviously need, in order to leave Woody Creek now and then—to New York, New Hampshire, New Orleans, Nome, Hong Kong, Bangkok, or even Paris.

My proposal is that *The Syndicate* will guarantee to cover the first $1,000 in travel expenses for any week that I choose to go ANY-WHERE FOR CLEARLY PROFESSIONAL REASONS . . . and that *The Examiner* will "guarantee" the next $1,000, if necessary.

If I want to go to Cairo, for instance, I would have a guaranteed credit line (or a *draw,* as they say in the trade) of $2,000—which is a reasonable figure, for most trips (but not all), and anything above $2K per week will be subject to negotiation . . . or I might cover it, myself, for my own reasons, pending settlement (with the SFX)—on all legitimate claims above that $2K number.

We have, as I presume you know, reached an unacceptable impasse with regard to the "HST expenses" question. . . . *There are none.* . . . And not even a vague explanation or response in any way except dead cheap silence whenever I submit *any* bill at all, at *any* time, for *any* reason at all. It has come to the point where I now list my *Examiner* expense bills on my 1040 forms as "uncollectible debts." And we now have a column that will never be written from anywhere more than 2.1 miles from the Post Office in Woody Creek.

2. PIGS . . . if *you* can't arrange a state-of-the-art Pig Hunt at your place down there on the South Coast, I will arrange it on my own, at Jo Hudson's place just south of the Hot Springs in Big Sur. We have killed many of those filthy black bastards down there, and I suspect we can kill many more. MANY. They are a menace, and they are breeding faster than rabbits. . . .

But if I have to arrange my own Pig Hunt, I won't invite you—and you will hear about it for a lot longer than you'll want to, and I will make sure you get at least one fine, fresh, blood-soaked trophy head right flat on the middle of your desk one bright morning—and then I will write a column about it.

3. I *must* have some kind of computer access to news and information: *The New York Times, Washington Post,* and mainly a LEXIS-NEXIS connection. This is *absolutely necessary.* I can't even presume to *compete* with other big-time political columnists without a massive and constantly available information base that is at least equal to theirs.

No argument about *this,* eh? *Only a matter of money* . . . so please arrange it and let me know ASAP. I *need* it. . . . Deduct the cost from my weekly expense tab, if necessary (at least on weeks when I *don't travel*) and please advise Mr. Severance that if he continues to kick my expense bills into the trash can and assume I won't notice, he is misinformed. . . . I am gearing up to a flogging mode on this one, and if I can't get my expenses paid I am going to rip the brains and the flesh of anybody who wants to sign the *Refusal Memo.*

When the Old Man sent Jack London and Frederic Remington to cover his war in Cuba, I doubt if he told them to pay their own travel and work expenses. We are, after all, professionals. And my name is not Bucky Walters.

4. Where is my *$11,000 Performance Bonus* that was supposed to come with delivery of SFX/hst#100? It was never mentioned or even noticed by you or anybody else who just sold me into some kind of "national syndication." . . . And $11,000 is *cheap,* given that some of the "insider" trade gossip said the 100th column bonus would be at least $22,000, or even $33,000.

5. Yeah . . . and so what?

Well . . . try this: if you keep loading McCumber with more and more big work (whoops—trying to change ribbons, here; my ancient and honorable IBM Model T got bashed around in the back of the Jeep last week, while I was in the hospital for surgery. It was the Silk Ribbon—continuous model, which never ran out—but it went into the shop for General Repair yesterday, and I will send the repair bill to the *Examiner* . . .).

And I will expect to have the goddamn thing *paid*—along with my long-lost "Phoenix Expenses"; my recently submitted "Houston Tracker" (TV/Dish receiver) bill; and whatever other pitifully small amounts that I've dared to send in, for things like paper and ribbons and stamps and other mundane things. . . .

I don't cheat on expenses, Will—and I don't expect to be cheated when I send in legitimate bills for out-of-pocket cash. And especially not by some slit-eyed yuppie who gets his salary paid out of *Chronicle* ad revenues and wallows (at company expense) in *white wine and pesto* in the finest high-dollar spots in San Francisco, Sonoma, and Tiburon.

Or even Oakland.

Jesus! Did *Arthur Brisbane* have to slink around town with a fistful of one-dollar bills and not even a formal *Examiner* press card to halfway pay for his lunch?

Probably not. The Old Man was a monster, but nobody ever accused him of skimming nickels and dimes off his best writers' expense accounts—and it wasn't his cheapjack *accountants* who made him a legend in American journalism and the highest roller of his time.

Right . . . and all I meant to say here was that if Dave Mac moves to another paper any time soon, I will want to *go with him,* if the New Boys can buy out my contract. As it were.

And *it won't take much,* will it? Burgin would snap it up about twenty-nine seconds into the first phone call. . . . And it *was Burgin,* in fact, who advised me (at the very beginning) to "never let your expenses (for the week) run more than $999. . . . Keep it *under four figures,*" he said, "and you won't have any problem."

Ho, ho . . . probably he was too busy to get to know Mr. Severance, at the time.

But *not me,* Willy. I got that nickel-and-dime drift a long time ago, and it has never really amused me. My mood is nasty tonight, and with nothing to lose I don't mind saying that it could *get nastier* very soon. I'll write one more column (or maybe two more) on this no-money, no-expenses, alleged "syndication" basis—but *it will not go beyond Halloween.*

Yeah. I can handle a few more weeks of this thing, as is—but at midnight on Halloween, I will

What?

Well . . . we will have problems beyond our ken. Our gig will turn queer. Ugly things will happen—some of them utterly brainless, like the craziness of an egg-sucking dog suddenly put on a chain that stops him with a terrible throat-jerk, just three feet short of the chicken coop.

Indeed . . . let us back off and stare at this thing (for a moment) and then move swiftly and smartly to cure it.

I *need* information, I *want* money and expenses from the syndication deal, I *must* kill pigs—and if I'm going to be a goddamn syndicated columnist on a level that we can put up against *anybody* else in the nation, *I want to be treated like a wizard and a main player and the best political columnist in America or anywhere else.*

What the hell, Willy? Give it a whirl. We've done okay so far. Send me the $11K bonus, *all* my back expenses, fix my credit line with the syndicate, stop loading McCumber like he was some kind of camel or mule and give him some room to work or even to think like a human being, and get back to cranking up the paper to where we said we were going, all along or *back then,* as it were.

Why not? Winning can be fun. And fuck the nickels and dimes. Let's get on with the real business.

OK,
Hunter

San Francisco Examiner Columns

How long, O Lord. . . . How long? Where will it end? The only possible good that can come of this wretched campaign is the ever-increasing likelihood that it will cause the Democratic Party to self-destruct.
—FEAR AND LOATHING ON THE CAMPAIGN TRAIL, 1972

THE NEW DUMB

SIXTEEN YEARS IS plenty of time for even dumb people to learn just about anything they need to, especially when the difference between winning and losing is usually a matter of life or death, professionally, in the business of big-time politics. It is a question of enlightened self-interest—learn quick or die.

But there are exceptions, as always, like Joan of Arc, Lyndon LaRouche, and even Gary Hart—which is not really fair in Gary's case; it was not that he couldn't learn, he just had different priorities. They jeered and called him crazy when he quit, but polls taken immediately after the election had him as the Demo front-runner for 1992.

It was the kind of news that nobody wants to hear, like having your pre-marriage blood test handed back to you in a lead bag, or getting a job as the next sheriff of Sicily. . . . Richard Nixon might handle a horror like that, or maybe William Burroughs, but no other names come to mind. Some things are too ugly to even gossip about.

Gary was unavailable for comment on the '92 poll, and his former campaign manager, Bill Dixon, has long since moved to Bangkok. Other Democrats wept openly at the news, but most just stared blankly. "The front-runner for '92?" one asked. "Are you crazy? I'd rather have a truckload of pig entrails dumped in my front yard by some of those tattooed guys from Yakuza."

It is an ancient and honorable method of collecting debts in Japan, but not yet chic in this country. The Yakuza, however, are said to be infiltrating American cities at a rate that will soon make them the second most powerful political organization in this nation, behind only the Republican Party.

The Mafia ranks No. 3—followed by the Roman Catholic Church, the IRS, the U.S. Congress, and the American Marijuana Growers' Association.

Indeed. There are many rooms in the mansion. James Angelton said that back when the CIA was still a ranking power. . . .

The Democratic Party is not even listed in the top twenty, despite a number-four ranking two years ago. It was a shocking plunge.

"The Democrats shouldn't even be listed in the top forty," said political analyst Harold Conrad. "They have become the party of Losers."

That is probably wishful thinking—but at ten to one it might float, even in Las Vegas. The last time a major political party self-destructed was in 1853, when the Whigs went belly-up despite the leadership of Henry Clay, Daniel Webster, and John Quincy Adams. They had ceased to stand for anything except pure politics.

"They refused to learn," says Conrad. "They became the New Dumb, and then they died."

If that is the only issue, the Democrats appear to be doomed. They have not learned anything about presidential politics since 1960, and they have lost five out of the last six elections despite a consistently powerful showing in state and local elections. While Dukakis lost in forty states, the Democratic Party added to its control of Congress with a net gain of five seats in the House and two in the Senate.

The dumb are never with us for long, and there is a lot of evidence to suggest that Republicans learn faster than Democrats. . . . Consider the crude learning experience that fell like a huge snake around the neck of the national Republican Party in 1964, when they were forced to go public as the party of Dumb Brutes and Rich People, and then see themselves flogged in the general election by 16 million votes.

When Goldwater was forced to wallow in the horror of public defeat, many experts said he was not wallowing alone, that the whole Republican Party was wallowing with him. The GOP was doomed, like the Whigs, to a cheap and meaningless fate.

But not for long. Four years later, Richard Nixon came back from the dead and ran the Democrats out of power with a 500,000-vote victory over the wretched arch-liberal, Hubert Humphrey. . . .

It was 1968—the Death Year—and this time it was the Democrats who ran amok. If the campaign had been conducted under the Rules of War—which it *was:* a *civil* war—thousands of hate-crazy young Democrats would have been tortured to death by their own kind, or killed in the streets like wild animals. Both Johnson and Humphrey would have been executed for treason.

We were all crazy, that year, and many people developed aggressive attitudes. When I packed my bags for Chicago, there was nothing unusual about including a Bell motorcycle helmet, yellow ski goggles, a new pair of Chuck Taylor All-Stars, and a short billyclub. Packing for Chicago was not like taking off for Club Med.

The Democratic Party has never recovered from that convention. It is a wound that still festers, and these people are not quick healers. They have blown five out of six presidential elections since then, and their only victory came after a criminal Republican president was dragged out of the White House in a frenzy of shame.

It was no big trick to beat Gerald Ford in 1976. He was clearly Nixon's creature, and the GOP was massively disgraced. It was a friendly preacher from Georgia against a gang of crooks. . . . And even then Carter blew a big lead and won by only two points.

Four years later he was crushed by Ronald Reagan, a goofy version of Goldwater, who ruled for two terms and then anointed his successor while Democrats embarrassed themselves once again.

Party Chairman Paul Kirk should be whipped like a red-headed stepchild, and the others should be deported to Pakistan. Any major opposition party dominated by shaggy whores and failed dingbats not only cripples the two-party system but insults the whole democracy.

Woody Creek, 1989

FEAR AND LOATHING IN SACRAMENTO

IT WAS JUST BEFORE noon when I walked into Ricci's down on J Street in Sacramento. The lunch crowd was not in yet, but a bunch of the boys were whooping it up down at the dark end of the bar, where they appeared to have a woman cornered in a big leather booth.

It would have passed for a yuppie lunch club anywhere else in the valley, but Sacramento is a political town, and I could see at a glance that Ricci's was a full-on political bar. Most of the gents mauling that woman down there in the booth were wearing neckties, but they had a vaguely seedy look about them, as if they had slept in their suits on a musty couch in some lobbyist's condo with a condom machine in the lobby and rubber palm trees in the elevators. . . . They were unemployed lawyers, pimps, and stockbrokers: *Politicians* in a word. . . .

I tried to ignore them, but the shrieks and cries of the woman they were passing around like a cheerleader made me jittery.

I watched for a while, then I stood up and eased down the bar to have a better look. The bartender eyed me, but said nothing. None of the wild boys noticed me at first, but when I passed closer to the booth on my way to the men's room the girl suddenly quit everything else she was doing and locked her eyes on me.

It was dark back there, or at least dim, but in the green glow of the EXIT light she seemed to smile like she *recognized* me and was about to cry out my name.

At first glance she was a stunningly beautiful woman—red hair and long legs in a tight-fitting business suit that looked almost prim, except that the front of her linen skirt was slit straight up to her groin.

Hands were grasping and groping at her; and suddenly, she kicked off her high-heeled Capezios and jumped up on the red leather seat, shrieking and kicking at her tormentors.

It was all in good fun; they were all laughing—but there was a strange high edge on the laughter that made me uneasy . . . or maybe it's just *me,* I thought. I had just averaged 88.26 miles an hour between the Bay Bridge and the Sacramento River in a custom-built 1969 mandarin-red V-8 427 Chevy convertible with a Turbo-Latham supercharger, and it had left me a little tense. My forearms were still vibrating crazily from the rolling vise grip I'd been keeping on the wheel. My fingers were so numb that I had to flex my whole hand a few times before I could lift the margarita glass to my lips.

"Bad business," I said to the bartender. "What's *happening* down there? A gang rape?"

He flinched, then he smiled professionally and said, "Naw, that's just a bunch of the local hustlers havin' a birthday party. Sorry. I'll tell 'em to hold it down."

"Nonsense," I said. "There's all kinds of rape going on these days. It's normal. We'd be *crazy* to complain about it." Then I seized him firmly by both shoulders. "But let me ask you something," I said. "Do you remember Kitty Genovese?"

"Not really," he said. "Did she work here?"

I stared at him for a moment. "They stabbed her forty-seven times," I said. "It was in a public place like *this* and many people watched her being killed by a gang of street thugs. . . . But nobody tried to help her. They just *watched.* They said they didn't want to interfere in her personal life. . . . Some of them said she looked like she was having a good time."

He shook his head sadly. "Jesus!" he said. "I'm really *sorry.*" Then he nodded at my glass. "Are you ready for another one?"

"Sure," I said. "This violence is making me sick."

Just then we heard a burst of wild laughter and breaking glass from inside the ladies' room. The red leather booth was empty.

"You crazy bitch!" the bartender screamed as he ran back and kicked the door open. . . . Seconds later he emerged, dragging the red-headed woman by one arm. "You slut!" he was yelling. "You're finished in this place. Get out, and stay out!"

He had her almost through the front door when she broke out of his grip and rushed over to me. "Please help me!" she begged. "Please take me away from here."

I grabbed her by the arm. What the hell? I thought. I'm leaving anyway. We ran outside to where my heavy red convertible was parked next to a fireplug. She jumped into the front seat while I swooped a traffic citation off the front window. "Hurry!" she yelled. "Let's get out of here. I can't be *seen* with you."

We boomed away from the curb in a long screech of rubber.

The girl was laughing, and I noticed she was sitting pretty high on the seat for somebody who didn't want to be seen with me. Suddenly she reached over and snatched the traffic ticket off my lap. "Don't worry about this thing," she said. "My boyfriend will take care of it," and she stuffed it into her briefcase.

"Wonderful," I said. "He must be a nice guy."

"He is," she chirped. "He's a very powerful man in the capital."

I glanced across at her. We were still rumbling along J Street in first gear, coughing up fuel mist and occasionally backfiring long blasts of flame out of the tailpipe.

"I like this car," she said, as we screeched onto the freeway and the supercharger kicked in.

"Yeah," she said dreamily. "This is more like it. I want to drive fast!"

"Where?" I asked.

"Reno," she said quickly. "Let's go to Reno and get married." She slid across the seat and grasped my leg. Then she sat up higher, and her hair blew straight back in the wind as we eased into the fast lane. At the next exit we passed under a big green sign that said, "Reno— 133."

STRANGE RIDE TO RENO

On the way out of town the car radio said it was 90 below zero in Butte, Montana, on Groundhog Day, which meant thirteen more weeks of winter and deep snow in the Rockies until June. . . . It was hideous news, but my fiancée was laughing wickedly.

"Perfect," she exclaimed. "The perfect honeymoon—snowed in for thirteen straight weeks."

I drove for a while and said nothing, just feeling her breathing and jabbering and vibrating like a strange instrument against my ribs as she curled up next to me and punched in a savage Warren Zevon tape—"Lawyers, Guns and Money"—an old tune, mean and crazy, but somehow it was right. . . . I felt fine.

It was a good day to be driving fast and happy, booming up the mountain in a hot-rod Chevy with a beautiful girl wrapped around me and headed for some all-night marriage parlor in Reno.

Earlier that morning, I was just another mean drifter speeding across the Bay Bridge in a flashy car with a brown bag full of hundred-dollar bills. . . . Heading east and over the hump to Colorado, fleeing the city and definitely not looking for anything strange—then I'd stopped for lunch and wandered straight through the looking glass. It was free-fall now, like one of those sudden Acid Flashbacks that they've been promising us all these years.

We were almost to Loomis when Jilly remembered that she had left her purse back at the bar in Sacramento. "Goddamnit," she moaned. "We'll have to go back for it. We have to turn around."

"Forget the purse," I said. "I have plenty of money." I reached under the seat and grabbed a fistful of hundreds out of the rumpled lunch bag. "Look at this," I said. "We're richer than Judas."

She shook her head. "No, I need my ID," she said. "You can't get married in Reno without ID."

So what? I thought. From what she'd told me about her boyfriend, I figured he would have his people after us by now—maybe even the highway patrol—for kidnapping.

I had understood from the start that I had some kind of bomb on my hands. It was not like I'd picked up a hitchhiker.

No, this was a very expensive woman—and I had, in fact, grabbed her out of a downtown political bar at lunchtime and run away with her. There were many witnesses, and my car was very visible. . . . And now we were on our way to Reno to get married.

That is not the kind of news any big-time powermonger wants to hear when he gets back from lunch in the governor's dining room: *Pardon me, sir, but the whole town is humming with the news about your girlfriend disappearing out of Ricci's with a bald drifter in a hopped-up Chevy convertible with Colorado plates. . . . The phone is ringing off the hook. What should I tell them?*

What indeed? And what should *I* tell them when we are stopped at a CHP roadblock on the outskirts of Truckee and her boyfriend swoops down in a helicopter and orders men in black suits to beat a confession out of me?

And what would *she* say? That we had fallen in love at first sight in the midst of an orgy at lunchtime and she had suddenly changed her mind about everything in her life?

Probably not. They would drag me away in steel-mesh animal net and execute me like Caryl Chessman. Any story I told would mean nothing, compared to hers. My fate was in her hands.

Feeling crazy has never really worried me. It is an occupational hazard and on some days I even get paid for it—but there are some things that even crazy people can't get away with, and this idea of turning around and driving back to Sacramento to pick up Jilly's birth certificate seemed to be one of them.

"Don't worry about *him*," she said. "He's having dinner with some tax lobbyists tonight. I'll just run in and get a little suitcase. It won't take two minutes."

I shrugged and turned around. What the hell? I thought. Buy the ticket, take the ride. There was madness in either direction. And besides, I was beginning to like the girl.

She was a dangerous dingbat with a very pure dedication to the Love and Adventure ethic—but I recognized a *warrior* when I met one, and on the way down the mountain I knew what Clyde must have felt like when he first met Bonnie.

OMNIA VINCIT AMOR

"We that are true lovers run into strange capers."
—Shakespeare

My heart was full of hate as we zoomed back down the hill to Sacramento, but I couldn't quite put it in focus. George Bush was on the radio, talking to Congress about justice for Puerto Ricans . . . but the sound of his voice was like Lithium Grease in my ears and my fiancée was babbling incessantly about her money-mad brute of a boyfriend.

"He watches me like a hawk," she was saying. "He clings to my back like a tick. I can't escape."

I laughed harshly and gave her a hard slap to the throat that caused her eyeballs to roll back in her head. She tried to screech, but no sound came out of her mouth . . . and just as I started to smile I saw her fist right in front of my face and then felt a whack of bone against bone that made me go blind.

There was a crazy look in her eyes for a moment, then she laughed and stretched out on the seat with her head in my lap. "Let's get some whiskey," she said. "There's a liquor store up here on the next corner. I can *charge* there."

We were almost to where she lived, she said, but she wanted to have a few drinks before slipping into the house. "I'm sure he's not there," she said, "but I still feel nervous."

We pulled into the parking lot of the liquor store and she gave me a long kiss before we went inside. The top was down and the bright red Chevy seemed to glow like a rolling bonfire. I felt a little queasy about necking openly under a street light in her own neighborhood, but she said it didn't matter.

"Who cares?" she giggled. "We're almost newlyweds."

Another wave of queasiness rolled over me, but I ignored it. . . . The store was full of rich-looking men fussing over the fine wine selection, but we went straight to the whiskey rack. It looked like a long night coming up, so I got two liters of Royal Salute, a tall bottle of 110-proof green Chartreuse, and a half-gallon of Chivas for backup.

At the cash register I noticed a tabloid with a big headline saying:

VULTURES ATTACK FUNERAL
AND EAT THE CORPSE

It was a heinous story: "Relatives and friends were sickened as they watched the fierce predators tearing away at the flesh of their loved one."

It happened in Poland, where a flock of huge meat-eating birds circled over the cemetery, squawking and croaking ominously as the casket was carried toward the grave—then suddenly swooped down and attacked the six pallbearers so savagely that one man had his scalp clawed off and another lost an eyeball. They panicked and fled, dropping the casket on the street and letting the corpse roll out. Stunned townspeople stood by helplessly, weeping as a horde of bloodthirsty birds carried the corpse away. . . . One relative said the vultures were squabbling hysterically over chunks of loose flesh.

• • •

I have always admired Polish journalism. There is a different rhythm to it, a brazenly off-center point of view that allows for unique perceptions. . . . But there was no time for scholarly reflection now: we were out on the boulevard again, driving slowly toward Jilly's house.

It was on a tree-lined street in a high-rent district not far from the Capitol—a brick townhouse with white pillars. I found a dark spot across the street and parked in the half-shadow of a big elm tree, then I felt her tongue in my mouth.

We were making so much noise that I decided to put the top up—which seemed to offend her. "I *told* you," she snapped. "He's *gone*. He's sniveling around at one of his goddamn *business dinners*. That's all he cares about."

"Not like us," I said. "We hear the *real* music."

She slid across the seat and got out. "I'll be right back," she said. "This won't take a minute."

I watched as she pranced gracefully across the lawn in her high-heeled shoes and disappeared through the front door. . . . Well, I thought, this must be what General MacArthur had in mind when he made his famous speech about the "Pitfalls of Unrealism."

For the first time all day I realized that this woman was serious. I was about to get married to a total stranger. She had made me drive all the way back here just to get her birth certificate.

I relaxed and turned up the radio. It was George Bush again—a news rehash of his speech about shame in Puerto Rico and the need to strip elderly welfare cheats off the Medicaid dole.

That swine! I thought. He's sleazier than Nixon. . . . Never mind that giddy swill James Baker puts out about how George loves to hum Dylan tunes while racing his Cigarette boat across the waters. . . .

Probably John Tower likes to go out with him. Load up on booze and a gaggle of wild women, then crank up the speakers and make a berserk run on the dock at 90 mph . . . scare the landlubbers into a coma.

Good old George. You can take the boy out of Yale, but you can't take Yale out of the boy. It's the same goatish attitude that got him mixed up with a loose cannon like Oliver North in the first place. Just an ungovernable hunger for life.

Suddenly, I heard a wild outburst of shouting from the direction of Jilly's house. "You drunken bitch!" a man's voice screamed. "You can't get away with this! I'll have you both locked up!" Then I heard a babble of cursing and her spike heels clattering on the asphalt as she sprinted across the street and jumped into the car.

"Let's go!" she yelled. "He's gone crazy! He grabbed me by the neck!"

The man was still screaming as I hammered the car into gear and roared away from the curb with my lights off. What the hell? I thought. Let's go to Reno.

THE DEATH OF RUSSELL CHATHAM

My fiancée was laughing hysterically as I flogged the car at top speed through the quiet streets of her old neighborhood, with my headlights off and the white canvas top flapping wildly out behind us like a ripped spinnaker. A green mist flared out of her mouth and blew back in her long red hair as she collapsed in the seat and sucked frantically on the bottle of green Chartreuse.

We were going to stop at Ricci's on our way out of town, to pick up her purse. She had managed to grab her birth certificate out of the house, but her boyfriend jumped her before she could pack any clothes.

"He tried to choke me," she said. "He was like a maniac. He bit me." I looked over and saw that her elegant silk blouse was shredded almost down to her waist and the once-stylish slit in the front of her skirt was now a gaping hole.

Going back to Ricci's made me nervous—especially with the berserk screams of her boyfriend still ringing in my ears—but she insisted on getting her purse.

It made sense, at the time. We were gripped in the throes of a very fast day—one of those rare little humdingers that comes along once in a while and scares you all the way out to that delicate point where fear turns into fun. . . . And now I had a *partner,* a full-bore whacko who was definitely prepared to rumble. And also to *prevail.*

That is a special attitude which not everybody understands. . . . But I did, and by the time we got to Ricci's I understood our situation well enough to know that my real problem was that I'd fallen in love with this woman, and that the next few minutes or hours or maybe even weeks of our life would be like rolling thunder and far too fast for logic.

I pulled up in front of Ricci's. The only other car parked nearby was a queer-looking, hump-back truck with huge wheels and black windows. I made a quick U-turn and tucked the convertible in right behind it, trying to stay in the shadows.

It was a Lamborghini Jeep with no color at all—a stainless-steel brute of a machine with six wheels and bulletproof windows and a .50-caliber machine gun mounted behind the cab.

Jilly leaned over and kissed me—then she slid across the seat and opened the door.

"Don't worry," she whispered. "Dave's working tonight. He's a friend. I trust him completely."

Just then, a huge Japanese gentleman stepped out of the Lamborghini—and Jilly went wild. She leaped back in the car and screamed, "O God! It's *them!* The *Yakuza!* They know me. They work for *him.*"

I slammed the car into low and took off, once again for wherever we were going . . . and the Lamborghini pulled out right behind me.

I knew the Yakuza: they were a gang of tattooed thugs out of Tokyo who got into the Power Business by offering a debt-collection service that included dumping a truckload of pig entrails in the front yard of anybody who owed money.

They made no secret of their skills—if only because they *worked.*

There are a lot of ways to fend off the bill collector, but getting nasty with people who are about to dump 600 raw swine bladders on your front porch is not one of them.

Jilly was hysterical as the huge Lamborghini pursued us through one red light after another along J Street at 90 mph . . . and I knew they were only in third gear. A recent road test on the "Lambo" said it will do 109 in fourth and 133 on a downhill glass road in fifth. . . .

So I knew we were doomed when the brute came up beside me at 110.

On the Road to Reno, 1989

Editor's Note

At this point in the editorial process Dr. Thompson was tragically interrupted by a telephone call regarding the horrible death of his long-time friend and spiritual adviser, Russell Chatham, the famous Montana artist.

Thompson went immediately into seclusion after hearing the news and we were forced to suspend publication of Part IV in his long-awaited classic: *Jilly and the Night Manager.*

The saga will continue whenever Dr. Thompson is able to conquer his grief and write professionally once again.

Close friends say he is "feeling fine," but doubts remain in the journalistic community about Thompson's ability to shrug off the shock of Chatham's ghastly death.

First reports said the artist was fly-fishing in a river near his home when he was accidentally hooked by a trolling boat and dragged away into deep water—then stabbed to death by members of the boating party who "reeled him in and gaffed him like a big catfish," they said—unaware that they were slaughtering a famous human being.

Meanwhile—at Thompson's crude and disturbing log home in Woody Creek, Colorado—his crafty executive counselor, Semmes Luckett, stunned a hastily called press conference by confirming that Dr. Thompson will be formal executor of Chatham's earthly estate and sole trustee of a bizarre handwritten scroll of "Personal Bequeathments" by the artist, long known as "profoundly eccentric" and a hillbilly dilettante who somehow accumulated great wealth.

Thompson's fee alone—as executor—will be 22 percent or $22 million, whichever is greater.

Luckett also confirmed that Dr. Thompson will leave "very soon" for an extended tour of Australia.

WHISKEY BUSINESS

IN A RECENT attempt to avoid the hellish clamor of my nine telephones, I became secretive and added a fourth private line, with yet another secret number—which resulted almost immediately in a tragic misunderstanding.

One of the first calls on the new line was a harrowing piece of news about the public murder of my old friend Russell Chatham, the legendary Montana artist, which soon proved to be utterly unfounded and caused outbursts of hysterical grief among many of his friends and business associates.

The story was so gruesome that only a fiend could have dreamed it. . . . The artist was said to have been seining for gold nuggets in a river near his home, wearing a black-rubber hooded jumpsuit, when he was accidentally hooked by a passing trolling boat and dragged for several miles upriver before he was reeled in and stabbed repeatedly with gaffing hooks and spears by members of the fishing party.

"He fought like a two-thousand-pound marlin," one was allegedly quoted as saying, "but he only weighed two hundred pounds. It was scary. We thought we'd hooked one of those goddamn sea monsters that you always hear about. It took us almost an hour to get him into the boat—and then I heard him yelling and snarling in English, which drove us all crazy with fear—and then, O God, the hood slipped back on his head and we saw it was not a fish!"

The origin of the rumor is still a mystery, although many in the art world suspect it was a plot by Korean speculators to drive up the price of Chatham's work—already skyrocketing—and then sell it back for huge profit to grieving friends and market-conscious collectors.

The artist himself was unavailable for comment, except through a battery of tort lawyers who were said, last week, to be busy taking orders for his new series of large oils on dead and dying animals, rendered in miniature against dismal winter backgrounds.

"Russell has gone beyond himself, this time," said one friend. "He is a thousand years old, but he has the heart of a fawn."

The phone rang again just before midnight. Semmes picked it up and muttered something about "decent people being asleep at this hour." A long silence followed, and then I heard him cry out, "Good God almighty!"

"What now?" I asked, as he turned to hand me the phone. I figured it was another whack of bad news.

The blood had drained out of his face and his eyes had narrowed to slits. "You better get some whiskey," he said. "This one is over the line."

I grabbed a bottle of pisco, then took the phone. It was a lawyer from Washington, who said he was part of the Bush transition team and could speak with me only if I swore I would never mention his name. The message he was about to give me, he said, was "Top Secret and extremely volatile."

"How did you get this goddamn phone number?" I shouted. "I've had it for only eight hours."

"It was easy," he said calmly. "There *are* no secrets—not for *us*."

"OK," I said. "What do you want? I'm innocent."

He laughed. "I know that," he said. "That's exactly why I'm calling. We have a job for you."

"Wonderful," I said. "How much does it pay?"

"Never mind that," he said. "This is a crisis. The president is about to dump Tower and he needs another nominee by morning. . . . And you're it," he hissed. "Are you ready to be secretary of defense?"

I felt sick, although it came as no surprise. Revenge is one of the few things in politics that never gets lost in the mail or written off for a dime on the dollar like losers' campaign debts or pledges to help the Poor.

No. Revenge is a timeless mandate in that world inside the Beltway. . . . Ask John Tower. He spent twenty-eight years in Washington, but he never paid his dues. So when he came back to take over the Pentagon, his old buddies in the Senate treated him like a skunk. They called him a sot and a whore-hopper, a walking booze-barrel with three legs. . . .

And now they wanted me.

"You evil bastard!" I shouted. "They'll rip me to shreds."

He chuckled. "Don't worry," he said. "George will defend you all the way to the end. You know how *loyal* he is—he read that piece you wrote about him being so *misunderstood,* and he feels he *owes* you something."

Indeed, I thought—a public flogging on national TV, then getting shipped out of Washington in a body bag while the president shakes his head sadly and bemoans the new wave of puritanical hysteria that is wrecking the lives of so many true patriots by dwelling on their vices instead of their virtues. . . .

It was brilliant strategic thinking—a naked pitch for the Whiskey Vote, for the one huge constituency that he will need for reelection in 1992 if the Democrats manage to nominate anybody who seems human: he will have to run against a sitting president who secretly weeps for the boozers he did everything in his power to include in his inner circle, because of their brilliance and their doomed humanism.

I almost felt a lump in my throat. "Remember the cruel purges of '89," they will ask, "when the wild boys were put on trial? Who was it, back then, who came down on the side of Sex, Drugs, and Rock and Roll?"

Ye gods. It was George Bush, the ex-wimp who once ran the War on Drugs and who refused to give up the one split of wine cooler that he always drinks after dinner.

Res Ipsa Loquitor.

Woody Creek, March 6, 1989

I KNEW THE BRIDE WHEN
SHE USED TO ROCK
AND ROLL

EVIL DAYS ARE common in this world, and they always draw blood in one way or another—but there are some days that draw more blood than even a human tick or a pimping bankrupt eunuch from Sacramento can afford to lose.

It is like being caught in a bad surf and banged off the bottom so many times that after a while you start thinking you can actually *breathe* the salt-water foam that you are thrashing around in when you finally erupt into what looks like real air.

But "there are many Coons in the Wilderness," as the Prophet Booar has said; "and Coons feed like vultures and cannibals on failure and broken dreams."

"There are no switchbacks on the road to Truth and Beauty," said Booar, "and there is no path so high or so secret that it will not lead, in the end, to some Final Doorway guarded by a vicious Coon full of Mandrax who will never open the Door."

It is a baleful vision—despite Booar's status as a guru to the financial community—but it is no less baleful than the new wave of rigid *Boy in the Bubble* zeal that is sweeping the nation today.

The fallout is all around us in the form of rubbers, reformers, and overcrowded jails—but it can be a very nasty tide to go against. The body Nazis *are* out there, and even the preachers in prison for compound sodomy and child rape are compiling lists of names.

One of these who will be called soon enough to the tribunals is a hoary political philosopher from Salida, Colorado, named Ed Quillen, who recently published a screed on Morality at the End of the Eighties.

"No one seems to have noticed that the most powerful force in American society these days must be the Purity League," Quillen wrote. "The Purity League believes that people who are not in a state of perfect grace have nothing to contribute. Our society now judges people not by what they do, but by what they don't do. Any mediocrity who can pass a urine test somehow becomes superior to a talent who can't. . . .

"Ray Charles did his most brilliant work during the years he was addicted to heroin. Keith Richards has confessed that he was a total junkie, living from one fix to the next, when "Exile on Main Street" was recorded, and that album has more great loud and dirty rock and roll on it than any dozen recordings by people who could pass blood tests.

"And it isn't just musicians. . . . Do we want to ignore the contributions that were made by William Stewart Halsted to medicine? Sterile operating rooms, thin rubber gloves, residencies for training—most of what we think of as modern surgery was invented by Halsted at Johns Hopkins from 1890 to 1922. During that entire time, Halsted had a morphine habit.

"Should we go without electric lights, phonographs, motion pictures, fluoroscopes, alkaline batteries, and dictating machines? Those were among the inventions of Thomas Edison, a man who slept only two hours a night and gladly endorsed a concoction whose major active ingredient was cocaine.

"Who contributed more to the political structure of America: Jimmy Carter, pure in all things great and small? Or Franklin D. Roosevelt, with his daily nip, his jutting Camel, and his mistresses?"

Last year was not a good one for The Moral Majority and others of the *Cleaner Than Thou* ilk—but the weight of their sleazy, hypocritical bullshit is still heavy on the scales of our time.

No once-wild "party" in Hollywood or Aspen or even Greenwich Village is complete, these days, without the overweening presence of superwealthy, hard-hitting ex-addicts, "recovering alcoholics," and beady-eyed fat women who never let you forget that they "used to hang out" with doomed friends and dead monsters like Janis, Jim Morrison, The Stones, or John Belushi, or even me. . . .

They roam the chic anterooms of movies and music and publishing like vengeful *golems* from some lost and broken Peter Pan world of Sex, Drugs, and Rock and Roll, and other unspeakable tragedies that crippled the lives and crazed the souls of . . . *so many.*

Yes, so many. . . .

So many.

Indeed, we were *all* snapped like matchsticks in that terrible conflagration—and the unexplainable few who survived, somehow, are now like the victims of some drunken golfing foursome that got so wiggy and disgusting by the time they finished the First Nine that God sent a lightning bolt down from the black cloudy heavens to hit them like a bomb while they gamboled like maddened sheep on the big wet green on No. 16.

Their flesh and their brains and their precious bodily organs were burned to cinders and black-chalk skeletons that will never again have *real strength.*

They will walk in the world forever like some strung-out collection of Ming vases that might crack any time they are touched.

Woody Creek, 1989

COMMUNITY OF WHORES

"Just how weird can you have it, brother— before your love will crack?"
—MIKE LYDON, in *RAMPARTS*, March 1970

SPRING IN THE Rockies is an ugly time. People get weird and embittered from too many months of winter. Especially in Aspen, where absentee greedheads are taking over the town like a pack of wild dogs, reducing the once proud local population to shame and degradation.

"We are all like whores now," said one ex-rancher who had just sold his land to a combine of Arabs. "First they suck up your land, then they force you to bend over."

Ten years ago, you could run a political campaign in this town for $1,100 and still be accused by your opponent of acting like a Texas-style vote buyer. But things are different now. Aspen is a big-time tourist town, and only two kinds of people live here—the Users and the Used—and the gap between them gets wider every day.

What was once the capital of Freak Power has rolled over and is now a slavish service community of pimps and middlemen where the only real question in politics is "How much money do you have?" The prices are so high that even Donald Trump was run out of town when he tried to muscle into the new high-dollar high-rise hotel industry.

"I used to live in a brick ranch house on top of Red Mountain that had four fireplaces and a pond ten feet deep," said the ex-rancher, "but now I live forty miles down valley in a trailer court. Every day, we drive two hours in a traffic jam just to get to work. And when we drive back down valley at night, the cops wait for us in the shadows."

His eyes were like two kiwi fruits jammed into a face gray and swollen with drink. He was a defeated man.

"They took my license a long time ago and I know I'll never get it back. . . . They have us in a vise and it's hopeless."

Most people have given up on politics entirely, but there are still a few diehards who will manage to grab a public office now and then like the sheriff, and the mayor, who was chairman of some sort of campaign committee for Jackson last year. He raised large amounts of money, but it was chicken feed compared to the contributions raised here by Ollie North for his defense.

My friend Cromwell is not running for office this year, but he is deeply involved in the City Council election this week. Cromwell hates greedheads, and his hatred keeps him in politics.

I was feeding the peacocks last week when he called me from the tavern and said he needed help.

"Get down here quick," he said. "I'm in trouble. Bring your cameras. There'll be a fight. And bring that rocket bomb gun. You may have to fire it into the crowd."

When I got down to the tavern I found Cromwell at the far end of the parking lot in the cab of his huge black power wagon drinking whiskey. He was hunkered down, muttering to himself as he carefully traced the words ---- EXXON on a tear-gas bomb. He was acting furtive.

"What's wrong with you?" I said. "Who's after you? We'll crush the buggers." I was in a giddy sort of mood, feeling suddenly mean.

Cromwell was gazing across the street at a crowd of giggling jabbering bicyclists swarming around on the patio.

"Look at those bastards," he snarled. "They're like gold-plated rats. We should round them up like sheep and send them to Alaska to clean up that oil spill."

His heart was full of hate and he had a serious attack plan. The beast in him was coming out. I knew he hated bicyclists and everything they stand for. And he was violently mad about the monstrous Exxon oil spill up in Prince William Sound.

I filmed the whole thing, more or less for posterity. But it was really not much. Just a lot of green smoke and people groping around in the fog and screaming at each other about "poison gas" and "call the police."

The bicycle people were bitter about having their lunch meat turned green, but they never got the point. It was a *political protest*—against them—but the next day a paper quoted one of their spokesmen as saying a maniac did it "to liven the place up."

Cromwell called it a failure and blamed himself for "not strangling one of those yuppie newts" before he herded them all inside and secured the front door—from the outside—with a Harley-Davidson chain lock, after tossing the bomb inside. . . . I had already jammed the back door shut with a snow shovel, and by the time I got the F1000 rolling out in front, thick green smoke was pouring out both windows and the people inside were making a lot of noise as they battered the door open with heavy wooden bar stools.

It was hard to see, but I let the camera roll anyway as the angry mob spilled out. They turned on me after Cromwell fled, so I drove back home and put my new video film on TV, just to see what I had.

The F1000 had seen a few things that I'd missed: mainly faces, and some were very clear. . . . And then I saw *her,* moving through the smoke and staring straight into my lens, and she was smiling the same crazy smile that I remembered from the first time I met her.

Ye gods! It was *her!* Jilly! My long-lost bride from Sacramento.

Woody Creek, May 1, 1989

RETURN TO THE RIVIERA CAFE

CHARACTER IS DESTINY

RICHARD NIXON TOLD me that, the first time we met, and I have never forgotten it. He was wrong from the start, but he won constantly at the polls. Nixon was elected to every office he ever ran for, except the governorship of California, which he lost in a frenzy of rage that caused him to quit politics and screech at the press: "Okay, you sons of bitches. This is *it*. You won't have Richard Nixon to kick around anymore!"

It was, of course, a lie—the first of many huge ones, and the bugger is still at it: now he is telling Selected Insiders that George Bush will soon offer him the ambassador's job in China. . . .

But that is nonsense. George will send *me* to China before he will send Nixon. I have never claimed to have a secret grasp on the complexities of the Oriental mind, but I am somehow in perfect tune with the Chinese sense of humor. . . . They laugh *with* Nixon—which is hard work—but they laugh *at* me, which is fun; and in truth I have never met a Chinaman I didn't like. I have traveled extensively in the Orient—usually on the Chinese Network—and I have always been treated graciously, on a level of communication far deeper than any language. If it is true that Character is, in fact, Destiny, then I will end my political career as the U.S. Ambassador to China . . . much in the manner of former Senator Mike Mansfield (D–Mont.) who finally saw the light: after running the Senate in his own image for thirty-three years, he quit and moved to Tokyo and lived like an emperor on the roof of the U.S. Embassy, like an echo of Douglas MacArthur. . . .

Or almost. MacArthur ruled the Japanese, and now the Japanese rule the world.

What? Is that true?

No. It is a classic Political Exaggeration. . . . But so what? The diplomatic business is always a two-way street, and since Mansfield went to Tokyo the Japs have been persuaded to abandon their traditional low sense of self-esteem and somehow purchased Rockefeller Center, The Bank of America, etc., etc., etc., and Mike will be buried in Kyoto.

Shit happens.

But never mind. I digress. We were talking about Sheridan Square and the many beatings I received there, for no good reason at all. The Riviera Cafe has been a main anchor of my socio-political universe for many years. I used to get my mail there, in one of the pigeonhole boxes next to the bulletin board just inside the front door. . . . That was when I was just another one of the neighborhood kids, a dumb brute with a huge brain and no money.

Indeed. But we overcame that. I picked up the torch dropped by Kerouac and went on to become rich and famous, more or less. . . . That is the conventional wisdom, and I have done my best to honor it and lend it credibility for lo these many years.

The truth is that I am still poor as a church-house rat and I have been severely beaten many times, just for trying to tell the truth. My life has been a series of tragic misunderstandings and my body is covered with scars—many of them incurred within crawling distance of the front door of the infamous Riviera Cafe. . . . The most recent incident, a clash with a gang of skinheads while I was on my way to Washington, happened within weeks of the thirtieth anniversary of the night when I tried to deliver a fifty-pound bag of what they called "lye" to the executive bar manager and was beaten stupid for my efforts. That is a true story, and so is the next one, which I wrote under an assumed name in an unpublished novel titled *Prince Jellyfish,* in 1959 when I lived in an illegal sub-basement at 57 Perry Street and learned most of what I know today, in re: Personal and Professional Relationships, from the relentlessly brutal Superintendent, a sixty-year-old black man named Sam who ran his building the same way Ronald Reagan ran the world. . . .

It was mainly a matter of illusion, but they both got away with it . . . so far, at least: Sam is dead and Reagan, if there is any justice in the world, will soon be forced by our spastic court system to yield up his personal diaries and be impeached *in absentia,* along with his creature, George Bush.

You bet. One of the first things I learned at the Columbia Law School is that "justice is the whim of the judge," and I have never forgotten it—along with Mr. Nixon's wisdom about Character and Destiny.

The world is still a weird place, despite my efforts to make clear and perfect sense of it. I have been cheated, beaten, and duped for thirty-three straight years, since Sam sent me out on the Proud Highway with his one main whack of advice: "We are *right,* and we *must* have our way."

I have tried to do this—just as the hapless Welburn Kemp (see "Prince Jellyfish") was right in his brain and pure in his heart when he followed that woman home from the subway station, because he sensed she was lonely. . . .

Res Ipsa Loquitor.

Woody Creek, 1989

AVERY: MAKING SENSE OF THE '60s

EDITOR'S NOTE

In response to numerous inquiries as to the whereabouts of Dr. Thompson, we reprint the following intercepted communique from the doctor's private secretary in reply to an invitation to be interviewed for a PBS documentary on the meaning of the '60s.

To: Carol Rissman/Character Research
From: HST/Avery
Re: "Making Sense of the '60s"

WE RECEIVED YOUR Fax message about the Doomed Generation '60s program and Dr. Thompson was profoundly excited by it. You'll be happy to know that he is recovering satisfactorily from his recent accident, when he was run over by a tractor pulling a Bush Hog.

We can only pray that his memory returns by Labor Day. But in any case he is eager to talk with you. . . . Indeed, he speaks of little else, and he has asked me to give you a list of high-powered electric gimcracks that he hopes you can locate and bring with you on the first major shoot. I will send you the list just as soon as we get a grip on Dr. Thompson's projected *role* in this saga. . . . He has his own notions, of course, but I no longer fear them and I know we can all work together on a plane of perfect happiness.

Don't worry. I can handle him.

You're aware, I'm sure, that he has recently become an avid polo player and also an award-winning male model in both Europe and the U.S.—none of which will be affected in any way by his persistent abulia and memory loss, although at the moment he remembers *nothing* prior to July 1, 1989. Only music can reach him now, but his physician, Dr. Walker, assures us that total restoration is inevitable, and that it might occur at any moment.

Don't worry. We are not talking about a normal human being here. Dr. Thompson once had his whole right hand cut off by a Cigarette Boat propeller, and then grew another hand back in its place before they could get him to the hospital.

It was eerie, but it worked, and nobody ever mentioned it again. The hand is his only vanity. And it still works perfectly. He has amazing Feel-and-Fling with the polo mallet, and it is well to remember that, in his youth, he was a famous local jockey at Churchill Downs, where he began as an exercise boy.

Yeah. And that's about it, Carol. I am not prepared, at this time, to get into the *character* issue. There are some things you just don't need at this hour of the morning, and discussing that evil bastard's *character* is one of them.

Only one person has ever dared to do that in public—and that was the eminent White House factotum, Patrick Buchanan, who will go down in history as the man who first introduced Dr. Thompson to Richard Nixon and also arranged their famous *Midnight Summit Conference on the Nature and Fate of Football in America* in a yellow Mercury on the Mass Turnpike in March of 1968.

(Jesus! Is that *true?*

Yeah. It is. That bastard! That swinish pig-eyed bully! To throw a cub reporter from Haight Street and Berkeley, wearing a ski jacket and a red SDS button, into a personal no-exit pit with Richard Nixon in the sudden full flower of his comeback. . . .

That is *mean*. That is extremely bad karma. . . .)

And Buchanan had better hope that God is not really a Buddhist like they say, because he will come back in the Next Life as a dung-eating rat in Calcutta, scuttling around the garbage heaps on drenching monsoon nights with only a dim genetic leak in his memory to remind him of those days of power and glory when he walked tall like a yeti in Washington and wrote speeches for Spiro Agnew and counseled Nixon to burn all his Watergate tapes and even taught Ronald Reagan how to deal with the media forever and George Bush how to act innocent in front of a TV camera. . . .

Good old Patrick. He thought Goldwater was a pansy and confiscated mini-bottles of gin out of Nixon's shaving kit. . . . It is horrible, but true: The Black Irish will always be with us. Like hyenas. Cruel and Besotted. Always with blood under their fingernails and their eyes crazy for revenge. . . . How long, O Lord, how long?

Ah, but I digress. It is late, and the sudden sight of The Doctor loading his ponies into a long silver trailer has made me giddy. . . . There is a woman with him, but I can't see her face. She has long blonde hair and laughs constantly while he does most of the horse-work.

I think he is crazy. How can a person be sane when a Bush Hog cuts off one leg and half of your skull? The leg grew back immediately, but the skull is a different matter. There is only so much magic in the world. . . .

Yes. Never doubt it, Carol. The fat can go into the fire at any moment, and we will all be fried like offal. I look forward to working with you, but I fear it—as I fear almost everything these days, and just because I'm religious doesn't mean I can't get weird.

Sincerely,

Avery
Woody Creek, 1989

GERMAN DECADE: THE RISE OF THE FOURTH REICH

A TALL BLOND MAN with flashing blue eyes came into the Riviera Cafe and started slapping people around. "Sieg heil!" he screamed. "Ich bin ein Berliner!"

It was midnight on Saturday in Greenwich Village, and I was hunkered down at the bar, watching the news on TV—gangs of wild Germans swarmed over the Berlin Wall. A huge crowd on both sides of the Brandenburg Gate was singing "Deutschland über Alles" while others waved fistfuls of money.

"Free at last!" a man screamed. "Down with the Communist pigs! We will march on a road of bones."

Indeed the war was over. The Red Menace was on the run. Total victory and no blood. The beast with two backs had finally come together.

A woman sitting next to me dabbed at her eyes with a handkerchief and said, "I wish I could be with George Bush tonight."

"Why?" I asked. For some queer reason, I had been thinking the same thing myself.

"You know why," she said, a faraway look in her eyes. "There is something magic about the man."

Which was true. George is a winner. He had triumphed—and now he was presiding over the collapse of the whole Communist empire. Sieg heil, democracy! They laughed at Woodrow Wilson.

Bush has inherited the wind once again. He is a human windsock. Whatever happens in Germany or anywhere else can never be blamed on him. George has been a success in every job he's had. He's a damage-control expert, a very good driver in a very fast lane, and we haven't given him credit for that.

The woman leaned over and seized me by the arm. "Let's go to Washington!" she said. "I want to be with him."

Why not? I thought. I was, after all, a charter member of the Presidental Task Force. It was time to call in some chips. The woman had her own reasons, but so what? We were patriots, and I had a fast car.

Suddenly a fight broke out in the doorway. The tall blond man had the manager in a headlock and was screaming in German.

We fled, but there was another fight in the street. A gang of skinheads had attacked some elderly Jews and was trying to shave their heads. Others were painting swastikas on parked cars.

The woman was dragged away by strangers. I tried to help her but I was clubbed on the head and fell unconscious.

Later, from jail, I spoke directly to the White House and had many people arrested. But I never saw the woman again.

CROMWELL'S FEARS

The incident traumatized me, and by midnight I was back home in the mountains. To hell with these trips to the East Coast, I thought. The whole place is a festering chancre. I chained my front gate and swore to lay low for a while.

Then my old friend Cromwell showed up with his son, Manqué, and bashed the lock off the gate. It was long after midnight, but he was desperate, he said. Nazis had burned his house. His eyes were small and red from driving for hours through a blizzard on a Fat Bob Harley, and I could see that his nerves had gone raw.

"We will soon be the Germans' slaves," he said. "This is the time of the Living Dead. We are doomed."

"Nonsense," I said. "Come inside. I have a fire and whiskey and powerful music. We will crank up the speakers and torch the propane tank. Never mind Nazis. This is the American Century."

Cromwell was a warrior, a true wild boy. We had been friends for many years and many savage moments. But now he seemed demoralized, which made me nervous.

He'd broken his back twice in the past months driving on black ice, but he'd taken little notice of it. His wife had been fingered in a federal murder investigation, and her life had been repeatedly threatened by criminally insane thugs.

But these things had not fazed Cromwell. He had no fear of men or murder or laws. But he was desperately worried now about the fate of his son and himself and the nation, and everything he loved and trusted and stood for.

It was the end of the decade that terrified him. It was like the coming of the midnight hour, with the screaming of the banshee and graveyard bells and the stench of the shroud all at once. It was not just the end of another failed decade that made him whine and quiver like Jell-O. No. What he feared was the final decade—the 1990s—and his horror of seeing his son a slave to Germany.

"The U.S. will become a colony—a cheap labor pool for Europe and a tree farm for Japan. The Chinese will take over Mexico and Canada will seal its borders. We will be a nation of unemployed refugees. My son will be standing in line at the German Embassy, begging for a work visa like all the others." He hurled his whiskey into the fire and cried out:

"Oh God! It's too horrible! He'll be better off if I put a bullet through his brain right now!" He jerked a stainless-steel .45 automatic out of a kidney holster on his belt and cranked a slug into the chamber, then aimed the gun at his huge blond son, sleeping peacefully in front of the fire.

I seized him by the neck and clamped my thumb on the hammer of the .45. "Be calm," I hissed. "George Bush is in charge now. Your son is safe. We are still Number One."

He went limp and meekly surrendered the weapon. I was lying, but it seemed necessary. I didn't need a murder in my house. I handed the .45 to his son. "Here, hold this," I said. "It's loaded."

"Good," said the son, then pointed the weapon at Cromwell and pulled the trigger. Nothing happened. It misfired. Old .45 ammo is like that.

New York City, 1989

TURBO MUST DIE

"Champion bull doomed in $10 million sperm bomb sacrifice
at famous sporting club"

By Raoul Duke

THE WORLD-FAMED WOODY Creek Rod and Gun Club will host a combined bull-sperm auction and prize animal sacrifice on January 26–

27, in conjunction with the annual Unlimited Class Firepower Demonstration at the club's secluded Bomb and Blasting Range on unpaved dead-end Lenado Road in upper Woody Creek.

According to press spokesman Semmes Luckett, who announced the event yesterday in a brief statement that was hailed by local cattlemen as "heroically brilliant" and "a masterpiece of understated genius."

The unprecedented sperm auction is expected to attract exotic cattle breeders from all over the world and climax with a record-setting $10 million sale bid for the sperm of Grand National Champion breeding bull "Turbo," who will die in a spectacular "sacrifice explosion" at the end of the auction ceremony personally performed by the bull's owner, Woody Creek rancher George Stranahan, who says he will donate all profits from the historic auction/sacrifice of his prize animal to the club's prestigious Bomb Research Endowment Fund.

Stranahan, a nuclear research physicist and dominant breeder of the ancient Limosin beef line, is the famed sporting club's vice-president for experimental explosions and a ranking expert in bull marketing strategies.

His neo-priceless Limosin strain dates back 20,000 years to the Bull Worship Era in the Limoges province of France, when bulls allegedly ruled the world.

Stranahan, a misogynistic recluse whose personal fortune has been estimated at $44 billion, said the public will not be invited to the bizarre auction/sacrifice and "if any intruders are captured, they will be chained to the neck of the doomed bull at dot-zero in the bomb area and will never be seen again."

The auction, he said, will begin with a catered lunch of wild lichen and gallbladders of recently killed bears—and will end only after a limited edition of one thousand vials of the prize bull's sperm are sold off to bidders at no less than $10,000 each.

"I feel wonderful about this thing," Stranahan said. "It's the smartest idea I ever had. With one jerk on the fuse puller we will finalize Turbo's price at ten million dollars and then blow him to smithereens."

The guest list of profoundly wealthy bidders expected to attend the event, said Luckett, "was top secret until yesterday," when a disgruntled animal rights activist revealed the names of Donald Trump, publisher Rupert Murdoch, Prince Bandar of Saudi Arabia, U.S. Secretary of State James Baker, and actor Jack Nicholson, a long-time member of the defiantly secretive club and a vocal defender of its frequently criticized traditions.

Membership in the Woody Creek Rod and Gun Club is so exclusive that no list of members is believed to exist, and the name of the club's president has never been revealed. Members communicate with each other by code names, and monthly gatherings are shrouded in secrecy and conducted in what spokesman Luckett described as "effectively utter darkness."

"Many of the two hundred twenty-two members are prominent and extremely beautiful women," he said, and "privacy is our dominant ethic."

"Loose lips are sealed quickly," he added, "by fire and other methods, which we will never admit or explain."

Woody Creek, 1989

MEMO TO JAY JOHNSON, NIGHT EDITOR, *SAN FRANCISCO EXAMINER*

To: Jay Johnson/Night Editor, *San Francisco Examiner*
From: Doctor Thompson
Subject: Why there will be no column this week/Kill it
Comment: Sorry/Extreme domestic violence/Police and jail/Attacked by The New Rich/Send money/Thanx

WELL . . . I COULD start off with that old-timey bullshit about "You'll never believe this."

But I have a feeling you *will,* once you check the Sunday AP wire out of Denver. . . .

Or maybe Monday—on the slim chance that the local police spokesperson might keep a lid on the story until then; but in fact I figure you've already seen it by now.

I refer, of course, to the shit train of eight (8) felony-assault, etc., charges that were brought against me by a maniac neighbor at dawn on Saturday morning, not long after he tried several times to strangle me for poisoning his dog, shooting his mules, and trying to force him to eat cocaine after spraying his trout ponds with gunfire while in the throes of a lethal psychotic episode that caused him to fear for his life.

Indeed. It was a king-hell bitch of a wrong Friday night in Woody Creek, and it ain't over yet. The fool wants to take the whole berserk package into court—where he spends about half his waking hours, anyway—to win a landmark decision establishing the right of a millionaire thug from Miami to move north and create a bastard replica of Disneyland and East St. Louis in a once-peaceful valley 8,000 feet up in the Rockies where he claims he can't sleep at night because of a cruel angst brought on by his new neighbors calling him a White Trash Swine behind his back and salting his pastures with Agent Orange to poison his water and kill off his mules and mock The American Dream.

Yeah, Jay—this is true.

Welcome to Floyd Watkins country. He is like the whole Manson Family compressed into one person like a huge tube of blood sausage with a head and two legs. . . . Not even Thomas Edison could have invented this monster. If you saw him in a crosswalk you would instinctively step on the gas.

Anyway, that's what happened with Friday night. It was like being on that DC-10 that went into Sioux City. About 10:30 on Saturday morning I heard many voices outside my bedroom window, croaking: "It's all over now, Doc." . . . "They're on their way out here with a warrant to search your house from top to bottom for guns, drugs, or anything else."

"Wake up and run *now*. Your only hope is to get to Moab by noon." "Get out of the state." "Never mind clothes and give us all your money and drugs." I lost a pound of weed, four guns, and $1,500 to a lawyer in less than forty-four minutes, before we fled along back roads in a Yugo toward the border.

All day long. Hiding in picnic areas with the lawyer who kept asking for $100 bills and telling me I was doomed unless I hid out in Moab all weekend with my new secretary who was scheduled to go to Princeton in three weeks on a fellowship that might turn utterly queer when this thing hits the front page on Monday: "*Sex and Violence in Woody Creek: Crazed Gonzo Writer Flees with Mystery Woman After Midnight Gun Battle with Rich Miami Wife Beater; Cocaine and Whiskey Blamed in Orgy of the Doomed; Dogs Poisoned, Mules Slaughtered, Police Dragnet for Thompson in Three States as Noose Tightens on 'Last Dope Fiend.'*"

Yeah. So we didn't get much writing done. Terry almost died from eating rancid lox and bagels. My lawyer thinks I'm in Moab, but I slithered back home around midnight and chained the gate shut with Harley-Davidson locks.

Call me tonight. We can get the column done if these fuckers leave me alone for six hours. I feel like I was shot through the looking glass. OK.

Woody Creek, 1989

WARNING IS ISSUED ON COCAINE USE WITH SEX AFTER MAN LOSES LIMBS

by LAWRENCE K. ALTMAN
The New York Times, June 3, 1988

IN AN UNUSUAL WARNING, doctors have reported the case of a man who injected cocaine into his urethra to heighten sexual pleasure and then, through "extravagant complications," suffered gangrene that led to the loss of both legs, nine fingers and his penis.

The authors of the report, three psychiatrists from New York Hospital, said it was not clear how the unusual cocaine use led to the complications. The doctors, John C. Mahler, Samuel Perry and Bruce Sutton, described the case in a letter in the current issue of The Journal of the American Medical Association.

The use of cocaine in the belief that it enhances sexual pleasure has often been reported. Several experts on sexuality and on drug abuse said they had heard of people rubbing cocaine on genital organs or injecting it into the urethra, the tube that carries urine out of the body. But they said it did not appear to be a widespread practice.

Cocaine use has been associated with a variety of medical problems including heart attack, stroke and death. But Dr. John Money, an expert in sexuality at Johns Hopkins Medical School in Baltimore, said it would be unusual for cocaine alone to produce the extreme complications. Dr. Money questioned whether some other factor, such as an impurity in the cocaine, might have been at fault.

Dr. Mahler said his team had considered that possibility but had no evidence to document it. He said his team had also speculated that the man might have developed an undetected infection or that attempts to treat him might have somehow led to additional complications.

Experts said cocaine would be absorbed into the bloodstream through the mucous membranes of the urethra as it would through any other mucous membrane, such as the nose, and presumably would have the same effect.

Priapism, Then a Blood Clot

Dr. Mahler said the New York Hospital case involved a 34-year-old man who told doctors he occasionally squirted a cocaine solution into his urethra. The last time he did so, in June 1987, he suffered a persistent painful erection immediately after intercourse with his girlfriend. His priapism lasted three days and he sought medical help.

Soon afterward, he developed blood clots in his genitals, arms and legs, back and chest.

By the 12th day in the hospital, gangrene had developed to such an extent that the man lost his legs, nine fingers and his penis.

Welcome to the NINETIES

WELCOME TO JAIL

IV

The right of the people to be secure in their persons, houses, papers, and effects, against unreasonable searches and seizures, shall not be violated, and no warrants shall issue, but upon probable cause, supported by oath or affirmation, and particularly describing the place to be searched, and the persons or things to be seized.

This past term the United States Supreme Court held that police can:

> Search your home upon the consent of someone who has no authority to give same[1],

> Stop your car based upon an "anonymous tip," which the Supreme Court described as "completely lacking in the necessary indicia of reliability"[2],

> Subject a motorist to mandatory sobriety tests without any indication they have been drinking or their driving is impaired[3].

Almost 62 years ago, Justice Brandeis reminded us that

> "Experience should teach us to be most on our guard to protect liberty when the Government's purposes are beneficient. Men born to freedom are naturally alert to repel invasion of their liberty by evil-minded rulers. The greatest dangers to liberty lurk in insidious encroachment by men of zeal, well-meaning but without understanding" . . .

---

[1]*Illinois v. Rodriguez*, U.S. (June 21, 1990) [58 LW 4892].
[2]*Alabama v. White*, 110 S. Ct. 2412 (June 11, 1990).
[3]*Michigan Department of State Police v. Sitz*, U.S. 110 L.Ed.2d 412 (June 14, 1990).

EDITOR'S NOTE

THE 1990S HAD barely begun when Dr. Thompson was struck down, as if by lightning, and our whole book production process was derailed and utterly destroyed by a series of events that staggered the faith of millions all over the world and panicked our production department into sending this book to press immediately and marketing the first 100,000 copies in a plain black box.

Dr. Thompson was clearly doomed. He had been seized by the forces of Law and Order and was apparently headed for prison—a sad and ignominious fate for the so-called Prince of Gonzo Journalism, or whatever it is that the crazy criminal snake tries to call himself.

Publishing Dr. Thompson has never been an easy job, but this recent episode was over the line and sent demoralizing shock waves through the whole organization, which for many years has stood behind him like a tall and solid rock. We lived in his shadow and endured his terrible excesses—clinging always to the promise that he would sooner or later make sense of his original assignment: *The Death of the American Dream*. . . .

So it was with a sense of shock, fear, and betrayal that we received the news that he was about to go to prison for a sudden, unexplainable outburst of cheap crimes, misdemeanors, and stupid felony loss leaders that made no sense at all. And it made people *angry*.

Tom Wolfe, after all, had never disgraced his publisher by running amok in public or twisting women's nipples. . . . and Norman Mailer has stabbed more people than Brutus, and they never put *him* in prison.

In any case, we were *wrong*. Strange things happened with baffling speed and soon we lost touch with reality. Except to know that *we were wrong*. And our decision to terminate the Doctor's mythology and send the remnants to market in a cheap black box for 99¢ each also proved to be hasty and was eventually reversed, at great cost.

. . .

Meanwhile, for reasons that have not yet been made entirely clear, Dr. Thompson's *legal* position took a series of wild turns that made many people wish that they'd been stolen out of their cradles by wolves. The whole case flipped and took off so *opposite* that it was like a golf ball hitting a steel wall, and many were left in confusion.

Dr. Thompson somehow seized control of the legal machinery and turned it back on the prosecution. All charges against him were suddenly dismissed and his team of savage lawyers filed massive civil actions against everybody they could reach, including the district attorney, a judge, two cabdrivers, and even his own publisher.

Fortunately, our contract allowed us to go to press with whatever sections of the book we already had our hands on—despite the author's objections and bizarre motions filed by his attorneys in courts all over the country, including New York and Nevada. . . . So we were, therefore, denied access to all written material on Thompson's case except those documents entered in evidence as Matter of Record.

It was a meager yield, at best, but we got enough to slap a fast chronology of The Case together in time to make our press deadline and beat that cruel whiskey-dumb geek at his own game. . . . And we were also able to hire the services of a premier investigator, Raoul Duke, who spent forty-four days with no sleep while putting together his report, which follows. We make no apology for Duke's hazy, slipshod report, which is mainly a bag of news clippings, rumors, and tedious court documents. Because it was all we could get, at the time, and it was all we needed to know. *Res Ipsa Loquitor*.

NOTHING BUT CRUMBS

D. A. SNAGS THOMPSON IN SEX CASE

by DAVID MATTHEWS-PRICE
Times Daily **Staff Writer**

Aspen Times Daily,
February 28, 1990

HUNTER S. THOMPSON, in an episode reminiscent of some of his books, has been charged with sexually assaulting a woman writer who came to his house ostensibly to interview him last week.

Thompson, 52, surrendered at the district attorney's office on Monday and is free on $2,500 bond.

Thompson told the *Times Daily* he's innocent and believes the alleged victim isn't so much a writer as she is a business woman who wants publicity for her new venture, which is selling sexual aids and lingerie.

"She's a business person in the sex business," Thompson said.

He said he's also suspicious of the motives of the district attorney, who had six officers search his Woody Creek house on Monday for drugs. Officers said they found a small quantity of suspected cocaine and marijuana.

Thompson offered his own headline for the case: LIFESTYLE POLICE RAID HOME OF "CRAZED" GONZO JOURNALIST; ELEVEN-HOUR SEARCH BY SIX TRAINED INVESTIGATORS YIELDS NOTHING BUT CRUMBS.

Lab Results Pending

District Attorney Milt Blakey said he's waiting for the results of lab tests before deciding whether to bring drug charges.

Thompson is already facing charges of third-degree sexual assault for allegedly grabbing the woman's left breast and third-degree simple assault for supposedly punching her during an argument about whether the interview should take place in a hot tub. Both misdemeanors carry a maximum two-year sentence in county jail.

The woman making the allegations is a 35-year-old self-employed writer from St. Clair, Mich., who said she was visiting Snowmass Village with her husband last week.

The *Times Daily* was unable to contact the alleged victim on Tuesday. However, her story about the Feb. 21 incident was detailed in an affidavit for an arrest warrant written by the district attorney's investigator Michael Kelly.

Affidavit Tells Story

The woman said she had written Thompson before arriving in Snowmass to request an interview. Such interviews are the fascination of out-of-town journalists. Just last week *Time* magazine published a first-person account of another writer's attempt to interview Thompson, a columnist for the *San Francisco Examiner* and national editor of *Rolling Stone* magazine.

The woman said she arrived at Thompson's house in a taxicab, on Woody Creek Road, and was greeted by a woman named Kat who introduced her to Thompson and two of his friends, identified in the affidavit as Semmes and Tim.

Drug Suspicions

"Within a few minutes, the woman suspected the group had been using drugs," the affidavit stated.

"She suspected some members of the group might be using drugs because from time to time they would get up and go into the other room and then return in a minute or so," the affidavit stated.

Then, about three hours after arriving at the house, the alleged victim said she saw Thompson carrying a green grinder that produced a white powdery substance, according to the affidavit.

"This substance, which she believed to be cocaine, was then passed around to the group and that with the exception of Tim and herself each ingested (snorted) some of it into their noses by means of a straw," the affidavit said.

Paranoid Group

"She observed the group becoming increasingly suspicious and paranoid," the affidavit said.

The woman writer said she got up and called her husband, a move which made the group suspicious that she might be an undercover agent.

She assured them that she wasn't an agent, she explained. Then Semmes and Tim left the house and Thompson gave her a tour of the residence.

She said Thompson showed her his "favorite" room, which contained a hot tub, and he supposedly suggested that she join him for a dip in the water.

Next, she claimed that Kat attempted to persuade her to join Hunter in the hot tub by telling her things such as "He's a harmless guy"; "[He's] a little crazy at-times, but he will never hurt you"; "He'd really like you to get in the hot tub with him"; etc., according to the affidavit.

ARREST WARRANT AND CHARGES

IN THE DISTRICT COURT IN AND FOR THE COUNTY OF
PITKIN AND STATE OF COLORADO
ARREST WARRANT   Warrant No._____

THE PEOPLE OF THE STATE OF COLORADO

TO: ANY PEACE OFFICER IN THE STATE OF COLORADO, INTO WHOSE HANDS
THIS WARRANT SHALL COME, GREETING:

WHEREAS, MICHAEL J. KELLY has made an Application and Affidavit for
the issuance of an Arrest Warrant:

AND WHEREAS, the Application appears proper, and this Court is satisfied
that there is probable cause to believe that the person named in the application
has committed the offenses of: SEXUAL ASSAULT IN THE THIRD DEGREE in
violation of C.R.S. 18-3-404, as amended, and ASSAULT IN THE THIRD DEGREE
in violation of C.R.S. 18-3-204.

YOU ARE HEREBY COMMANDED to arrest HUNTER STOCKTON THOMP-
SON and bring him without unnecessary delay before the nearest available
Judge of the County or District Court.

IT IS FURTHER ORDERED that Bond is set in the amount of _Two thousand_
dollars, the Bond to be approved by the Sheriff of the County wherein the arrest
occurs, or other Officer authorized by Law to admit to bail.

DONE this _23rd_ day of _February_, 1990
BY THE COURT

_____
JUDGE

STATE OF COLORADO   )
) s.   RETURN OF SERVICE
)

I duly served the within Warrant by arresting HUNTER STOCKTON THOMPSON
as required therein, on _MONDAY 26 FEB 90_

Michael J. Kelly
INVESTIGATOR NINTH
Title: _Judicial_ DISTRICT ATTORNEY

HUNTER S THOMPSON: *Those Charges in Full*
IN THE DISTRICT COURT, COUNTY OF PITKIN, STATE OF COLORADO
Criminal Action No. 90-CR-40

INFORMATION
THE PEOPLE OF THE STATE OF COLORADO

vs.

HUNTER S THOMPSON
Defendant

COMES NOW MILTON K BLAKEY, District Attorney in and for the Ninth Judicial District, State of Colorado, in the name and by the authority of the People of the State of Colorado, and informs the Court that:

COUNT ONE
On or about February 26, 1990, in the County of Pitkin, State of Colorado, HUNTER S THOMPSON did unlawfully, feloniously and knowingly possess a Schedule I controlled substance to-wit: Lysergic Acid Diethylamide; thereby committing the crime of UNLAWFUL POSSESSION OF A CONTROLLED SUBSTANCE SCHEDULE I, in violation of C.R.S. 12-22-309 and 18-18-105(1)(a)(2)(a)(I), as amended, contrary to the statute in such case made and provided and against the peace and dignity of the People of Colorado.(F-3).

COUNT TWO
On or about February 26, 1990, in the County of Pitkin, State of Colorado, HUNTER S THOMPSON did unlawfully, feloniously and knowingly possess a Schedule II controlled substance, to-wit: Cocaine; thereby committing the crime of UNLAWFUL POSSESSION OF A CONTROLLED SUBSTANCE SCHEDULE II, in violation of C.R.S. 12-22-310 and 18-18-105(1)(a)(2)(a)(I), as amended, contrary to the statute in such case made and provided and against the peace and dignity of the People of Colorado.(F-3).

COUNT THREE
On or about February 26, 1990, in the County of Pitkin, State of Colorado, HUNTER S THOMPSON did unlawfully, feloniously and knowingly possess a Schedule IV controlled substance, to-wit: Diazepam, thereby committing the crime of UNLAWFUL POSSESSION OF A CONTROLLED SUBSTANCE SCHEDULE IV, in violation of C.R.S. 12-22-312 and 18-18-105(1)(a)(2)(a)(I), as amended, contrary to the statute in such case made and provided and against the peace and dignity of the people of Colorado.(F-5).

COUNT FOUR
On or between February 21, 1990, and February 22, 1990 in the County of Pitkin, State of Colorado, HUNTER S THOMPSON did unlawfully, knowingly and recklessly cause bodily injury to Gail Palmer-Slater; thereby committing the crime of ASSAULT IN THE THIRD DEGREE, in violation of C.R.S. 18-3-204 as amended, contrary to the statute in such case made and provided and against the peace and dignity of the People of Colorado.(M-1).

COUNT FIVE

On and between February 21, 1990, and February 22, 1990 in the County of Pitkin, State of Colorado, HUNTER S THOMPSON did unlawfully and knowingly subject Gail Palmer-Slater to sexual contact knowing that Gail Palmer-Slater did not consent; thereby committing the crime of SEXUAL ASSAULT IN THE THIRD DEGREE, in violation of C.R.S. 18-3-404.

COUNT SIX

On and between February 21, 1990, and February 22, 1990 in the County of Pitkin, State of Colorado, HUNTER S THOMPSON did unlawfully, knowingly and feloniously use a controlled substance Schedule II, to-wit: Cocaine; thereby committing the crime of UNLAWFUL USE OF A CONTROLLED SUBSTANCE, in violation of C.R.S. 18-18-104(1), as amended, contrary to the statute in such case made and provided and against the peace and dignity of the People of Colorado.(F-6).

COUNT SEVEN

On or about February 26, 1990, in the County of Pitkin, State of Colorado, HUNTER S THOMPSON did unlawfully, knowingly possess more than one ounce of marijuana, but less than eight ounces of marijuana; thereby committing the crime of POSSESSION OF MORE THAN ONE OUNCE OF MARIJUANA BUT LESS THAN EIGHT OUNCES OF MARIJUANA, in violation of C.R.S. 18-18-106(4)(a), as amended, contrary to the statute in such case made and provided and against the peace and dignity of the People of Colorado.(M-1).

COUNT EIGHT

On or about February 26, 1990, in the County of Pitkin, State of Colorado, HUNTER S THOMPSON did unlawfully, feloniously and knowingly possess and control an explosive and incendiary device, to-wit; dynamite and blasting caps; thereby committing the crime of UNLAWFUL POSSESSION, USE AND REMOVAL OF EXPLOSIVES AND INCENDIARY DEVICES, in violation of C.R.S. 18-12-109(2) as amended, contrary to the statute in such case made and provided and against the peace and dignity of the People of Colorado.(F-4).

Dated this 6th day of April, 1990
Respectfully submitted
MILTON K BLAKEY
District Attorney

By:

Charles B. McCrory   Charles B. McCrory #10601
Chief Deputy District Attorney

BEWARE

Today: the Doctor
Tomorrow: <u>You</u>

The Hunter S. Thompson Legal Defense Fund
Box 274, Woody Creek, Colorado 81656
Paid for George Stranahan and Michael Solheim

THIS IS A POLITICAL
TRIAL . . .

A LOT OF PEOPLE are going to court these days and many are going to jail. Crime is rampant. The court dockets are overloaded and all the prisons are full. They are building more of them. Many more. The new prison business is booming, especially in the private sector.

Private prisons, free enterprise. If I were on better terms with the government right now I could apply to build a prison right here in my back yard. I might even get it. . . . Hell, I *should* get it. I am a solid citizen—a hard-working rancher. I am known as an honest man and a good neighbor. A pillar of the community, as it were. A gentleman and a scholar, with many friends in the valley.

I am a writer, a professional journalist with serious credentials in Crime, Craziness, and Politics. I have mingled with dangerous criminals and attended many trials. . . . from Hell's Angels, Black Panthers, and Chicano street fighters to Roxanne Pulitzer and even Richard Nixon, back in the good old days before he was run out of the White House for fraud, perjury, graft, and criminal negligence.

But they were always other people's trials. I have never been in the dock. I have never been on trial. Never accused of felonies.

All that has changed now. . . . Now I am under arrest and charged with eight felonies.

I am facing forty-four years in prison, sixteen with good behavior. *The New York Times* estimated, "If he is convicted, he could go to prison for decades." *The Village Voice* said " . . . next century."

These are ugly things to read over morning coffee, but these are eerie times. The hog is out of the tunnel. The dark underbelly of the American dream is beginning to surface.

Nobody seems to know what my crimes are. The Charges are vague, but . . .

I am actually on trial for Sex, Drugs, and Rock and Roll . . .

The too much Fun club

The Passing Lane

Queer Street

This is a Political Trial, and I am nothing if not a politician. I understand vengence.

This case is as important to me as it was that Nixon be impeached because they both involve abuse of political power for political reasons.

Nixon turned the White House into a national secret police headquarters; the hallways teemed night and day with hired burglars, political hitmen, and vengeful thugs who had a license to so anything the White House wanted done.

This time I am looking forward to going to court. . . .

Woody Creek, April 1990

THOMPSON HIT WITH 5 FELONIES

by DAVID MATTHEWS-PRICE

Aspen Times Daily
April 10, 1990

"THIS IS A LOW-RENT, back-alley cheap shot," Thompson muttered about the charges. He observed that many defendants get religion when they want mercy from the court. "When you see me coming out for Jesus you'll know they really have something on me," Thompson told the *Times Daily*.

MEMO TO HAL HADDON:
ATTACK NOW

To: Hal Haddon
From: HST
Date: May 6, 1990

Never mind that bullshit about "The Scopes Trial of Drug Use in the Home." No, counselor, that is *wrong*. . . .

The only mention of drug use in this case comes from a browbeaten female witness who was drunk at the time and dopey with fear and booze and bad nerves.

This is a *Fourth Amendment* case. It is not about sex or drugs or violence. It is about police power.

Do the police have a right to search my/your home tomorrow on the word(s) of three kinky complainants who flatter the Three Stooges and who lie to each other by accident and who now say the "victim" would rather flee than testify? And who then had their sordid squabble taken out of their hands by vengeful cops and Jesus freaks who would never have touched the case in the first place if they hadn't been convinced somehow by incredibly bungled investigatory procedures by the Pitkin County Sheriff's Dept., who then dumped it on the DA's doorstep as a sure-fire arrestable Felony Menacing case (". . . drew a gun on her") that turned out to be utter bullshit unless they could somehow make it stick with some kind of *guaranteed* whack—like a search that *could not fail* to turn up something. Even .09 grams.

By Friday afternoon at least three sheriff's deputies had made such a Three Stooges–style mess of "The Thompson Crime(s)" that Sheriff Braudis was frantic to get it off his hands and into the hungry maw of the DA *at all costs.* Even if it meant lying briefly to the DA's investigator, Mike Kelly, about the bogus "gun to her head" charge against me that went up in smoke before sundown and left the DA no option except a 100 percent sure *search.*

Indeed—Kelly had been hung out to dry again: unless he could come up with at least one felony, and never mind that rumor about use in the home. It was too flimsy. Only a search would do the trick—drive a stake through the monster's heart.

Yeah, it was *you,* Charley. I'm going to send Braudis forty silver dimes wrapped up in that nice new corduroy sheriff's hat he gave me.

Indeed—and don't even think of making me a doomed symbol of some giddy liberal crusade for "Your Right to Use Drugs in the Home," etc.

Not me, Jack. All I care about is not being raided by cops for provably wrong and evil reasons that still fester in the once-righteous heart of Mike Kelly. He knows he was suckered by Braudis and now yearns for a chance to roll over and confess.

Let me remind you, counselor, that John Scopes lost the "Monkey Trial." He was convicted and fined $100—then released on probation to a chain gang near Waycross, Georgia, where he soon ran afoul of the rules and was red-flagged and stabbed to death by a liberal prisoner who claimed to love him like a brother against all odds and forever. . . . But what the hell? Forever is like a dime in the fast lane, and the Times, of course, were changing. . . .

This low-rent treacherous case should be thrown out in the first twenty minutes of the preliminary hearing. Judge Crater should croak it in ten. . . . No guilt, no business, *No Pasaran*. . . . Thanx.

—Doc

THE ART OF HITTING THE ONE IRON

"Not even God can win a preliminary hearing."
—HAL HADDON, May 22, 1990

I CURSED HADDON when he told me this. "You lazy money-mad bastard," I shouted. "Lee Trevino said not even God can hit a one iron . . . which proved to be true, in his case—but so what?

"I can hit a one iron," I said. "I can *kick the shit* out of a one iron."

Which was true, for some reason. The Ping Eye 2 Beryllium One iron is my favorite club. All golfers fear and hate the One. It has no *angle,* no pitch, no loft. . . . It is straight up and down, like a putter, and the chances of a normal person getting a ball up in the air with it are usually about 1,000 to 1 against. . . . The one iron is a confidence-crusher, a Fear Trip, an almost certain guarantee of Shame, Failure, Dumbness, and Humiliation if you ever use it in public. Few PGA pros ever touch the One, and most amateurs won't even carry it in their bags. The One is so ugly, they will tell you, so evil and wrong by nature that its mere presence in the bag poisons all the other clubs. A used One is usually the cheapest club in the "33 Percent Off" barrel at any pro shop. Charles Manson once said he would rather use a wooden-shafted Frances Ouimet Two iron than a Ping Eye 2 Beryllium One.

So it was weird when I picked up the Ping One and lashed five or six straight balls off the tee like line-drive homers at 240 yards each. . . . A deathly silence fell on the crowd at the driving range. They watched in amazement, and said nothing, as I continued to bash low-rising 240-yarders like a golf robot who couldn't miss.

Hot damn, I thought. This is wonderful. These people are frozen and stunned, like members of a vision . . . they have made me an object of worship, a Hero of Golf. . . .

They were like law students watching my old friend Ed Williams (deceased) win five (5) preliminaries in a row, always in the face of huge odds. . . . Indeed. One of my first Combat Memos on this case asked, "Where is Edward Bennett Williams? Now that I finally need him?"

Ed could not hit the One, but he was hell on wheels in a courtroom.

Woody Creek, May 1990

MOTION AND ORDER TO DISMISS THE CASE

IN THE DISTRICT COURT, COUNTY OF PITKIN, STATE OF COLORADO
Criminal Action No. 90CR41

MOTION AND ORDER TO DISMISS CASE

THE PEOPLE OF THE STATE OF COLORADO
    vs.
HUNTER S. THOMPSON
    Defendant.

COMES NOW MILTON K. BLAKEY, District Attorney in and for the Ninth Judicial District of the State of Colorado, and moves this Honorable Court to dismiss this case and as grounds therefor states that:

· The People would be unable to establish guilt beyond a reasonable doubt.
   Dated this 30th day of May, 1990.

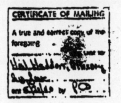

Respectfully submitted,
MILTON K. BLAKEY
District Attorney

by: _____
Charles B. McCrory; #10601
Chief Deputy District Attorney

ORDER

The People's Motion to dismiss this case is hereby granted this __30__ day of __May__, 1990.

BY THE COURT

J. J. Crater
District Court Judge

HUNTER HAILS LEGAL TRIUMPH FOR AMERICANS

by MARK HUFFMAN
Times Daily Staff Writer

Aspen Times Daily
June 1, 1990

HUNTER THOMPSON apologized Thursday for mumbling when he denied drug, dynamite, and sex assault charges in February.

But he wasn't sorry for anything else.

Thompson, the Gonzo journalist of Woody Creek, was triumphant Thursday as prosecutors who tried to nail him formally dropped the charges. Thompson proclaimed his victory a victory for all Americans, a victory for the Constitutional right to privacy in a person's home.

"I've been accused of mumbling. I didn't mean to mumble when I said, 'Not guilty,' " Thompson mumbled to Judge Charles Buss. "I should have said it more clearly."

Selective Prosecution

Thompson called himself "a victim of selective, malicious prosecution.

"I'm the point man for a lot of people," he said. "This is just part of what I think is a long series of abuses of the Constitution, the Fourth Amendment, which guarantees all of us, even judges, the right not to be subjected to unwarranted search and seizure."

Judge Buss accepted the motion from Chief Deputy Attorney Chip McCrory to drop the charges, but wasn't very happy with the timing.

"Why couldn't you have made this decision before you filed?" he asked McCrory.

McCrory told him a wavering witness and new findings about just how difficult it would have been to get a conviction against Thompson came only after last week's preliminary hearing.

Thompson was bound over for trial on all but a single count of cocaine use at that hearing.

Fight for Rights

Denver attorney Hal Haddon, Thompson's main defender in the case, called dismissal of the charges a significant Constitutional development.

"In this country privacy is only as safe as we are willing to fight for," Haddon said from the courthouse steps after the 10-minute session. "That's why this is an important case, why Hunter Thompson is important—because he fought for it."

Houston attorney Gerry Goldstein, a Constitutional expert in town to lend a hand, said Americans today are "alarmingly anxious to throw away their rights" and that it was "important to see someone like Dr. Thompson fight for his."

Thompson, who emerged from the courthouse videotaping the crowd of photographers waiting for their own shots, told the crowd of press, well-wishers, and hangers-on that "we are all, in all of our houses, a little safer than we were yesterday."

Like Goldstein, he said he was dismayed that so many people seem unwilling to fight as he did.

"We've grown accustomed to letting anyone with a badge walk over us," he said.

She "Got Sloppy"

And, as he had earlier, Thompson denied charges by Gail Palmer-Slater that he'd assaulted her.

Her complaint to police after a visit to Thompson's house Feb. 21—when she said he used cocaine and threatened and assaulted her after she rebuffed his sexual advances—led to an 11-hour search that turned up a variety of drugs and explosives.

"I didn't beat that woman up," Thompson said. "She came to my house and got sloppy, got rude. I don't have a right to beat anybody up. I didn't."

Dismissal of the charges by Judge Buss "without prejudice" means they cannot be refiled.

The only possibility of another hearing is if there's a dispute between prosecutors and defenders about return of property seized in the search of Thompson's house. Everything except "contraband" will be returned, prosecutor McCrory said.

But when it appeared that deciding what constitutes "contraband" might be a problem, and McCrory said he wasn't prepared to argue the matter Thursday, Judge Buss said he would "find my way back to Pitkin County" if another session is essential.

"Let's have another hearing," Buss deadpanned. "That'd be fun."

PRESS RELEASE, OWL FARM,
5/31/90

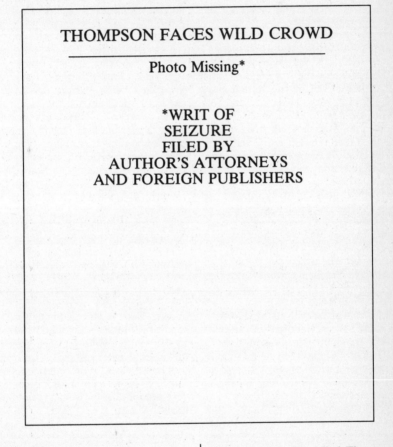

THOMPSON FACES WILD CROWD

Photo Missing*

*WRIT OF
SEIZURE
FILED BY
AUTHOR'S ATTORNEYS
AND FOREIGN PUBLISHERS

WOODY CREEK, COLO., May 31, 1990— Famed Gonzo journalist Dr. Hunter S. Thompson waves to a frenzied mob of his "supporters" at yesterday's press conference on the steps of the Pitkin County Courthouse . . . where all charges on Sex, Drugs, Bombs, and Violence crimes against The Doctor were *Dismissed With Prejudice* by District Court Judge Charles Buss, who called Thompson "a perfect gentleman" and excoriated the District Attorney for *Negligence, Malfeasance,* and *Criminal Abuse of Police Power.* Spectators applauded as Dep. Dist. Atty. Chip "Shiteyes" McCrory wept openly at the verdict and was led from the courtroom by bailiffs.

Thompson denounced the Dismissal as

"pure cowardice" and said he would "appeal it at once" to the Colorado Supreme Court.

Thompson described the District Attorney's "whole goddamn staff" as "thugs liars crooks" and "lazy human scum. . . . These stupid brutes tried to destroy my life," he said, "and now they tell me to just forget it.

"*Fuck that!*" he screeched. "They are guilty! They should all be hung by their heels from iron telephone poles on the road to Woody Creek!"

The crowd roared and surged forward, chanting, "*Yes! Now! Hang them now!*"

A man with a pitchfork rushed up the ancient stone steps and attempted to enter the courthouse, but he was hurled away by Thompson, who blocked the doorway and told the mob to "be calm."

"Not now!" he shouted. "Not *today!* But *soon! Yes!* We will PUNISH them! We will chop off their fingers and gnaw on their skulls and feed their flesh to our animals!"

The crowd responded by ripping up trees in the courtyard and hammering crazily on the hoods of nearby police cars. "Death to the Weird," they howled. "*They shall not pass!* PUNISH them!" At this point Dr. Thompson was seized from behind by his two high-powered attorneys and rushed to a waiting car, which departed at high speed.

Later, from his heavily guarded fortress called "Owl Farm," Thompson's lawyers issued a statement that called him "a hero, a saint . . . and the bravest man in America. . . . Dr. Thompson is a great poet," they said, "who often speaks in apocalyptic terms.

"His comments earlier today about Death, Cannibalism, and Vengeance should not be construed in any way as a threat to the physical safety of *any living thing.*"

The statement was hailed by the press as "further proof that Dr. Thompson should be awarded the Nobel Prize for Peace."

"The Doctor will have no further comment on The Case," his attorneys said, "for legal reasons stemming from his $22 million civil lawsuit against the District Attorney's Office, which will be formally filed next week."

Later that night, however, the restive Gonzo journalist issued a mysterious "personal statement" that local authorities called "very gracious, very strange, and very bloodthirsty all at once."

He spoke of a "historical mandate," citing mysterious blood feuds. He refused to talk about his rumored blood relationship to Genghis Khan, Cassius Clay, John Gotti, and other legendary warriors.

"But you forget," he said. "I am Lono. I am He. When the great bell rings, I will be there."

Thompson refused to elaborate on his claim to be Someone Else, and his aides brusquely turned aside press queries. Reporters who persisted were roughed up by burly "advisers" wearing bulletproof vests and "Owl Farm/Security" badges. One TV journalist, who begged not to be named, said he was taken to "a cistern somewhere in the compound" and forced to strip naked while standing knee-deep in "ice-cold water rushing up from an underground river." For "many hours," he said, he was tormented by drunken lawyers and mocked by what appeared to be naked women.

FINAL ANALYSIS: GERALD GOLDSTEIN, ESQ.

LAW OFFICES
GOLDSTEIN, GOLDSTEIN AND HILLEY
Eli Goldstein

29TH FLOOR TOWER LIFE BUILDING   Area Code 512
Gerald H. Goldstein   Telephone 226-1463
Van G. Milley   San Antonio, Texas 78205
Robert O. Switzer   Area Code 512
Patricia T. Peranteau   Telefax 226-8367
Cynthia Hujar Orr

June 2, 1990

Dr. Hunter S. Thompson
Owl Creek Farm
Woody Creek
Aspen, Colorado

Re: "Saving Us from Ourselves"
    Random Reflections on What It All Meant

Dear Doc;

   After dallying too long in your hospitality Thursday last, I gave some thought to what your ordeal has meant to me and others while en route back to Deep East Texas where the War on Drugs is currently venting its spleen over five black kids in an all-white courtroom.

   Your persecutor, muttering something about his ethical code, said he could not proceed with the hanging because he had little faith in the credibility of his sole source of information. The Judge gratuitously queried why he could not have made such a decision before dragging you through the streets.

   The real question that has to be asked is why the authorities cannot make such determinations before they break down a citizen's door and rummage through their homes and lives in the first place.[1]

IF THEY CAN DO THIS TO THE RICH AND FAMOUS

If they can do this to *you* over spilled cranberry juice, imagine what they must be doing to the poor and ignominious every day in courtrooms across this country.

What you did, Hunter, the reason I'd fly back halfway across the country to stand with you again, is that you had the *huevos* to fight back, to say you would not tolerate the system's intolerance. Things are not going to change in this country until the famous and not so infamous alike are willing to hold their ground and say enough is enough.

We cannot expect people to have respect for law and order until we teach respect to those we have entrusted to enforce those laws.

There is hysteria running rampant in our nation's capital and our local statehouses. Of late, it has been accompanied by serious talk of reducing citizen rights in an effort to combat the dreaded plague of drugs. To demagogue about drugs is certainly simpler, and much more popular, than the difficult task of balancing budgets. But escalating the punishment for drug offenders, bankrupting our state and national coffers warehousing these poor souls, will hardly solve our nation's social ills. It is only going to create more poverty. And poverty is a greater root cause of crime than drugs could ever hope to be.

In the late '60s and early '70s the law in my fair state provided life imprisonment for possession of one marijuana cigarette. In 1973 there

[1] *Who will protect us from our protectors?*
That is what Justice Jackson was talking about when he opined over forty years ago:

"[Fourth Amendment rights] . . . are not mere second-class rights but belong in the catalog of indispensable freedoms. Among deprivations of rights, none is so effective in cowing a population, crushing the spirit of the individual and putting terror in every heart. Uncontrolled search and seizure is one of the first and most effective weapons in the arsenal of every arbitrary government. . . .

"But the right to be secure against searches and seizures is one of the most difficult to protect. Since the officers are themselves the chief invaders, there is no enforcement outside the court." *Brinegar v. U.S.*, at 180–181 (1949) (Jackson, J., dissenting).

were thirteen individuals serving life sentences for possession of small quantities of that drug. Yet, during that same period of time, first-time use of marijuana rose at a greater rate than during any other period in our history.

The last five administrations have declared war on drugs. Last term in *Mistretta v. U.S.,* 109 S.Ct. 647 (1989), the Supreme Court approved the Federal Sentencing Guidelines which upped punishments, eliminated parole, and virtually did away with probation. The 1984 Incomprehensible Crime Control Act raised everything from minimum mandatory sentences to prosecutors' salaries. And the incessant Anti–Drug Abuse Control Amendments simply add insult to the injury. Under these enactments, many of our clients begin serving their sentences at the time of arrest, rather than conviction.

"No, no!" said Queen. "Sentence first—verdict afterwards." Lewis Carroll, *Alice in Wonderland.*

In *Solerno v. U.S.,* 481 U.S. 739 (1987), the Supreme Court upheld Bail Reform Act amendments providing for the detention of presumptively innocent citizens, without bail, prior to any trial or determination of their guilt. We often house these presumptively innocent citizens under deplorable conditions, without rehabilitation, education, or recreation. Then, after we convict them, send them to a "Club Fed" for punishment.

With many citizens not getting bail, none getting paroled, and all facing the prospect of higher minimum mandatories under the Sentencing Guidelines, there soon will be no more room at the Inn. The Federal Bureau of Prisons, now running at 150 percent of capacity, estimates that their inmate population will quintuple in the next five years.

The Fatal Shore, a popular book a few years back, depicted a period in English history when over two hundred property crimes carried the death penalty, yet they couldn't kill people fast enough. Prison overcrowding had become such a problem that "private" prisons were created to deal with the overflow. Ultimately they took 160,000 of their most incorrigible inmates, put them on "prison ships," and banished them to an island in the South Pacific, which Captain Cook had visited seventeen years before and no one had seen since. We do not have an Australia. And unless we intend simply to fence off Oklahoma, we are not going to be able to build prisons fast enough.

The Third Reich did not impose its will upon an unwilling, unreceptive public. Hitler rode into power on a groundswell of public opinion, fueled by law-and-order rhetoric and scare tactics, not unlike those being unleashed in our legislatures today.

What may appear to be innocuous incursions in the face of this perceived fear have a cumulative impact. None of us complained when our bodies and our baggage became the subject of scrutiny at our airports in the face of repeated hijackings and terrorist attacks. Yet, if our grandparents had been told their persons and personal effects would be searched before they could board a means of public transportation, they would have been shocked. And it was these very airport "security checks" that served as an example for the Supreme Court's approval last term of intrusions into our bodily fluids. See: *National Treasury Employees Union v. Von Raab*, 489 U.S. (1989) [approving urine tests of certain government employees]. Almost one hundred years before, that same Court had noted:

"It may be that it is the obnoxious thing in its mildest and least repulsive form; but illegitimate and unconstitutional practices get their first footing in that way, namely by silent approaches and slight deviations from legal modes of procedure. This can only be obviated by adhering to the rule that constitutional provisions for the security of person and property should be liberally construed. A close and literal construction deprives them of half their efficacy, and leads to gradual depreciation of the right, as if it consisted more in sound than in substance. It is the duty of the Courts to be watchful for the Constitutional rights of the citizen, and to guard against any stealthy encroachments thereon. Their motto should be *obsta principiis*." Boyd v. U.S., 116 U.S. 616, 635 (1886).

Last year, as if our skies were not unsafe enough already, Congress narrowly missed passing a statute permitting drug agents to shoot down suspected drug smugglers. And, exalting form over substance, recreated the federal crime of flag desecration. While encouraging the crass commercial and partisan political exploitation of our national symbol, our legislators have seen fit to criminalize its symbolic use by those with whom they do not agree. President Bush even ate an American flag birthday cake for the television cameras, and one must assume excreted what was left the following day. That would appear to make defecation of our flag a laudable gesture, while burning it, as a form of pure political speech, constitutes a federal crime.

However the public may view the so-called drug problem, stripping the citizenry of two hundred years of civil liberties is not the solution. And beating the public into a frenzy, willing to throw their own protections away, poses even greater dangers than whatever evil they seek to prevent. When the Supreme Court addressed our government's newfound interest in its own agents' bodily functions, it was surprisingly Ray-gun's appointee Justice Scalia who retorted:

"There is irony in the Government's citation, in support of its position, of Justice Brandeis's statement in *Olmstead* . . . that '[f]or good or ill, [our Government] teaches the whole people by its example.' Brandeis was there dissenting from the Court's admission of evidence obtained through an unlawful Government wiretap. He was not praising the Government's example of vigor and enthusiasm in combating crime, but condemning its example that 'the end justifies the means.' An even more apt quotation from the famous Brandeis dissent would have been the following:

"[I]t is . . . immaterial that the intrusion was in aid of law enforcement. Experience should teach us to be most on our guard to protect liberty when the Government's purposes are beneficent. Men born to freedom are naturally alert to repel invasion of their liberty by evil-minded rulers. The greatest dangers to liberty lurk in insidious encroachment by men of zeal, well meaning but without understanding. . . .'

"Those who lose because of the lack of understanding that begot the present exercise in symbolism are not just the Customs Service employees, whose dignity is thus offended, but all of us—who suffer a coarsening of our national manners that ultimately give the Fourth Amendment its content, and who become subject to the administration of federal officials whose respect for our privacy can hardly be greater than the small respect they have been taught to have for their own." *National Treasury Employees Union v. Van Raab,* 489 U.S. (1989) (Scalia, J., dissenting).

What you did was important. Thank you for letting me be a small part of it. As J. Frank Dobie said: "You'll do to ride the river with."

Sincerely,

Gerald H. Goldstein
for Goldstein, Goldstein and Hilley

A LETTER TO *THE CHAMPION:* A PUBLICATION OF THE NATIONAL ASSOCIATION OF CRIMINAL DEFENSE LAWYERS, KEITH STROUP, EXECUTIVE DIRECTOR

WELL, KEITH, WHAT can I say? Except *thanks* to you and your gang: The Long Riders from NACDL.

Your boys are OK. When the Great Whistle blew, NACDL members Gerry Goldstein and Hal Haddon were *warriors,* and saved me from going to prison

Which is no small thing in these times, as you know. That number "8" in *1984* was a typo. In the original manuscript Orwell wrote *1994,* but he was so far behind on his deadline that his publisher refused to let him make any changes.

Publishers are notoriously slothful about numbers, unless they're attached to dollar signs—unlike journalists, quarterbacks, and felony criminal defendants who tend to be keenly aware of numbers at all times.

The key number in my case was "8"—the number of crimes I was falsely and maliciously charged with—and the number of years I was expected to spend in prison seemed to go up in multiples of 8, depending on who was doing the math. Each felony charge, for instance, carried 16 years, which led *The New York Times* to estimate that I could spend 8 "decades" in prison, if convicted, and caused *The Village Voice* to guess that I would be behind bars "until well into the next century."

It was grim. Especially with a new D.A. who had come into office boasting that he was "going to hang [my] ass—a threat which I failed to take seriously since I knew the man to be a vicious, low-rent punk and dumber than nine chickens. Even grimmer was the fact that my original/erstwhile attorney (a local boy and former sheriff's deputy who had never tried a criminal case) was/is a crusading ex-drunk AA leader who didn't mind saying that Re-Hab was the best place for me anyway and was eager to begin the plea bargaining process ASAP in order to get me on supervised court probation and safely "within the system."

The story gets longer and uglier, but we have no time for it now. In a nut, I was doomed to the impossible life of a convicted felon, even though I'd committed no crime(s) and was clearly the victim of a greedy amateurish setup. Going to trial with a lawyer who considers your whole life-style a Crime in Progress is not a happy prospect.

Ah ha! But now the story changes. The worm turns, the wind shifts one-eighty, and the firestorm turns back on the arsonists, who had been operating with impunity for so long that they'd forgotten the feeling of Heat. The D.A. was a half-bright meatball who had run unopposed for reelection three times and had rarely been challenged in court; the judge was a Reformed Alcoholic who hated the sight of a drinker. The D.A. was a failed rodeo cowboy who is still trying to put a twenty-two-year-old girl in state prison for allegedly "slapping a jailer"; and the D.A.'s investigator was a born-again Christian. It was like going up against The Meese Gang, in their own court with their own rules and facing the rest of your life in prison if you lost.

Ho-ho. These lame cheapjack bullies had reckoned without the Long Riders from NACDL, who came over the horizon on both flanks and swept down on them like Jeb Stuart at the first Battle of Bull Run, and I will never forget the feeling of wild happiness and raw courage I felt when I saw them coming and knew that I finally had not just the troops, but Generals . . . and, Mother of Babbling Christ, I even had *credit.*

Try it sometime, folks, it's a rush you'll remember forever. They seemed to come all at once, in what clearly was my darkest hour. Mike Stepanian from San Francisco, Hal Haddon from Denver, Keith Stroup from Washington, and the ineffable *maestro of motions,* Gerry Goldstein from San Antonio.

Suddenly I had *my own gang.* My own *army,* my people, my friends, my warriors. . . . They came from all points of the compass and all points in time, and we stomped on the terra like champions. It was something to see, folks, and it was a beautiful war to be part of. . . . Haddon stomped through the courtroom like one of the Gallo brothers mashing grapes, and Goldstein gave them nightmares at high noon just by sitting at the Defense table with that fine cheetah's grin on his face and shooting his cuffs now and then with obvious impatience at having to wait so long for the meal he knew was coming.

It was a rout, folks. The D.A.'s cheap bunglers collapsed in a heap and fled like rats into whatever darkness they could find, which was not much. They are on the run now. Some are resigning and others are under arrest; the judge is finished, and the D.A's dream of a judgeship is now a bad joke.

And, yes . . . there is more to this hellish story, but the magazine is going to press and Keith is going crazy, so I have to quit *now;* but the tale is not finished. All I can say now is Thanks, once again. You boys are OK when you get the right music to dance to, and I was proud and goddamn happy for the chance to dance with you.

With great respect and affection, I remain, your friend,

Dr. Hunter S. Thompson

Woody Creek, July 1990

LATER THAT YEAR . . .

ON AUGUST 22, 1990, Dr. Thompson and his relentless criminal lawyer, Hal Haddon, made a formal appearance in the ancient brick Pitkin County Courthouse on Main Street in Aspen, Colorado, and filed Notice of Intent to whack the District Attorney's office, collectively and individually, with a $22 million civil lawsuit for *Malicious Prosecution, Gross Negligence and Criminal Malfeasance with Harmful Intent.*

Simultaneously, Haddon secured from the District Court a formal Purge and Seal order for all official records concerning Thompson's alleged connection with the ill-fated and ill-advised case brought against him by the D.A., who is currently under investigation by a Special Prosecutor, for Conspiracy to Commit Perjury, a felony crime carrying a 5-year sentence in the massively overcrowded State Prison at Canon City.

Dr. Thompson was more specific. "They are doomed," he said. "They will soon be in prison. Those bastards have no more respect for the law than any screwhead thief in Washington. They will meet the same fate as Charles Manson and Neil Bush."

AUTHOR'S NOTE

TIMES HAVE CHANGED NOW, but not much. Alphonse Karr was right: "The more things change, the more they stay the same." Jesus! Only a cynical Frog could have written a thing like that. . . . But he was right, I think, and his wisdom has shaped many lives, for good or ill.

But not mine. I have changed constantly all my life, usually at top speed, and it has always been with the total, permanent finality of a thing fed into an atom smasher. My soul and my body chemistry are like that of a chameleon, a lizard with no pulse. . . . People praise me for this, but they are all foreigners and they know nothing. When I go to Mexico or Germany they call me "Lizard Man," and I laugh smugly. . . . "To get along, go along." That's what I say.

Woody Creek, August 1990

THE HONOR ROLL

Ralph Steadman
Michael Solheim
Terry Sabonis-Chafee
David Matthews-Price
Jim Mitchell
Artie Mitchell
Jeff Armstrong
Virginia Ray Thompson
George McGovern
Jack Nicholson
Jesse Barron
Lyle Lovett
Julie Oppenheimer

Christine Nelson
Jay Johnson
Susie Sterling
Mark Breslin
Semmes Luckett
Tim Charles
Tony Yerkovich
Joe Bergquist
Andy Hall
The Cowboy Junkies
Warren Hinckle
Dr. Bob Geiger

And all the others who ride for the Gonzo Brand. Responsibility for any and all errors found in this book will be shared among them.

"I turn to simplicity; I turn again to purity."
—GENGHIS KHAN, 1221

The first and greatest of all the Khans had these words carved on a simple stone pillar somewhere between Persia and Mongolia as he and his victorious troops rode home along the same invasion route that they'd been using for decades to conquer the entire Middle East, and that his generals would soon be using again for the invasion of Russia and then Europe. . . . But his stunning conquest of Muhammed Ali Shah's whole empire in less than a year had left the Khan weary of war. He had proven his point and now he was going back home, leaving his generals, Jebe and Subedi, to pillage the rest of the world in his name. The splendors of the fallen Persian empire had amazed him at first, he said, but he soon tired of one golden temple after another full of veiled dancing girls and endless feasts in his honor. "My sons will live to desire such lands and cities as these," he said, "but I cannot."